A SOCIOLOGY OF OF WOMEN

The Intersection of Patriarchy, Capitalism, and Colonization

SECOND EDITION

Jane C. Ollenburger

Boise State University

Helen A. Moore

University of Nebraska

PRENTICE HALL
Upper Saddle River, New Jersey 07458

Library of Congress Cataloging-in-Publication Data

OLLENBURGER, JANE C.
   A sociology of women : the intersection of patriarchy, capitalism,
and colonization / Jane C. Ollenburger, Helen A. Moore. — 2nd ed.
      p.   cm.
   Includes bibliographical references and index.
   ISBN   0–13–671637–7 (paper)
      1. Feminist theory.   2. Women—Sociological aspects.   3. Women—
Social conditions.   I. Moore, Helen, A.   II. Title.
HQ1190.055   1998
305.42'01—dc21   97–24490
                                                             CIP

Editorial director: Charlyce Jones Owen
Editor-in-chief: Nancy Roberts
Associate editor: Sharon Chambliss
Project manager: Joan Stone
Prepress and manufacturing buyer: Mary Ann Gloriande
Marketing manager: Christopher DeJohn
Copy editor: Rebecca J. McDearmon

This book was set in 10/12 New Baskerville by The Composing
Room of Michigan, Inc., and was printed and bound by Courier
Companies, Inc. The cover was printed by Phoenix Color Corp.

 © 1998, 1992 by Prentice-Hall, Inc.
Simon & Schuster/A Viacom Company
Upper Saddle River, New Jersey 07458

Printed in the United States of America

10 9 8 7 6 5 4 3 2 1

ISBN 0-13-671637-7

PRENTICE-HALL INTERNATIONAL (UK) LIMITED, *London*
PRENTICE-HALL OF AUSTRALIA PTY. LIMITED, *Sydney*
PRENTICE-HALL CANADA INC., *Toronto*
PRENTICE-HALL HISPANOAMERICANA, S.A., *Mexico*
PRENTICE-HALL OF INDIA PRIVATE LIMITED, *New Delhi*
PRENTICE-HALL OF JAPAN, INC., *Tokyo*
SIMON & SCHUSTER ASIA PTE. LTD., *Singapore*
EDITORA PRENTICE-HALL DO BRASIL, LTDA., *Rio de Janeiro*

Contents

TWO

Feminist Approaches
to the Study of Women, *16*

THREE

A Sociology of Women, 35

FOUR

Feminist Methodologies, 57

FIVE

Women and Work,   *69*

SIX

Women and Schooling, *117*

SEVEN

Women and the Law,   *159*

EIGHT

Women and Aging,   *194*

NINE

The Intersection of Gender, Class, and Race, *215*

Preface

We define a *sociology of women* as a comprehensive perspective on the diversity of women's experiences of structured inequality. This is an integration of the micro- and macrosociological enterprises and is informed by feminist theory. By defining a sociology of women in terms of structured patterns of inequality, we incorporate the framework of sexual stratification. In addition, however, we explicitly integrate progressive sex-roles research from the discipline of sociology. We move toward a systematic assessment of all women, including women of color, working-class women, elderly women, and lesbians. In sum, what we do is explicate a sociology by, for, and about women.

FEMINIST SOCIOLOGY AS SYNTHESIS

Chapter One begins with the thesis of traditional sociological theory and its application to women in society. We review the works of Herbert Spencer, Auguste Comte, Jane Addams, Emile Durkheim, Karl Marx, and other prominent sociologists. The major theoretical perspectives are presented, including functionalist theory, role theory, and conflict theory.

Chapter Two presents the antithesis to this theoretical tradition in sociology–feminist theory derived primarily from the disciplines of women's studies and ethnic studies. We include the women's studies frameworks of the sociology of law and women's place within it. We trace the historical influence law has had on women, illustrating the point with a description of protective labor legislation. Next, we look at women's marginality as criminal justice professionals, focusing on women as lawyers and police officers, and then as criminals. Gender issues specific to women's criminality are addressed, including the invisibility of the female actor, the roles of the status offense in female delinquency, the history of the sexualization of female crime, and survival in a world of physical and sexual abuse.

In Chapter Eight, we focus on women and aging. First, we present a general overview of the discipline of gerontology. Then, we turn to five issues specific to elderly women: culture and body image; marriage, widowhood, and divorce; housing; sexuality; and physical and mental health. The final section is devoted to the intersection of race, class, age, and sex. We deal with issues specific to elderly minority women and aging lesbians. We also include an overview of economics and aging, and caregiving among elderly women and their daughters.

Chapter Nine summarizes our propositions for each of the four areas of social organization covered in the book. We address the issue of "but what about men?" and conclude with a statement about praxis and policy.

ACKNOWLEDGMENTS

A Sociology of Women is a book about women, for women, and written by women. There are many people we wish to acknowledge who have assisted us in this project. First and foremost, we wish to express our sincere gratitude to the women who have educated us by their experiences of racism, classism, sexism, and heterosexism in the educational, criminal justice, and economic systems. In addition, Darlene Lind deserves our heartfelt thanks for her dedicated work of typing the original manuscript even when faced with extremely tight deadlines. Cori Barrera and Jan Cannata, working as research assistants, provided extensive assistance in updating the tables and text for the second edition. We have benefited from the advice of a number of our colleagues including John Hamlin, Danny Hoyt, and Kathy Ward, and we appreciate their insights into earlier versions of the manuscript. Part of Chapter Four on feminist methodology appeared in *Feminist Ethics in Social Science Research,* and we would like to acknowledge the work of Beth Hartung and Mary Jo Deegan in that collaboration. In addition, we would like to thank the first-edition reviewers from Prentice Hall: Kathryn Ward, Southern Illinois University at Carbondale; Linda Grant, University of Georgia; Jennie J. McIntyre, University of Maryland; and Rosalind Gottfried, Albuquerque Technical Vocational Institute, for their helpful suggestions, as well as reviewers Polly F. Radosh, Western Illinois University, and M. Cathey Maze, Franklin University, for the second edition. Our editor, Nancy Roberts, has been a delight throughout this process, and we appreciate her time and the attention she gave to answering our questions and concerns. Finally, we extend our thanks to Nancy Bowen, who put up with us throughout the long haul, and to Mark Nicholas for his patience and editing assistance.

Jane C. Ollenburger
Helen A. Moore

A Sociology
of Women

ONE

Sociological Approaches to the Study of Women

WOMEN'S PLACE IN THE HISTORY OF SOCIOLOGY

Philosophical concerns about societal problems and the rise of rational/scientific analyses for solutions to such problems provided the impetus for the birth of sociology. Within sociology, the study of women has been subsumed under the general headings of family, sex, and gender studies, while the substantive work in the field has focused on men and men's lives (Smith, 1974; Nebraska Sociological Feminist Collective, 1983). "In sociology, woman as an object of study is largely ignored. Only in the field of marriage and the family is she seen to exist. Her place in sociology is, in other words, the traditional one assigned to her by the larger society: women's place is in the home" (Ehrlich, 1971:421). This is not surprising given the influence of science, with its patriarchal foundation, on sociology. By referring to women only in the narrow context of family and reproduction, sociology was, and is, in the mainstream of social thought.

In this chapter, we present an overview of historical sociological theory and women's place in it by outlining some of the major assumptions and propositions of a select group of major sociological contributors. The first of these are the positivist, functionalist theorists, who assert the "natural" order of male dominance as a contrast to arguments for women's "rights." The second are the conflict theorists, who describe systems of oppression that systematically restrict groups, and at times include women as one of those groups. Finally, we assess the contributions of alternative perspectives, including activist models such as social work and interactionist perspectives.

1

POSITIVIST/FUNCTIONALIST THEORISTS

Auguste Comte—Sociology as Social Science

Auguste Comte, often referred to as the founder of sociology,[1] is important to the analysis of sociological history because he took the intellectual ideas of such writers as Saint-Simon and Montesquieu and combined them into a comprehensive work. He then claimed that we can study human nature using the same techniques as those of the natural sciences: "The main weight of Comte's argument rests in the assumption that there is a natural order that human beings can comprehend" (Rossides, 1978:130). Prior to Comte's work, the study of society as a historical and empirical entity began in the eighteenth century in France and Scotland (Swingewood, 1984). However, these earlier works simply introduced sociological themes; later Baron de Montesquieu and Giambattista Vico established key foci, such as social change and social class issues, for later sociologists.

Women were addressed in these earliest works only within their familial role because the family was viewed as an institution exemplifying larger social processes. For example, in early analyses of society, the family was considered the most fundamental unit of society, parallel to the biological concept of the cell. Women were discussed only in their relation to this unit. The Italian philosopher Giambattista Vico wrote in *The New Science* that

> Men mean to gratify their bestial lust and abandon their offspring, and they inaugurate the chastity of marriage from which the families arise. The fathers mean to exercise without restraint their paternal power over their clients, and they subject them to the civil powers from which the cities arise. (1744/1948:425)

According to Auguste Comte, women are "constitutionally" inferior to men because their maturation ends in childhood. Therefore, he believed that women become subordinated to men when they marry. Divorce was denied to women since they were simply the pampered slaves of men. Comte claimed that in order for proper societal order and progress to occur in France, it was necessary to have both patriarchal authority and political dictatorship. His *positivism* was a philosophy of stability, based on the permanence of the "true" family unit. He posed the model as an alternative to the "negative" critical, egalitarian philosophy of the Enlightenment and the French Revolution (Kandal, 1988:74), and he concluded that sociology was a method to halt the drift to "a savage communism" and "degrading equality" (Comte, 1854/1877; Schwendinger and Schwendinger, 1974).

Beginning with the work of Comte and others, the study of society shifted from the realm of social philosophy to that of social science. These sociologists

---

[1]He is also referred to as the "father" of sociology, emphasizing the patriarchal history of the discipline.

considered themselves to be scientists of the human order. Part of their responsibility was to define and analyze the mechanisms that organize social order and the people within it. To carry this out, the techniques of the natural sciences were applied to the study of society. Comte drew many comparisons between biology and sociology because he viewed both as *holistic* sciences: Society was a collective organism whereby each of the independent parts served to benefit the whole. This view reflects his perception of social statics and social dynamics.[2]

Comte led the way in sociology, setting the groundwork for a positivist bias by focusing on empirical observations of cause-and-effect relationships. Positivism is illustrative of "normal" science with its claims to objectivity and rationality. However, this science does contain gender biases. To counter the nineteenth-century argument that women were more stupid than men because they had smaller brains, Virginia Wolf commented that "Science, it would seem, is not sexless, she is a man, a father, and infected too" (as quoted in Sydie, 1987:204). This distorted "genderization of science" means that the discipline is dominated by male thought and male activity. When positivist sociology took science as its example for the discipline, it took with it all the difficulties and biases of "normal" science (Sydie, 1987).

Sociological positivism made significant progress following Comte in the works of Herbert Spencer and John Stuart Mill. Mill, in agreement with Comte's pro-science stance, argued that fundamental differences between the natural and social sciences did not exist. In fact, he argued that the goal of social science was the analysis of the laws of society through reverse deductive methods (Mill, 1965).

> The universal laws of human nature are part of the data of sociology, but in using them we must reverse the method of the deductive physical sciences: for while, in these, specific experience commonly serves to verify laws arrived at by deduction, in sociology it is specific experience which suggests the laws, and deduction which verifies them. (Mill:85)

If one had access to the empirical laws, then predicting social outcomes would be possible. Mill's influence on sociological theory was limited, although he and Harriet Taylor Mill strongly influenced the development of liberal feminism (Anderson, 1988).[3] This influence is discussed in more detail in Chapter Two. Herbert Spencer, however, took on a more prominent role in contemporary sociological theory through an emphasis on positivist organicism.

---

[2] *Social statics* refers to the study of how societies survive or remain the same and *social dynamics* is the study of how societies change.

[3] Although many attribute the publication of *The Subjection of Women* (1792) to John Stuart Mill, a convincing argument has been made that, in fact, it was a collaborative effort with Harriet Taylor Mill (see Rossi, 1970). This is an example of women's contributions being made invisible through history by subsuming the wife's identity and productivity under her husband's name.

Herbert Spencer—Evolution/Organicism

The concept of *positivist organicism* centers on the construct of social evolution. According to Spencer, individuals within societies, social institutions, and societies themselves evolved from the simple to the complex just as a single-celled amoeba evolved into an animal, or a more complex organism. His model is termed *organicist* as all parts function to the benefit of the whole organism. This is why it is considered a *functional* argument. The interdependence of the parts makes up the whole, as with a living organism. Some of Spencer's key sociological concepts such as *function, system, structure, equilibrium,* and *institution* (Swingewood, 1984) became the bases for the later theory, structural functionalism.

Two aspects of Spencer's positivist organicism provide early models for the sociological analysis of women. First is the concept of *organicism* itself, which implies an equilibrium or a balance. When all parts work to benefit the whole, society maintains an equilibrium. Women are often analyzed in terms of their "place" in society—that is, their function in the family. As women maintain their place in the institution of the family through their social roles of mother and wife, they help to integrate the family as a unit. This balances the unit in two ways. First, the woman brings female expression into the family unit while the male serves as the link between the family and the other social organizations in society. These paternal and maternal roles and functions create social adaptations in male and female physical and psychic roles and behavior. Positivists argued that women become differentiated, with smaller brains, less intellectual capacity, and more emotional focus than men. Second, it places the family and its members in equilibrium with other institutions. Social action or movements that attempt to eliminate personal or class oppressions, such as feminist movements, are disruptive forces creating social disequilibrium. If change occurs, positivists argued it should come slowly through social evolution.

The second aspect of Spencer's organic equilibrium model as applied to women is the assumption of *linearity*. Given the focus on social evolution within the functionalist framework, these theorists assume that what exists now is an improvement on what came before. Because societies evolve in a linear fashion (from simple to complex), it is dysfunctional to interfere with this evolutionary process through social action, revolution, or other activities aimed at changing the social order, or the status quo. These social actions lead to social disequilibrium.

In his earlier writings, Herbert Spencer did champion laissez-faire rights for individual women and argued that women's nature was not fixed or immutable (Spencer, 1851). As did Mill, he claimed that women had the right to compete freely with men. However, in his later writings, which were influenced by social Darwinism, he argued that women should be denied the right to compete for occupations with men and that it was foolish to educate women to compete for business and political careers because of their smaller brains and weaker bodies (Schwendinger and Schwendinger, 1974). Spencer believed that "if women comprehended all that is contained in the domestic sphere they would ask no other" (1876/1894:774).

Emile Durkheim—Rules for the Sociological Method

The French sociologist Emile Durkheim is best known for applying the scientific method to the discipline of sociology. Although his theory of sociology developed initially along the evolutionary frameworks of Comte and Spencer, with the publication of *The Rules of the Sociological Method* Durkheim went beyond their work. In 1897, he applied the scientific method to the study of suicide (Durkheim, 1897/1963).

Durkheim defined *sociology* as "the science of institutions, their genesis and their functioning" (1982:45). Within this tradition lies the foundation of sociological positivism in contemporary sociology.

The concepts of *social solidarity, cohesion,* and *anomie* and their relationships to an increasingly complex division of labor in society are at the core of Durkheim's analysis. Although Durkheim rarely addressed the specific issue of women's labor, the concepts of *anomie* and *social cohesion* can be applied to the contemporary issue of women's labor-market participation.[4]

Durkheim did include discussions of women in two narrow contexts. The first was the positive nexus of marriage and family: Women fulfilled traditional roles he perceived as functional to the family. The second was the negative nexus of suicide/divorce and sexuality, in which women's sexuality played a role in suicide and divorce (Lehmann, 1991). In each of these connections, Durkheim perceived women as inherently inferior to men—as part of nature, not of society, or perhaps part of a more primitive society.

Within the family, men assume authority, according to Durkheim, because the family is in need of a "chief" (Lehmann, 1991:33). This authority includes control over economic resources and a sexual division of labor within the family. Women's roles are restricted to private activities, which Durkheim imbeds in the inherent (lesser) abilities and the asocial nature of women. He also opposed sexual equality, which he believed was unnatural and primitive (Lehmann, 1994:53). Durkheim then explains the lower suicide rates of women as evidence that they are less involved in public arenas of activity (as are the elderly and children) (Lehmann, 1991:12).

In his arguments on suicide and the beneficial functions of the family, he ignores his own findings that unmarried women have lower suicide rates than married women. This pattern remains today, as does the pattern that unmarried men have higher suicide rates than married men. Lehmann concludes that Durkheim views marriage as upholding the interests of men (high au-

---

[4]Durkheim defined *mechanical* and *organic solidarity* as the forms of social cohesion holding together small simple societies with a simple division of labor (mechanical solidarity) and large complex societies with a complex division of labor (organic solidarity).

thority and low suicide rates for men) and divorce as opposing the interests of men (raising male suicide rates and challenging natural family forms). Durkheim presents women as unaffected or disinterested by the social arrangements of events such as suicide or marriage, but his model in fact argues for the precedence of men over the interest of women (Lehmann, 1994:80).

To each of the functionalists reviewed here—Durkheim, Spencer, and Comte—the inherent, natural state of being a woman creates a division of labor, a hierarchy of male authority, and a structure of morality. This natural state places women under the logical control of men within a patriarchal family and social structure. Patriarchy, then, is assumed as a natural evolutionary form of social organization that protects women from their own nature and enhances the functioning of society.

CONFLICT THEORISTS

Karl Marx—Early Conflict Theories and the Dialectic

Whereas Durkheim focused attention on cohesion and societal solidarity, Karl Marx viewed society as composed of antithetical forces generating social change by the tensions and struggles between conflicting classes. Social progress, therefore, consisted of struggles and strife, making social conflict the core of the historical process. Whereas Durkheim wrote about the influence of a complex division of labor on social solidarity as that solidarity progressed from mechanical to organic, Marx wrote about the exploitation of labor leading to alienation and the formation of antagonistic classes.

The development of Marxism was strongly influenced by the growing labor movements in England and France, as well as the rapid growth of industry combined with capitalist production. Marx's writings introduced many key concepts to the discipline of sociology, including *alienation of labor, materialism* and *dialectics, class formation,* and *class consciousness.* He also addressed the issue of ideology in relation to social, political, and economic conditions and the potential for change.

Marxian writings do contribute to the study of women. Key concepts used in the analysis of the oppression of women include *alienation, economic oppression, use value, reserve labor,* and *dialectic* (Benston, 1969; Rowbotham, 1973). In *Capital* (1849/1949), Marx discussed the general effects of machinery on family life in the domestic industries. In the *Communist Manifesto,* Marx and Engels wrote about women as instruments of production:

> But you Communists would introduce community of women, screams the whole bourgeoisie in chorus. The bourgeoisie sees in his wife a mere instrument of production. He hears that the instruments of production are to be exploited in common, and, naturally, can come to no other conclusion, than that the lot of being common to all will likewise fall to the women. He has not even a suspicion that

the real point aimed at is to do away with the status of women as mere instruments of production. (Marx and Engels, 1847/1970:39)

Frederick Engels, in *The Origin of the Family, Private Property and the State* (1884/1972), did write specifically about the oppression of women within the family:

> Today, in the great majority of cases, the man has to be the earner, the bread-winner of the family, at least among the propertied classes, and this gives him a dominating position which requires no special legal privileges. In the family he is the bourgeois and the wife represents the proletariat. (Engels, 1884/1972: 81–82)

This theme was evident in the 1844 Paris manuscripts, in which Marx criticized the existing forms of marriage as maintaining the basic position of women as property. In *The German Ideology*, Marx (1818–1883/1960) again cited the "natural division of labor" in the family as the basis of property and inequality.

In Marx's writings, women's oppression is an economic factor shaping the political and social structures and women's lives within them. By prioritizing the economic infrastructure of capitalism as the source for social change, Marx is open to critiques of theoretical narrowness. A contemporary theorist to Marx, Max Weber, proposed a set of dimensions in addition to economics that may underlie systems of inequality and create potential for social change.

Max Weber—Status Conflict

Max Weber's writings focus on the interrelationships among class, status, and power. To Weber, *class* is the economic basis of inequality, loosely organized around classes of "haves" and "have-nots." To this he adds social *status*—the notion of honor or prestige that can be bestowed by family background, occupational activities, or consumption patterns. His third dimension, *power*, refers explicitly to political rights and resources. These dimensions overlap significantly in advanced industrial societies, but Weber was interested in the variations among them. For example, a woman may be held in low status by virtue of her gender and have few economic resources or political rights. However, her occupation as nurse may bestow her with a certain amount of status honor in communities that value the nurturing, caretaking roles of women.

For the analysis of women in society, this was an important development because status, or one's position in a social order, is related to power. Women's status in society can be analyzed for disadvantages in both economic and social power, and for the construction of social prestige as it relates to gender and occupational roles. These multiple dimensions are not prioritized by Weber, although he notes the importance of economic resources as a means of accessing the other two dimensions.

Weber also argued for a value-free sociology, or a sociology with a focus on objectivity. In contemporary sociology, this emphasis on objectivity enabled the discipline to adopt scientific models that establish positivist methods and scientific observation. Historically, both the status of observer and the definition of scientific norms have been monopolized by men, and this can trivialize or make invisible women's experiences. This focus on objectivity and the certification of observers excludes women's subjective experiences, making them either "invisible" or "nonscientific" (Nebraska Sociological Feminist Collective, 1983).

ALTERNATIVE MODELS IN TRADITIONAL SOCIOLOGY

Jane Addams—Social Work Model

Although rooted in these historical theories, sociology in the United States developed differently from its European counterpart. Sociology in the United States emphasized ways to redress social problems such as urban crime. This is best exemplified by Jane Addams with the settlement house, Hull-House, in Chicago's West Side slums during the late 1800s and early 1900s (Addams, 1910). A leader in the American social settlement movement, Jane Addams opened Hull-House in 1889, predating the opening of the University of Chicago in 1892. The model for the settlement was, according to Deegan (1988), egalitarian, female dominated, and pragmatic. The networks of social activists and academics that frequented Hull-House, including John Dewey and George Herbert Mead, contributed greatly to the development of *Chicago pragmatism,* which combined "scientific and objective observation with ethical and moral issues to generate a just and liberated society" (Deegan, 1988:6).

Addams published eleven books and hundreds of articles, including five articles in the *American Journal of Sociology.* Most notable was the publication *Hull-House Maps and Papers* in 1893 by the residents of Hull-House, which later influenced many of the male sociologists at the University of Chicago. Addams was what Deegan calls a *cultural feminist* who asserted that female values were superior to male values and that a society built on feminine values would be more "productive, peaceful and just" (Deegan, 1988). This belief was based on the premise that women were biologically superior because of their maternal instinct. These ideas were a strong impetus for Addams's pacifism, which eventually resulted in her receiving the Nobel Peace Prize in 1931.[5] Her emphasis on philanthropy and moral reform highlights her connection with the *social feminists* in France during her lifetime as well as today. The emphasis on women's suffrage, educational access, and pacifism opens this model to the criticisms of class-based theorists—these are the issues of a relatively privileged

---

[5]Two notable women sociologists have won Nobel Peace Prizes, Jane Addams of Chicago and Alva Myrdal of Sweden.

group of "other" women who perform their philanthropic work for women who lack their "advantages" (Kandal, 1988:65).

The academic separation of social work from sociology legitimates the detachment of many sociologists in universities from their research "subjects." Though the topics of research for sociologists often encompass the social problems of the day (e.g., AIDS and prostitution, poverty, health care for the elderly), it is rare that sociologists "do" anything to ameliorate these problems for groups or individuals through their direct sociological action. The split of sociology from social work is a rationale for the scientific, objective claims of the former. The social worker is left with the task of ameliorating individual problems on a temporary basis, given the structural factors that guarantee the continuation of the social problem (Adams, 1971).

The split between social "science" and social "work" is exacerbated by the gender differences in the occupation and the struggle over the definition of the profession that followed in Addams's footsteps. Social work is identified in the mind of the public and in the mind of the academics as a feminine occupation; the helping, nurturing roles of the social worker are associated with traditional parenting roles for women (Toren, 1969:56). Sociologists who study occupations and professions have assigned social workers to the status of "semi-professionals" who labor under increased supervision, recruit members from the lower classes, and work for low wages. In addition, some sociologists argue that social work has no developed theoretical knowledge base. In sum, the historical split of social work, marked by low wages and a largely female workforce, has created a social status in which the contributions of Jane Addams are considered anomalous or an "add-in" to the "great white men of theory" in the sociological discipline. Because Addams's work was based on the everyday lives of immigrant women, she was trivialized and omitted from the canons of the discipline; her ideas of a normative structure based on peace and justice, derived from a feminine norm, have been largely ignored.

George Herbert Mead—Symbolic Interactionism

Symbolic interactionism, and specifically the work of George Herbert Mead, has its roots in the same Chicago school that ignored Addams's work, and dominated sociology in the United States for the first part of the twentieth century. W. I. Thomas influenced the Chicago school and is probably best known for his quote that describes the individual response to the world: "if men [sic] define situations as real they are real in their consequences" (Thomas and Thomas, 1928:572).[6] *Symbolic interactionism,* often referred to as *microsociology,* is a perspective focusing on the relationship between the personal and the

---

[6]It is of some interest that the famous W. I. Thomas quote later coined by Robert Merton in "The Thomas Theorem" in 1938 was initially published in *The Child in America,* a book coauthored with Dorothy Thomas, whose name was dropped as an originator of this quote.

structural. Symbolic interactionism focuses on the interplay between social structure (macrosociology)—defined as process and habits or patterns of interacting—and personality (microsociology) (Mead, 1934). This theme emphasizes human society as being in process, rather than as static. Symbolic interactionists also recognize that individual acts and interpretations take place within the context of groups and institutions and that individuals have varying resources within those settings to create change (Manis and Meltzer, 1978). This interpretative approach highlights the symbolic meaning attached to social life and has profound implications for understanding women in society. For example, Kathryn Pyne Addelson (1991, 1994) uses the analysis of the abortion debate and a combined feminist–symbolic interactionist definition of ownership to illustrate some of the moral issues in public problems. Kristin M. Langellier (1994) uses phenomenology and feminism to analyze the complex communication involved in quilt making.

CONTEMPORARY THEORETICAL APPROACHES TO THE STUDY OF WOMEN

Three contemporary approaches in sociology specifically address women in society: the structural-functionalist approach, the sex-roles perspective, and the conflict perspective, each of which is linked to a sex-roles model. The social work and interactionist frameworks also provide models for addressing the practice of a sociology by and about women. Later, we argue for developing a dialectic between these approaches and feminist theory to propose a framework for a sociology of women.

Functionalist Theory—Study of Men's Culture

Functionalist theory in sociology is inherently conservative and associated with the works of Auguste Comte, Herbert Spencer, and Emile Durkheim. Contemporary functionalist theorists emphasize social stability and harmony, specifically those factors contributing to the maintenance of societal stability or to gradual social change. Social change is framed as a natural evolutionary response to imbalances between functions and the structure of social roles. Social factors that encourage stability are considered functional and factors that promote rapid social change are considered dysfunctional.

In this framework, the focus on women is on their functions and roles in society. As women's roles contribute to stability, they are seen as functional; as they contribute to rapid change, such as entering the paid labor market in ever-increasing numbers, they are seen as dysfunctional (Park, 1967).

In his classic work on prostitution (1937), Kingsley Davis provides a functional analysis of women. Davis analyzes prostitution in terms of its functions and dysfunctions in the social order. He concludes that prostitution serves the sexual needs of masses of men including armies, the perverted, and the ugly. He classically ignores the issue of why women are prostitutes and the everyday lives of prostitutes, including the oppression, violence, and victimization of these women. He assumes that women exist to serve the sexual needs of men and focuses on the function of prostitution, not the individual experiences of prostitutes. This is consistent with the functional analysis framework where the function takes on more importance than the individual. The potential dysfunctions of a social activity remain unexamined if it is part of the status quo.

Perhaps the most influential sociological writing about women from a functionalist perspective is by Talcott Parsons. Parsons saw the nuclear family as inevitable in an industrialized society due to isolation of the family: the social differentiation that arises from the isolation, geographic mobility, and the needs of an industrialized nation for a trained workforce. From this isolation arise two distinct roles for men and women, with men taking the active instrumental role and women primarily taking the socioemotional role in the family (Parsons, 1949; Parsons and Bales, 1955). Role theory is a refinement of this traditional orientation.

Sex Roles—A Focus in Sociology of Women

Talcott Parsons paved the way for discussing the sexual division of labor in terms of a language of roles:

> the influence of functionalism is apparent in widespread, uncritical use of terms like "sex roles," "the female role," and "the male role," terms that obscure not only differences of power between women and men but also the presence of conflict. (Thorne, 1982:8)

The sex-roles tradition in sociology primarily focuses on men's worlds and women's places within these patriarchal spheres.

Arlie Hochschild (1973) identifies four types of research in the sociology of sex roles. First, research focuses on sex differences, analyzing emotive and cognitive differences between men and women such as spatial ability or levels of self-esteem. Often psychologists conduct this research, and then sociologists refer to it. Second, there is research that analyzes role strain. For example, Talcott Parsons's work differentiates sex roles and then delineates the norms that define these roles (Parsons, 1949). Both of these research models assume the division between men and women is functional and look to explain differences from a balance perspective. Type three includes sex-roles research analyzing women as a minority group, especially in terms of discrimination, prejudice, and women's social and economic marginality (Hacker, 1951). The fourth type is the "politics of caste" perspective, which is similar to the minority perspective but focuses on the differences between men and women in terms of vested interests and power struggles. These last two types take the differences between men and women as a problem to be explained (Hochschild, 1973), and areas for potential social change. They do not explain how these changes occur.

Types three and four "radicalize" sex-roles research and are a result of the influence of feminist theory on sociological thought (Rossi, 1969). Alice Rossi claims that female graduate students bridge the disciplines of sociology and feminist theory because "feminist writings from Kate Millet and Shulamith Firestone to Juliet Mitchell have been making their way into Sociology through recent generations of female graduate students" (1969:3).

Conflict Theory and the Relationship Between Sex Roles and Sex Stratification

Sex stratification theory concentrates on women's position in the paid labor market, in contrast to the sex-roles research model (Chafetz, 1988). This raises the possibility of a conflict approach to explain the origin, maintenance, and change of women's position in society. One example of a status-conflict model that draws on Weberian notions of multidimensional inequality is represented in the work by Randall Collins.

Randall Collins argues that gender inequality varies across societal types but posits three constant social facts that fix women as the sexual property of men. *All* human beings have (1) a strong drive for sexual gratification and (2) a strong resistance to coercion. The third fact is that males are usually larger and stronger than females: "males thus become the sexual aggressors, and females generally adopt a defensive posture" (Collins, 1975:231). The basic feature of sex stratification, then, is the institution of women as sexual property, and not inequality in the labor market, with a relatively permanent claim by men to exclusive sexual rights to particular women.

Collins further argues that gender inequality and coercion will vary according to two social structures: constraint by the political organizations of a society (e.g., family, law) and the market positions and resources of men and women. In the first instance, Collins proposes that the greater the concentration of force and political power within the household, the greater the power of men over women "in terms of menial labor, ritual difference and standards of sexual morality" (Collins, 1975:283).

Collins thus sees domination of females as rooted in biology—but a biology linked to sexual access as opposed to reproduction and private property. Economic and political structures mediate the extent of this subordination, with the highest dominance/subordinance inequalities existing in the households of preindustrial, stratified societies. The lowest rates of inequality are in affluent market societies, depending upon the extent of the equalization of women's economic positions. Collins notes that women continue to be in subordinate economic and political enclaves in these affluent market societies, but this varies over time and geography.

Conflict Theories and the Use of the Dialectic and Feminist Theory

Conflict theory, with roots in the writings of Karl Marx, maintains that social change occurs through a dialectical process. Many of the conflict theories in sociology developed in opposition to traditionally held beliefs. This process itself illustrates the dialectic. The dialectic describes inevitable contradictions and conflicts that lead to change. Given any thesis (e.g., inequality), an antithesis will develop. The contradiction between unequal groups based on day-to-day differences in interests creates the conflict between the thesis and antithesis. From this a new synthesis will emerge, which is not necessarily equality. This synthesis then becomes the new thesis with an ensuing antithesis, and so forth.

We can use the concept of the dialectic to portray changes in society, theory, organizations, groups, and so on. For example, as shown in Figure 1-1, in sociological theory the traditional Parsonian approach to gender roles can be viewed as a thesis from which an antithesis—radical-feminist theory—would stand in contradiction. From this, sociology developed sex-roles research. This new synthesis would become the new thesis, and a feminist critical response to sex-roles research would become the new antithesis. The development of a sociology of women could then be perceived as a more recent synthesis of ideas.

As groups in society come in conflict over scarce resources, or even over ideas, this conflict produces change. The focus in conflict theory is on the eco-

FIGURE 1-1   The Dialectic

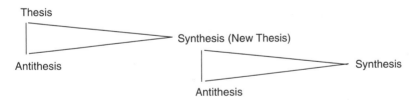

Thesis

Synthesis (New Thesis)

Antithesis

Synthesis

Antithesis

EXAMPLE:

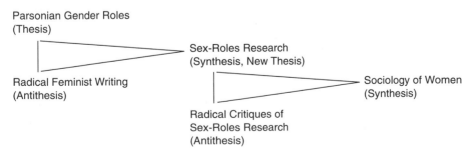

Parsonian Gender Roles
(Thesis)

Sex-Roles Research
(Synthesis, New Thesis)

Radical Feminist Writing
(Antithesis)

Sociology of Women
(Synthesis)

Radical Critiques of
Sex-Roles Research
(Antithesis)

nomics, specifically the competition for scarce resources among groups and its influence on all other social relationships. Contemporary conflict theories often expand this focus to include multidimensional components to describe conflict and inequities in societal structures. The work of Max Weber with his focus on power, status, and wealth as they describe societal inequalities exemplifies this position (Weber, 1947), as does Collins's emphasis on sexual access and division of power.

In conflict theory, we assume that women's position in society is derived from unequal distributions of wealth and power. As stated earlier, sex stratification theory concentrates on women's position in the paid labor market (Chafetz, 1984). Because of the focus on a patriarchal/capitalist economy, much of women's work (caretaking, volunteerism, etc.) becomes invisible. Women's labor has been analyzed primarily in relation to the wage economy, ignoring the nonwage economy. When nonwage work is analyzed, it is often in terms of its contributions to the paid economy (i.e., women's work in the home as it contributes to providing a comfortable atmosphere for the proletariat, or to consumer patterns). Conflict theorists consider how unpaid labor serves the needs of the bourgeoisie through the production of surplus value and the protection of profits. However, they often ignore the life-span issues for women of day-to-day caretaking, including the effects on family life, self-esteem, sexuality, and so on. Collins ignores the heterosexist assumption in his work: that all women and men engage in roles defined by the heterosexual norms. How, then, does his model explain the lives of lesbians? How does his work contribute to an understanding of relations among women and men who stand in opposition to the status quo?

LIMITATIONS OF TRADITIONAL THEORIES

There is an inherent flaw in using only the historical views of women. These theories are based on male experience, patriarchal structure, and a masculine paradigm. Women are "fitted" into a theoretical model that developed without women's experiences as a framework or validation point.

> The problem here is not a simple one, because liberal political theory and its empiricist epistemology, Marxism, critical theory, psychoanalysis, functionalism, structuralism, deconstructionism, hermeneutics, and the other theoretical frameworks we have explored both do and do not apply to women and to gender relations. On the one hand, we have been able to use aspects or components of each of these discourses to illuminate our subject matters. . . .
>
> On the other hand, it has never been women's experiences that have provided the grounding for any of the theories from which we borrow. . . . When we begin inquiries with women's experiences instead of men's we quickly encounter phenomena (such as emotional labor or the positive aspects of "relational" personality structures) that were made invisible by the concepts and categories of these theories. (Harding, 1986:646)

In the next chapter, we develop a theory of women's lives and women's experiences. This framework is not merely a remodification of old sex roles. Instead, we look for feminist antitheses to sex-roles, traditional functionalist, and conflict models and propose a sociology of women as a synthesis. We draw on a range of women's studies, ethnic studies, symbolic interactionist, and social work models to posit an antithesis.

TWO

Feminist Approaches
to the Study of Women

The women's movement and the discipline of women's studies led to the development of feminist theories that influence the way in which sociologists analyze women's position in society. Feminist theories are very diverse and have changed dramatically since their beginnings. What follows is a systematic review of major feminist theories, drawing on the conceptual framework outlined by Jaggar and Rothenberg in *Feminist Frameworks* (1984).

THE DEVELOPMENT OF A FEMINIST THEORY

In the 1960s, feminist political goals focused on establishing women as equal to men. After centuries of being ignored, excluded, and trivialized by patriarchal disciplines, women sought inclusion as the objects of investigations. Traditional theories were often modified by feminists to account for women's oppression. By concentrating on women's equal inclusion into these past theoretical frameworks, women's similarities to men were emphasized (Gross, 1986).

A shift in feminist politics occurred when feminists directed their theories to account for women's autonomy—"that is, to women's right to political, social, economic and intellectual self-determination" (Gross, 1986:193). Gross outlines five points where feminist theories of autonomy contrast with earlier theories of equality. First, women become the subjects as well as the objects of knowledge. By producing knowledge, women's ways of knowing are validated. Second, the methods, procedures, presumptions, and techniques of previous

16

theories are put into question. Third, using the theory of autonomy, feminists develop perspectives not just on or about women and women's issues but about a wide range of topics, including other theories. Fourth, they do not simply assert either/or alternatives but instead work through patriarchal texts. They no longer simply condemn or accept given discourses. These existing discourses are now analyzed, examined, and debated. Finally, feminist theory emphasizes social institutions and social action, presenting alternative frameworks for social change (Gross, 1986:194).

FEMINIST FRAMEWORKS

Women's studies approaches that some sociologists include are the liberal-feminist tradition, Marxist feminism, radical feminism, socialist feminism,[1] and to a lesser extent, the newer concepts of cultural feminism and poststructural feminism. These theories are similar in that they focus on the oppression of women in society; however, they differ in their definition of the causes of women's oppression as well as in the solutions they offer for societal or individual change.

Liberal Feminism

In the liberal-feminist tradition, the cause of women's oppression is rooted in individual or group lack of opportunity and education. The solution for change is for women to gain opportunities primarily through the institutions of education and economics. The focus of liberal feminism is on the individual and on equality. The social groundwork for this theory arose during the French Revolution and the Enlightenment in Western Europe. These massive social changes provided both political and moral arguments for the ideas of "progress, contract, nature, and reason" that broke traditional social ties and norms (Kandal, 1988:5). The assumption is that if women are allowed equal access to compete, they will succeed. Liberal feminists typically omit a systematic analysis of recurring structural factors and assume that societal barriers can be overcome by individual effort and governmental intervention. They also ignore the ways in which societal and institutional discrimination can influence individual choices to reproduce patterned inequality.

The liberal-feminist tradition dates to 1779 when Mary Wollstonecraft published *A Vindication of the Rights of Women* (1779). This was the period of the great "liberal thinkers" and the development of social contract theories. Philosophers such as Rousseau argued for the rationality of *man*, holding that all *mankind* had the capacity to reason but that women, by nature, should be

---

[1]This categorization of feminist theories into four frameworks was developed by Jaggar and Rothenberg in *Feminist Frameworks* (1984).

confined to domestic education and tasks. Mary Wollstonecraft, Aphra Behn, and other writers of the time asserted that women also had the capacity to reason and, therefore, should have equal rights with men (Spender, 1983). Wollstonecraft further maintained that women's inferior intellect was due to the lack of quality education, which resulted in unequal opportunities.

The liberal-feminist tradition was further influenced by the works of Harriet Taylor (*The Enfranchisement of Women*) and John Stuart Mill (*The Subjection of Women*). Taylor eventually married Mill and coauthored many of the works that are central to his reputation. Taylor, however, died before Mill published *The Subjection of Women* and he dedicated it as "a memento for Harriet." In fact, it was a reworking of *The Enfranchisement of Women*, but it was a narrower and less consistent argument than the original essay written by Harriet Taylor (Schwendinger and Schwendinger, 1974).

The focus of these works was on the equal capacity and capability of women. They contradicted theories that women were inherently inferior or superior and that differences between men and women were attributable to individual intellectual and emotional differences. Specifically, in *The Subjection of Women,* Mill made a plea for women's suffrage and argued for women's equal claim to their children, for the equality of married women before the law, and for the right of married women to control their own property (Mill, 1792/1983).

Mill traced the causes of women's oppression to the customary attitudes of individual men. Here the focus was on male oppressors—their improper moral education led them to develop selfish desires for power. This created a *political man* with desires for power in political, economic, and family relationships. It is not surprising then that Mill's solution to women's oppression was legalistic and moral. He promoted the education of women and appealed to male compassion. It is interesting to note that when Mill published *The Subjection of Women,* the information he presented was fairly well known. The ideas, however, did not receive attention until he published them.

There are many limitations to Mill's arguments. He did not support divorce laws, yet he saw the marriage contract as a patriarchal form of control. He ignored class and race differences among women. By raising the economic demands of equal pay for equal work, he represented the interests of middle-class women. By arguing that married women and single women should work, both Taylor and Mill failed to address the problems of the "double day" for childrearing women. Mill assumed that individual men achieved their social and economic status in free competition with each other in a capitalist society. Therefore, women should also have the opportunity to achieve status by their efforts—that is, a right to compete, with an emphasis on legal equality and access to rights. Mill assumed that fair competition would lead to equality, although he ignored other structural constraints such as the lack of safe and accessible birth control or the vulnerability of women to sexual assault both at home and in the public sphere. Finally, Mill claimed that women's *nature* included a lesser ability than men's to engage in abstract reasoning. He argued that male and female roles were complementary in the ideal relations for men and women (Schwendinger and Schwendinger, 1974).

Liberal feminism in the twentieth century. Many of the criticisms of Mill's and Taylor's work remain unresolved by contemporary liberal feminists because much of twentieth-century liberal feminism incorporates similar ideas. Some have even asserted that many of the goals expressed in the nineteenth century, including the need for equal education and the right to vote, have been attained. This has led some to conclude that women are no longer oppressed.

Alice S. Rossi, in "Sentiment and Intellect" (1970), dismissed structural analyses of economic oppression for women in favor of Taylor's and Mill's arguments for legal rights. In *The Feminine Mystique* (1963), Betty Friedan highlighted the restrictive roles for women in marriage and motherhood, pointing out the dissatisfactions of suburban, white, educated, middle-class, heterosexual "housewives" in the United States. She urged women to leave the home and find meaningful work in the labor force and public sphere. Writing in the 1980s, in *The Second Stage* (1981), Friedan finally examines the problems in these multiple roles for women and exhorts women to work with men to change public values, leadership practices, and institutions, with the goal of personal fulfillment. Each of these liberal feminist approaches questions the boundaries of gender differences but is unable to articulate a direction for societal change.

Contemporary liberal feminists in politics are probably best exemplified by such organizations as the National Organization for Women (NOW). NOW's primary purposes are to promote education and equal access to employment and to challenge gender roles that restrict women's opportunities. Much of the criticism of liberal feminism focuses on white, middle-class women's roles and the goal of assimilation into the status quo.

However, there has been a radicalizing of the liberal tradition (Eisenstein, 1981). "Although all liberal feminists adopt the ideas of freedom of choice, individualism, and equality of opportunity, they differ on how self-conscious they are about the patriarchal, economic, and racial bias of these ideas" (Eisenstein, 1981:229). As liberal feminism develops along more radical lines, it begins to adopt some principles of the Marxist and radical feminists, focusing on the area of economic rights. Without a clear statement of social change, particularly for women of color, lesbians, and poor and working-class women, only individual women can benefit from the liberal-feminist social change model.

Marxist Feminism

Traditional Marxist feminists trace the oppression of women to the beginnings of private property. The cause of women's oppression is linked to social organization of the economic order. The private ownership class system is inherently oppressive and white males hold the privileged positions within it. The component that distinguishes Marxist feminism from other feminist theories is that capitalism or class oppression is the primary oppression. Class oppression is specifically related to the way in which capitalism works to hold women in degraded positions. Within capitalist systems, women are used as a cheap pool of reserve labor that deflates overall wages and establishes a sex-segregated workforce with differential pay scales. In addition, through free labor in the homes, women provide a free service to capitalists, which becomes a hidden tax on all wage-earning workers. In addition, women reproduce the labor force within the private sphere of the home. Women are also consumers who purchase capitalist products over which they have little control, thereby reinforcing their own oppression.

Marxist feminists presume that only after economic oppression is resolved can patriarchal oppression be eradicated. Therefore, in order for society to change, it will require radical social change of the economic structure and destruction of class-based inequality. The focus here is on structural factors of oppression as opposed to individual opportunities.

An example of classic Marxist feminism is Friedrich Engels's *The Origin of the Family, Private Property and the State* (1884/1972), which outlines the link between the introduction of private property and women's oppression in a class society. He describes the connection between the patriarchal oppression of women in the family and the oppression of the proletariat by the bourgeoisie. Sheila Rowbotham also reflects on the connection between patriarchy and capitalism in *Woman's Consciousness, Man's World* (1973). In capitalism, the ability to impose the notion of the family, childhood, femininity, and sexuality reinforces and maintains the power of bourgeois man.

Benston's (1969) work also reflects the early Marxist feminist tradition, as she emphasizes the importance of *exchange value* of labor, which is defined as wages in a market economy. Exchange value, or the value of work, is determined by the capitalist system as the bourgeoisie seek profits. The profits of capitalism come from the production of *surplus value*—that is, the gap between workers' wages and the market price for a product, which owners collect as profits. Owners' attempts to control this surplus value put them in conflict with the workers, who seek to maximize their own wages. Given this conflict, the notion of exchange value takes on special significance to women because of all their unpaid labor within the family, including reproduction, child care, and household labor. In the chapter on work (see Chapter Five), we discuss the effects of nonwage labor on the exchange value of women's work in greater detail.

More recently, von Werlhof (1988) and Mies (1988) have expanded Marxist definitions of class to incorporate women. Claudia von Werlhof argues that housewives and peasants are systematically excluded from definitions of the economy in traditional Marxism. She proposes that more attention be paid to imperialism in non-European, Third World nations that affects the labor of the nonwage workers, especially peasants. She questions the two-class scheme in Marxist analyses of exploitation and accumulation and proposes three tiers. The first tier consists of capitalists, including those who use imperialism to expand their sources of accumulation, not only through wage labor but also through expropriation of nonwage work and material resources. The second tier consists of wage workers, mostly white and male. Finally, the third tier is composed of nonwage workers, mostly female, and including housewives, and in Third World countries, subsistence producers in colonized territories (male and female) (von Werlhof, 1988). Because many of the women bridge both the second and third tier, this often requires more complex analyses.

Maria Mies examines the effects of capitalist development on the conditions of poor rural women in India. The penetration of capitalism has often separated women from their traditional production activities and has instituted a disadvantageous change in the sexual division of labor. First, the market roles of women have been undermined because the exchange roles are taken over by nontribal men. Second, the introduction of new technologies often geographically uproots women and their families. The move to new environmental niches may undermine women's traditional production activities (they lack materials for making traditional baskets or mats) and make them economically vulnerable (Mies, 1988:39).

In both of these adaptations, sex inequalities are rooted in capitalist intervention. Whether through imperialism or the export of technology, the capitalist drive for profit is a mechanism of oppression. Mies argues that it is inadequate to pose the question of priority of "class contradictions and the man-woman contradiction" (Mies, 1988:45). She suggests that traditional Marxist approaches defining women's liberation as only a tactical goal in the process of class struggle misses the main point of both contradictions.

Radical Feminism

Within the many radical-feminist perspectives, most fundamental of oppressions is patriarchy. Multiple oppressions such as racism, able-bodiedism, heterosexism, and classism also take on significance in their relationship to patriarchal oppression. In order for women to be free of oppression, the patriarchal structure of society must be changed.

According to Jaggar and Rothenberg, radical-feminist theorists argue the fundamental nature of the oppression of women (patriarchy) over other forms of oppressions (race, class) in a variety of ways:

1. Women were historically the first oppressed group.
2. Women's oppression is ubiquitous, existing in all societies.
3. Women's oppression is the hardest form of oppression to eradicate, and it will not be eliminated by other social changes such as the abolition of class society.

4. Women's oppression causes the most suffering to its victims; however, this suffering may go unrecognized.
5. Women's oppression provides a conceptual model for understanding all other forms of oppression. (1984:86)

Shulamith Firestone's *The Dialectic of Sex* (1970) illustrates this last point. Firestone argues that women's oppression is biologically based since women are tied to the childbirth and childrearing processes, which continually place them in positions of dependence on men to survive. Firestone calls for the women's movement to participate in a "biological revolution" freeing women from their biological oppression. She also makes the argument that the analysis of women's oppression gives us the tools to understand all other forms of oppression, including racism and classism.

A key component of patriarchy within radical-feminist analysis is the control of women through violence. Carole Sheffield (1984) argues that violence and the threat of violence against women by men represent the need of the patriarchal system to deny women control of their own bodies and lives. This violence takes place in the forms of sexual assault, incest, battering, and sexual harassment of women by men. The notion of *sexual terrorism* as a tool of the patriarchy was introduced in its powerful cross-cultural and military forms in Susan Brownmiller's groundbreaking work, *Against Our Will* (1975). Sheffield further documents the ideology of male superiority and control in the propaganda of the popular media and academic "sciences" and identifies other components of terrorism as the indiscriminate and arbitrary aspects of violence (all women are potential victims) as it is institutionalized through family socialization, formalized education, and legal processes.

Suzanne Pharr analyzes the combined effects of sexism and homophobia through heterosexism. She defines *heterosexism* as the systematic display of homophobia in the institutions of society, such that they enforce compulsory heterosexuality, especially in "that bastion of patriarchal power, the nuclear family" (1988:17). The privileges accorded to heterosexual women and men, and denied to lesbians and gay men, include fundamental civil rights as well as social and emotional support systems. These heterosexual privileges commit women to the patriarchal family structure as a "safe" and rewarded status.

Lesbian feminism as represented by the works of such authors as Andrea Dworkin and Charlotte Bunch also fits within the framework of radical feminism. Here women's oppression is seen as the first form of oppression as well as the deepest. The personal is political, and the politics of liberal feminists have often denied lesbian existence in an effort to gain support from men who hold power within the patriarchy. Women who share their lives and their emotions with their oppressors (inherent within heterosexual lifestyles) are unable to confront their oppressors because of their economic and social vulnerability. Lesbian feminists argue that one's freedom to make choices in the personal sphere, such as sexual preference, creates possibilities for eradicating individual oppression as well as the oppression of others. The overall assessment of radical feminists is that patriarchy is universal and provides insights into the oppression of women in all cultural and political settings. They assert that women's oppression as women is likely to continue in liberal or Marxist state systems through the connections of sexual violence, struggles for control of women's bodies, and the push for heterosexual and male privileges.

Socialist Feminism

Among socialist feminists, both patriarchy and class are regarded as primary oppressions. One form of oppression does not take precedence over the other. Socialist feminism involves the

> refocusing and redirection, by feminism, of the historical Marxian approach . . . toward understanding the structure of women's oppression, particular in terms of the sex-class structure, the family, and the hierarchical sexual division of labor. (Eisenstein, 1979)

For example, the introduction of private property was associated with both class oppression (control of property and production resources by the bourgeoisie) and the oppression of women (patriarchal laws that grant men control of women's property through marriage).

Within a socialist-feminist framework the solutions for change involve radical social changes of all societal institutions. Juliet Mitchell's book, *Woman's Estate* (1971), laid the groundwork for socialist feminism. In it, she describes the politics of oppression as a consequence of both patriarchal and class oppression. She identifies the central socialist-feminist constructs for analyzing the dimensions of oppression as production, reproduction socialization, and sexuality. In her later work, *Psychoanalysis and Feminism* (1974), Mitchell clearly juxtaposes the concepts of patriarchy and capitalism. She rejects the notion that equal access or economic revolution or productive control alone will eliminate women's oppression. She identifies the ideological mode of patriarchy as separate and distinct from the economic mode of production. Both forms of oppression must be eradicated to liberate women.

Heidi Hartmann (1981a), another leading feminist in the socialist framework, claims that the basis of patriarchy is the sexual division of labor that exists in virtually all societies. The material basis of patriarchy—the control over women's labor—allows men to control women's access to productive resources. As childrearers, women reproduce patriarchal social relations, including intergenerational male-female relationships. Through this familial socialization process, the partnership of patriarchy and capitalism is legitimated. Capitalism joins forces with patriarchy to dominate women's labor and sexuality by reinforcing and developing the ideology that rationalizes women's oppression.

It may be that socialist feminism is "nothing less than the confluence of Marxist, radical, and more arguable, psychoanalytic streams of feminist thought" (Tong, 1989:173). Mitchell and Hartmann propose a dual systems approach, in which the parallel oppressions of patriarchy and capitalism are analyzed. Jaggar (1983) suggests a bridging of the insights of Marxist and radical perspectives through the concept of *alienation*. Marxists posit that work is the central human activity that becomes alienated under capitalism as workers are separated from control of their labor. This alienation extends to gender-specific work that is affected by both patriarchy and capitalism. Women are alienated from their bodies, their reproductive labor, and their mothering roles. Childbearing alienates through patriarchal and capital-producing birthing practices; motherhood becomes a nonwage labor that gives privilege to heterosexual women but only within the confines of the isolated nuclear family. Finally, women are alienated from their intellect by the control of the intellectual marketplace and the schools by the ideologies of capitalism and patriarchy.

Cultural Feminism

The focus of cultural feminism is that femininity is the most desirable form of human behavior. In a rejection of the masculine ideal and the devaluing labels placed on femininity by the patriarchal world, cultural feminists redefine femininity in a positive framework (Brownmiller, 1984). In early feminist work, this often takes the form of utopian theory, such as in Charlotte Perkins Gilman's *Herland* (1979).

Within sociology, Jessie Bernard's *The Female World* (1981) defines women's existence as a separate and unique reality from the male world, and although the male world and female world influence each other, the analysis of the female world is worthy of its own independent study. Bernard argues that women exist in a unique women's culture, or sphere, with its own governing values and norms. The female world is unique in that it includes (1) an integrating system, pivotal to kinship; (2) a love/duty ethos; and (3) a culture bounded by a distinct awareness of verbal and nonverbal behavior and distinctive technologies.

Research by Gilligan (1982) and Belenky and others (1986) focuses on the development of women's perceptions of the world, including both intellectual and moral development. They propose, in contrast to former male-focused normative models, variations of a process by which women develop their understanding of the world. This understanding takes place in the context of social institutions, including families and schools, that are based on male-defined norms. They each argue that most women (and some men) construct knowledge and decisions by integrating "separate" (e.g., linear, authority-based) ways of knowing with "connected" (e.g., empathic, person-based) modes. The fusion of these two processes leads to a constructed knowledge that is the basis for a female-normed model of development, which is posited as a more "authentic voice" for women and for society.

Cultural feminism often failed, however, to break from the tradition of using dichotomized definitions for gender. Merely specifying new women-oriented definitions and a different hierarchy of gender does not challenge those unequal power structures that control the cultural evaluations of masculinity and femininity; nor does it take into systematic account the patterns of ethnocentrism that distort the cultures of women in subordinate groups.

Poststructuralist Feminism

Until recently the poststructuralists were referred to as the French feminists because many of the writings were done in Paris and translated from the French into English. Simone de Beauvoir is a core figure in this field who, in *The Second Sex* (1952/1974), discusses how man has come to define himself as the "self" and woman as the "other." From this initial dichotomy woman is not only different from man but also inferior to man. According to Tong, "If woman (the other) threatens man (the self) then in order for the man (the self) to be free, he must subordinate the woman (the other)" (1989:202).

The poststructural feminists focus on individual solutions even though the key to oppression is often structural, such as economic discrimination. There is no escape from one's "womanness" and the limitations that patriarchal society has placed on women. If a woman wants to stop being the second sex, the other, she must overcome the forces of circumstance. De Beauvoir recommends three strategies: First, women must go to work even though working in a capitalist system is exploitative and oppressive. It is only through working that women will be able to control their own destiny. Second, women need to become intellectuals because intellectual activity involves thinking, looking, and defining as opposed to being looked at, thought about, and defined. Third, women should work toward a socialist transformation of society that will assist in addressing the subject/object and self/other conflicts (Tong, 1989:210–211).

Poststructuralist feminists reject traditional assumptions about truth and reality; in fact, they reject the possibility of defining woman at all. Simone de Beauvoir poses the classic poststructuralist question: "Are there women?" Cultural feminists affirm that there are women by defining women in terms of their activities or cultural attributes. Poststructuralists, in contrast, disagree and attack the category and concept of *woman* as reflecting the definitions of woman imposed by men. Their insight into the problems of creating overarching definitions of experiences, when faced with the cultural diversity of social categories, is an important contribution. The effort to critique liberal notions of the abstract "human" and to destabilize general categories of social identity, including race, class, and gender, are key processes (Bordo, 1990). Poststructuralists refer to this process as *deconstruction,* in which all concepts involving women are deconstructed or analyzed, presumably outside of the traditional biases and assumptions of the patriarchal language. According to the poststructural feminists, "any attempt to define woman is politically reactionary and ontologically mistaken" (Tong, 1989:212).

Women of Color and Colonization

An important part of our work is to examine theories in women's studies and sociology that can account for the experiences of women of color in the United States and throughout the world. Race and ethnic relations are often studied as a separate field within sociology, and the overlap with sex stratification has been largely ignored. In women's studies, the political concern for issues faced by women of color has not been systematically addressed in the theoretical models.

Zinn et al. (1986) argue persuasively that women of color and women from working-class backgrounds face barriers to their participation in the production or monitoring of knowledge in women's studies, as well as in the traditional disciplines. These barriers include underrepresentation as faculty, staff, students, and researchers in the elite institutions that carry on this work. Some of the many consequences of this underrepresentation include the uncritical development of concepts that distort the lives of women of color; the lack of editorial, review, and publication opportunities for women of color; and the development of curricula and pedagogical practices that exclude women of color as students and teachers (Zinn et al., 1986).

Zinn and her coauthors also critique the range of feminist theories for their lack of synthesis with race and cultural issues. They argue that the study of race and class in women's studies and feminist theory has three common dimensions: (1) the treatment of race and class as secondary to sex subordination; (2) the perfunctory treatment of race and class because we "lack information that would allow us to incorporate them in the analysis" (1986:296); and (3) a focus on descriptions of cultural norms and problems for women in subordinate race and class positions. They conclude that these are inadequate for developing feminist theory and argue for attention to the structural factors that intersect to create sex, class, and race inequality.

bell hooks argues that we must not abdicate responsibility for responding to theoretical and practical work by "different others" (1989:47). Such a stance implies that women of color represent a group so removed from the experiences of white women that we cannot address their work critically or theoretically. She further argues that the omission of work by women of color constitutes racist scholarship.

We find one useful structural theory in sociology, not yet discussed, that we incorporate into our sociology of women as an expansion of feminist theory—the colonization model of race and class inequality. Robert Blauner (1972) set out the initial framework of the model by describing African American oppression in the United States. He argues that racial oppression arises from the colonizing efforts of imperialism. For African Americans, this initial colonization from the United States took place not as a classic colonization or capture of home territory but as a colonization of groups of people through capture and transport to a slavery system.

The historical and contemporary variations in this colonization process must be emphasized. As both Mies (1988) and von Werlhof (1988) note in Marxist feminist analysis, the concept of imperialism can be traced throughout capitalist relations and may include ethnic as well as race relations. As Blauner argues, the concept of race imperialism can be applied in noncapitalist as well as capitalist economies.

Colonization is accomplished through three major steps. The first is the involuntary entry and subordination of one group by a dominant group. The enslavement of blacks by whites throughout the seventeenth, eighteenth, and nineteenth centuries in the United States was accomplished by capture in Africa and involuntary transport to the "New World." In general, this conquest of people (possibly including territorial capture) is driven by profit motives. The human labor or material resources of the indigenous group are expropriated by the dominant group through force.

The second aspect of colonization is the destruction of those cultural factors that might lead to resistance against the dominant group. For whites who dominated in the slave system, this meant the destruction of African institutions, such as religious organizations, the family, and the educational process. Those cultural norms and behaviors of the indigenous groups were broken up deliberately through the dispersal of slaves across plantations (Blauner, 1972). Thus family, religious, and linguistic ties were effectively broken. The dominant whites then replaced African tribal religions with a measure of Christianity, restricted education to those skills that would enhance profits, structured laws that placed power in the hands of all whites over all blacks, and distorted family relations to meet the reproductive needs of a slave-based economy.

The final aspect of colonization is the structuring of an economic and a social system based on race privilege. This race privilege constructs legal and economic barriers that restrict opportunities for the subordinate group in housing, employment, income, education, and lifestyle. In addition, it creates an underlying ethnocentrism that distorts the major social institutions, as well as day-to-day interaction. For example, ethnocentrism dictates that students will learn about the contributions of white Anglo Saxon literature, art, history, and customs, perhaps to the exclusion of all others. This education will also take place in the language of the dominant group and will be administered by representatives of the dominant group.

Mario Barrera (1982) expands the original colonization models to include several new dimensions. He discusses the colonization of Mexicans in the southwest United States as a form of internal colonization. This took place after the military conquest and forced incorporation of Mexico's northern territories and inhabitants into the United States, as ratified by the Treaty of Guadalupe Hidalgo. Thus, the colonization processes of expropriating human labor and material resources affect the economic and political status of Chicanos today. In addition, the ethnocentrism in educational and social processes reflects continued dominance of Anglo[2] customs, norms, and language, and creates issues unique to the Chicano experience.

Barrera also adds to this model an expanded definition of how economic structures reinforce racial and ethnic patterns of domination and subordination. Through the development of dual or split labor markets, differential resources and working conditions are attached to specific jobs and industries. In a colonized setting, the primary labor market with the highest reward levels and most advantageous work settings is reserved through discriminatory screening mechanisms for the dominant racial or ethnic group. The secondary labor market becomes a stagnant economic niche for the subordinate groups. For Barrera, these economic factors are reflected in other major institutions, such as the political, educational, and familial systems.

Maria Mies connects these and earlier Marxist models to patriarchy in her analysis of the international division of labor. To the economic expropriation of human and natural resources in the colonization process and the destruction of indigenous, nonwhite cultures she adds the colonization experiences of women. She highlights these experiences for women living in colonized areas, with an emphasis on the historical roles for women as producers and reproducers "based clearly on capitalistic cost-benefit calculations" (1986:90). She argues that fluctuations in the treatment of enslaved women as breeders, including times in which fertility was encouraged or discouraged, were based upon the comparative costs of purchasing and breeding slaves. The sexuality of colonized women was exploited, as was their labor power. Mies cites the development of prostitution, and later marriage reforms, as additional capitalist programs that used women to control the behaviors of colonized men.

Mies also discusses the changing roles of white Western women in concert with the exploitation of women of color throughout the colonial world. She posits two significant time periods for the subordination of Western women: one, during the witch hunts of the twelfth to sixteenth centuries, and the other, during the *housewifization* of the eighteenth century. The first phase was a response of the emerging bourgeois, male-dominated class system to the economic and sexual independence of women. The church acted in concert with bourgeois interests to decimate the rebellious female population. Mies perceives resistance among women in their religious, healing, and productive work as acts of rebellion against a new capitalist order. The second phase, housewifization, occurred as a counterpart to the degraded nature of colonized women: The Western woman is provided with luxury items to be man-

---

[2]In a recent article (Moore, 1989), the racial and ethnic terminology for defining Caucasians who dominate institutional resources was described as "white" by African American respondents and "Anglo" by Chicano respondents. In this manuscript, we use the reference that reflects the preference of the racial/ethnic group in the specific context. Respondents indicated that they consider each term to have both racial and cultural connotations.

aged and consumed and a "civilized" role within the emerging bourgeois family structure. The creation of the "private" family in contrast to the public economic and political sphere constrained women's independence, first in the
bourgeois family, and later in the proletarian family, to benefit the interests of
the state and the church in controlling women's bodies and labor.

WOMEN AND FAMILY THEORY: ILLUSTRATING THE DIFFERENCES

Liberal Feminism and the Family

Feminist theorists have approached the issue of family with varying assumptions, conclusions, and actions. Liberal feminism has focused on women's
entrance into the paid labor market and their ability to compete with men in
this sphere. Liberal-feminist theory has not attended to the value of women's
place in the family as an economic issue but has primarily focused on changing gender roles. Thus, liberal-feminist theorists examine the evolving nature
of the family from a patriarchal structure to an egalitarian or democratic family structure. They include the issue of unpaid labor in the home primarily as
an individual negotiation for more leisure time shared by partners. The economic value of unpaid labor, which is defined by the structure of patri-
archy/capitalism, is largely ignored.

The focus for liberal feminists is on the labor market, which is assumed
to function only outside the home in waged labor. The liberal feminist agenda
emphasizes women's entrance into the labor market and their ability to compete within it but also women's acceptance of the male patriarchal normative
structure. The relearning and valuing of male norms and ideals in order to
compete more successfully in the capitalist/patriarchal labor market takes
precedence. This is exemplified in the "dress for success" workshops held for
women entering or competing in the labor market or the emphasis on individual and family access to quality child care. Within the family, liberal feminists focus on reproduction and child care as hindrances to paid work. Many
of the liberal feminist calls for access to child care and reproductive freedom
ignore the economic conditions of child-care workers and teenage or surrogate mothers who provide infants for childless couples.

The whole range of feminist activism has refocused on reproductive
rights in the recent challenges to *Roe* v. *Wade*, but liberal feminists pay little attention to the issues of adequate, safe birth control and forced sterilization
among poor women and women of color in the United States. They are unable to politically or theoretically assess the ethnocentric norms for family
planning that ignore the child mortality rates and reproductive expectations
for women in Third World countries and the connection to autonomy and social standing.

In the last three decades, feminists used liberal principles to secure legislation and court decisions undermining the sexual division of labor (e.g., arguments for individual rights) (Shanley, 1983). This emphasis provided women with "the opportunity to participate in the society as it is currently structured, but [does] nothing directly about altering those aspects of those structures inimical to family well being" (Shanley, 1983:358). Legal reform will not necessarily transform family roles. According to Eisenstein (1983), the ideology of liberal individualism will conflict with male privilege and economic profit, and this conflict will be central to "pro-family" political policy.

Radical Feminism and the Family

Radical feminism focuses on the patriarchal system within the family that is pervasive throughout Western cultures. Women trade their autonomy for protection from a patriarchal and often violent world. The reduction of women to the status of sexual and reproductive property owned and controlled by men is accomplished through the social construction of the family and the family contract, and more recently through the state "in patria potestis" (Boris and Bardaglio, 1983).

The family is seen as an oppressive institution where women contribute to their own oppression as a group through socialization as sex objects and their symbolic equation as "mom" with "apple pie" patriotism. Dworkin (1983) notes that this is often a deadly negotiation, given the high rates of spouse abuse, marital homicide, and marital rape. Within the patriarchal family, men also control women's labor power in formal and informal ways, such that resistance by women has significant economic and social consequences for themselves and their children. State agencies that keep families together "at any cost" and the struggle to change laws, court procedures, and police interventions that favor men are evidence that the state is antagonistic to women's autonomy and safety (Grossholtz, 1984).

Suzanne Pharr (1988) sets the discussion of family in the context of heterosexist norms. She argues that the restrictive gender-role system of the nuclear family is reinforced through sanctions applied to lesbians and gay men. The fear of being denied economic or emotional support because women reject dominant heterosexual family norms ties women to the status quo. The social degradation ascribed to lesbians and gays by patriarchy and heterosexist institutions denies the reality of lesbian and gay households as "family" structures with emotional resources and legitimate economic and social consequences.

Many alternatives to confrontation with the patriarchal, heterosexist family are possible. Separation of women from violent homes is already a reality in many communities through safe houses and advocacy services that provide resources for personal and economic autonomy. The claim of legitimate lesbian and gay households, with economic and parenting responsibilities, is now recognized in some city ordinances that provide for housing, insurance, and employment rights to lesbian and gay household members.

Cultural Feminism, Poststructuralism, and the Family

Cultural feminists argue for the creation of a diversity of family structures by revising heterosexual families, enhancing single-parent families, and including lesbian and gay families. They focus on egalitarian, nurturing, or communal family processes. These alternatives confront what Bernard (1981) calls the "restraining myths" of the family, including the legal, reproductive, and productive restrictions attached to the family norms. She then outlines the historical changes in the cultural ideology of "women's family sphere" and suggests a new female subworld of the family, populated by

> still young, energetic women whose obligations as mothers are becoming attenuated, who are increasingly engaged in educational activities, political work, and the like, and increasingly subjected by consciousness-raising experiences to a perspective on their world which may reorient their view of themselves as well as their world. (Bernard, 1981:169)

She then notes the world of the widowed and divorced as increasingly frequent realities for these women.

Postmodernist theorists would advise against an analysis of either (1) historical and cultural categories such as "family" or (2) the consequences of family structure for female-dominated infant care or housework (Bordo, 1990). They argue against such metatheories and models because they obscure a potential "truth" or "truths." Bordo, in contrast, argues that most of the critical feminist analyses of these categories have barely begun to be recognized as modernist social criticism: "[I]t is too soon to let them [social institutions] off the hook via postmodern heterogeneity and instability" (Bordo, 1990:153). In sum, the postmodernist critique may lead us to reassess the overarching theories of family "functions" from both conservative and radical perspectives. However, cultural reformation of patriarchal attitudes or the postmodernist denial of cultural patterns are unlikely to address issues of family economic survival for poor women and women of color or to confront patterned violence in patriarchal family structures.

Capitalism and the Family

Marxist feminists have condemned the family as an economic, not an emotional unit (Tong, 1989:62). According to socialist feminists and Marxist feminists, economic dependence is part of the system that maintains marriage, the family (even single-parent families), and mothering (Eisenstein, 1983). Women as childrearers are socially and biologically reproducing patriarchal and capitalist social relations intergenerationally. Women become unpaid labor and ideological resources for the bourgeoisie within the family. In some analyses, bourgeois marriage is equated with prostitution, or perceived as being different in degree. In prostitution, women are "sold" as property in a piecework fashion; in marriage, women are bonded into a long-term slave relationship. As women take wage labor outside of the family, their obligations to provide home labor remain, to the benefit of the profit-making activities of men and employers (Cronin, 1987).

Rayna Rapp (1982) argues that household and family patterns of black Americans have been a response to both the dominant white class and regional patterns of family, and to the specific economic and political history of race stratification. In her review of research, she highlights the job market, welfare legislation, and segregated housing as they relate to female-centered households, kinship networks, and the roles of women in the black community. Rapp also notes the use of the black family as an ideological tool to "blame" the poor for their own condition. The focus on black families in poverty has played a political role in capitalism: It reduces the focus on the structure of the resource base, while welfare practices detract attention from the accumulation of subsidies by the elite.

Colonizing the Family

Colonization theorists would look to both the destruction and the distortion of indigenous family forms in a subordinated group (Mies, 1986). For most women of color, the definition of family has been colonized repeatedly by social scientists, including feminist social scientists who uncritically accept distorted family definitions. Maxine Baca Zinn (1990) addresses the revisionist interpretations of family presented by feminist and racial/ethnic scholarship. She notes, however, that revisionist research on minority families has remained marginalized, and issues of racial stratification are often ignored in feminist theory. She cites the development of the concept of the "backward and culturally deviant minority family" as rising from the assimilationist and Anglo-normative frameworks of the sociology of race relations. The result is that "racial meanings create a hierarchy in which some family forms are privileged and others are subordinated, even though both are products of larger social factors" (Zinn, 1990:69).

The Moynihan Report described the African American family as "disorganized" and "emasculating" due to a strong economic presence of women and an absence of economic roles for men. This is a classic example of distortion. Another distortion is the uncritical acceptance of the concept of *machismo* as an explanation for "dysfunctional" Mexican American families (characterized as lacking achievement, competitive independence, and self-worth).

In the case of black families, the omission of economic factors such as extremely high rates of unemployment among African American males and of social-welfare policies that demand the absence of males prior to providing assistance are clear indicators of a social science distortion (Davis, 1989). For Chicanos, the reluctance of social scientists or radical feminists to drop these stereotypes, in the face of research that indicates little inequality and rigidity, helps to maintain a colonized view of Chicano families (Mirande, 1985). Moreover, the stipulation that competition and achievement in the material world are paramount indicators of healthy, functioning families is also a suspicious norm in a colonizing framework. The uncritical acceptance of these views, based on Anglo-dominant norms for family structure and outcomes, should be a consideration in a comprehensive feminist theory.

This brief overview of feminist theory and the family highlights gaps in our current understanding as well as biases in the various feminist approaches. Liberal feminists, with their attention to individual rights, ignore the complications of patriarchy, capitalism, and colonization. Among radical, Marxist, and socialist feminists, the focus has been on the group roles of women within a larger sphere of social change. However, these theorists also focus on the labor market as the key to revolutionary, egalitarian, or cultural changes. Men are seen as either direct or indirect oppressors. These theories highlight various factors that may contribute to the origin, maintenance, or change in family structure from a feminist perspective.

The poststructuralist feminist asks whether a woman can truly know herself within the construct of the family, and this approach may undermine the feminist critical analyses of social structures and interpersonal processes that maintain family violence and restrictions for women. Cultural feminists propose utopian kinship structures as a solution to family tyranny, yet they have no specific directions for development toward those structures. Both of these perspectives fail to systematically address the dominant cultural norms of the family. Cultural feminist analyses dismiss the experiences of women of color and diverse groups of women (older, lesbian, differently abled, poor, and working class) by excluding them from specific consideration.

FEMINIST THEORY AND SOCIOLOGY

In general, we draw on both feminist and sociological theories to reframe our understanding of women's material and cultural condition. Feminist theories often omit women's contemporary position, concentrating on historical antecedents or utopian futures. The focus on praxis is often on creating revolution, egalitarian reform, or cultural utopias. Most sociology is grounded in what *is*—the relation of the individual to the world as it exists and is maintained. Feminist theory is an emancipatory theory focusing on the relation of the individual or group to the world as it can be conceived. Much of feminist theory, then, emphasizes a social philosophy of women as opposed to a sociology of women.

According to Janet Chafetz (1988), a feminist sociological theory is composed of the following elements:

1. Gender comprises a central focus or subject matter of the theory.
2. Gender relations are viewed as a problem.
3. Gender relations are not viewed as either natural or immutable.
4. The acid test is whether feminist-sociological theory can be used to challenge, counteract, or change a status quo that disadvantages or devalues women.

Chafetz deliberately omits activism as a central component of what makes a theory feminist. Earlier sociological theories, which were also feminist, claim that theory must involve praxis (Millman and Kanter, 1975; Cook and Fonow, 1988). The feminist sociologist is involved in changing society in the very process of doing sociology. Chafetz rejects this activist definition of sociology. To her, feminist sociology is one that can be used for activist purposes but is not by definition activist. "It is a judgment of the theory itself, not of the scholar who created it" (Chafetz, 1988:5).

However, theories that can be used for activism to assist some women may in fact be used to oppress others. For example, the oppression for women of color may be at the hands of white women for whom the theory holds potential for empowerment. Does the theory hold potential for middle-class women yet ignore the oppression of women on welfare? As the sociologist Dorothy Smith claims, a sociology of women necessitates a sociology for women (Smith, 1987).

THREE

A Sociology of Women

The feminist theories reviewed in Chapter Two present a number of options for organizing our model of inequality and empowerment for women. At times, they present mutually exclusive concepts or definitions or even causal factors. In this chapter, we draw on what we consider to be the most significant dimensions of these theories to build a theoretical model for the sociology of women.

Patriarchal and functionalist theories will not be used because they do not assess women's oppression and the effect of sex stratification without which women's reality cannot be accurately described. Functionalist sex-roles socialization theories can be criticized for having (1) an emphasis on finding a singular universal truth and verification method, (2) a commitment to objectivity and observer neutrality, (3) dichotomous classification of gender and other constructs, and primarily causal models, (4) ahistorical views, and (5) nonreflexive use of language as a medium for transmitting thoughts, concepts, and theories.

Both patriarchal and sex-roles models ignore the dependence of theoretical discourse on "particular positions established by particular modes of language" (Pateman and Gross, 1986:200). For example, sex-roles analyses use bipolar concepts such as masculinity and femininity as givens. Even models of androgyny anticipate the reality of a continuum with fixed masculine and feminine end points. Thus, the language used in creating patriarchal and sex-roles theories sets parameters that cannot be ignored or transformed by the models themselves.

FEMINIST THEORY AND SOCIOLOGICAL THEORY

A genuinely feminist approach to theory draws on concepts and analytic tools that are appropriate to the questions of women's experiences of inequality that promote activism. First, we can begin from an understanding of our own conditions (a sociology by women). This understanding need not depend on the concepts or definitions set by traditional research. We can develop models that use nonsexist concepts and language and move away from rigid either/or dichotomies. Instead of assuming a gulf between rational concepts such as the public and private spheres, or between the subject (researcher) and object (women respondents), feminist theorists acknowledge the continuity between them (a sociology about women). This new assumption reduces that bipolarity. Finally, the products and consequences of our thinking can be assessed against the probability of change for women (a sociology for women).

The reasons for such a feminist approach to theory move from the criticisms outlined in the earlier chapters toward an integrative model that allows us to

1. Examine the possibility of a theoretical integration
2. Account for historical fluctuation
3. Develop models that are testable and challengeable through the use of feminist methodologies and praxis

One caution for developing an integrative theory is that we not simply accept eclectic concepts and approaches such as gender roles in isolation from structural factors. Instead, we should draw together conceptual pieces into a web of ideas that transcend patriarchal theory building. But we must also struggle with the use of traditional sociological theory-building tools, including the language of theory building and the hierarchy of these constructs and propositions.

Why Build a Feminist Sociological Theory?

It is clear that earlier patriarchal and liberal feminist theories are inadequate to explain the development and maintenance of and the change in women's oppression in different cultures (Chafetz, 1988). The reasons for building a feminist theory or explanation derived from women's studies frameworks are clear. But why build a sociological theory? Are the problems created by patriarchal theory and liberal-feminist theory inherent to the sociological theory-building process? Theory as a practice can itself be examined from a feminist perspective, analyzed for potential consequences, and revised for its potential contributions to an understanding of women's lives.

Patricia Hill Collins points to those aspects of the white scholarly community that have excluded black feminist intellectual traditions. These aspects include the assumption that scientists are distanced from their values, vested interests, and emotions attached to their gender, race, or class situation (Collins, 1990). A primary characteristic of white masculinist epistemology is the distinction between wisdom and knowledge. Wisdom consists of "mother wit" and experience as a criterion of meaning. Knowledge consists of "book learning" and additive objective facts that are accumulated and legitimized through scholarly processes controlled by dominant groups. Collins notes that a black feminist epistemology rises out of an assertion that knowledge without wisdom is "adequate for the powerful, but wisdom is essential to the survival of the subordinate" (Collins, 1990:208).

Collins then challenges us to reject competitive, additive theory-building processes. She draws on the processes of dialogue to assess knowledge claims, a dialogue among women who share their wisdom about the world around them. She adds to this dialogue an ethic of care that includes personal expressiveness and emotions in the knowledge validation process.

Theory "seeks to explain why phenomena exist and why they reveal certain *processes* and *properties*" (italics added) (Turner and Beeghley, 1981:2). If, then, sociological theory building can be used to illuminate not only products, outcomes, properties, and classification schemes but also *processes*, then sociological theory retains utility for feminist purposes. Our purpose is to explain some dimensions of the following questions: Why does sex inequality exist? What are its origins and consequences? How is it maintained? What are the dynamics of change? These are basic questions outlined by Janet Chafetz in *Feminist Sociology* (1988), and expanded by the epistemological frameworks of Collins (1990) and Smith (1987), who argue for a dialogue grounded in women's experiences.

Currently, the process of building a theory in the social sciences involves a set of rational, objective steps. These steps must be questioned, evaluated, and revised to maintain integrity from a feminist perspective.

THEORY BUILDING AS A FEMINIST PROCESS

The goal of mainstream theory building is first to define important concepts and then to organize them (Turner and Beeghley, 1981). *Concepts* are systems of terms that allow us to understand what is being studied. These can be abstract or concrete terms that are expressed in language that should be accessible to some other audience. Often this language is understandable only to a small number of "experts," and we then label this terminology *jargon*. A frequent criticism of academics is that we use language that is unknown or inaccessible to other audiences, particularly the groups that we study. Feminists and other critics of academic work argue that this use of language is deliberate. It creates a barrier between the researcher and the subject and gives the person or group that creates the language more power, or at least an aura of "expertise" (Nebraska Sociological Feminist Collective, 1988).

Not only should a concept be accessible, by labeling phenomena in an inclusive context, but it should also inform us about differences in degree. Here lies the crux of feminist theory building. To identify variation, Weber developed the notion of the *ideal type,* which outlines a set of characteristics or aspects of past events or social actions (behaviors or attitudes). An ideal type should not have a fixed normative connotation but "has the significance of a purely ideal *limiting* concept with which the real situation or action is *compared* and surveyed for the explication of certain of its significant components" (Weber, 1949:93).

How these ideal types are constructed by the theorist is crucial to the debate over a "value neutral" perspective of sociology. Weber argued strongly that the use of the ideal type would allow the development of concepts and models that could parallel the natural science model to some extent. The ideal type describes abstract elements, and not all elements will exist at one point in time or in one social setting. It is a hypothetical definition. Yet, researchers often approach these concepts too concretely, as if we might find an ideal type of "anxiety" or "revolution" or "family" in existence. All too often, the discussion of the ideal type leads to evaluations and conclusions, including the findings that some groups or individuals do not reach *the* ideal type, as if it might be a moral goal or a socially necessary condition.

To Weber, any systematic approach to theory building also involves *verstehen* (translated by some into English as "understanding"). Weber outlined two different types of *verstehen:* "[T]he first is the direct, observational understanding of the subjective meaning of a given act" (Weber, 1922:8). This type of *verstehen* does not necessarily include extensive knowledge of the broader social context. The second type of *verstehen* involves explanatory understanding, where the researcher supplies an explanation in terms of motive or social context. Some theorists imply that the second type of *verstehen* provides a rational understanding of motivation that places the act in a more intelligible and more inclusive context of social meaning (Weber, 1922/1968:8–10).

To most feminists outside of the liberal-feminist model, "it is here that the problem of explanatory understanding arises" (Smith, 1987:120). The very process of observation builds a "one-sided" relationship between the knower and the known. The researcher (subject) has the power to impose a potentially biased framework over the respondent's (object's) own interpretation. This is not merely an intellectual power but also an institutional power, providing the researcher with access to books, media, and the role of "expert" on women's lives.

Dorothy Smith argues that we must begin any inquiry into women's lives from the standpoint of women (Smith, 1987:127). This requires beginning with what women know, by asking women to talk about their everyday lives and local practices. Feminist researchers should seek methods that preserve the standpoint of the women researched. This should include not only the definition of concepts but also the construction of research questions, the development of research instruments, and the drawing of conclusions. Smith suggests that we take particular experiences and embed them in the social organization of institutions: school, family, church, and so on. The process of building inquiry from the basis of women's accounts is discussed in Chapter Four.

Building Propositions in a Sociology of Women

In the preceding chapter, we identified a number of important concepts that contribute to inequality: sex roles, gender stratification, patriarchy, colonization, and oppression. In this chapter, we will add the concept of *value* as a crucial bridge between interpretive and structural discussions of women in society.

The next step in mainstream theory building is to organize concepts into propositions. *Propositions* are statements that relate phenomena to each other. In this case, we would organize the above concepts to map out a theory of women's oppression. We anticipate how variation in one factor might account for variation in another.

Shulamith Firestone (1970) studied the relationship between reproduction (how it is defined both biologically and technologically) and oppression (including economic, sexual, and familial inequality). To Firestone, the control of reproduction by women through technology would lead to reduced inequality. Thus, her propositional basis is an effort to build a theory describing how women's inequality is maintained and can be changed.

From these propositional statements we can derive hypotheses based on earlier observations. A *hypothesis* is an educated guess at the existence or form or direction of a relationship between two or more specific variables. For example, we might hypothesize that increased access to birth control information would increase educational commitment and self-esteem for teenage women. We might then test these relationships through repeated observations or with statistical tests, or with repeated dialogue with teenage women and men.

Let us use examples from Firestone's *The Dialectic of Sex* (1970) as a set of theoretical propositions. Firestone proposed that an increase in reproductive technology might be associated with an increase in women's paid labor-force participation and economic independence. Some historians use the advent of modern birth control methods, the rise of women's paid labor-force participation, and additional legal rights granted to women as observational indicators of the validity of such a theory. Advances in birth control technology were made possible by the new technologies utilizing rubber at the turn of the century and the development of chemical birth control pills that regulate women's hormonal levels and estrus cycles. Historians might then point to increased wage labor by women and parallel changes in civil rights for women workers as empirical verifications for Firestone's model. Clearly, other factors might be important and could be brought into the model to generate other specific hypotheses based on particular feminist perspectives. For example, the dumping of birth control devices that are banned in the United States into developing nations, with tax write-offs for pharmaceutical companies, must be considered in the contexts of patriarchy (the struggle for reproductive freedom by women), capitalism (the gain of profits at the expense of women), and colonization (the export of life-threatening products to a dependent nation, whose population growth may be of concern to the colonizing nation). Other factors might affect the relationship among reproductive technology, economic independence, and legal rights for women of various cultural backgrounds.

A THEORY FOR THE SOCIOLOGY OF WOMEN

A major challenge for feminist theorists is to bridge the structural and interpretive approaches available in the social sciences and in women's studies theory. An integrative theory of women's oppression should draw from all available models, not to construct a hodgepodge, but with an eye toward the patchwork quilt of women's traditional crafts. Such a patchwork would take the useful concepts of feminist models and draw them together to make a strong theoretical fabric.

We first draw on structural approaches that contribute generalizable concepts and an "anticipated social structure" (Glaser and Strauss, 1971). These generalizable concepts should not determine ahead of time the questions we ask of women or the answers we hear from them. Instead, these provide frameworks for anticipating those social structures and organizations that might influence women's lives. Interpretive approaches then can contribute meaning and process at the individual level (Smith, 1987).

In the next section, we outline how the concept of *value* can be used to frame women's experiences of oppression from a formal perspective. The poststructuralists argue that we cannot answer the question "Are there women?" or "What is value?" We believe that these questions must be asked, even if the medium of language will ultimately distort the reality of women's lives. In the next chapter, on feminist methodology and praxis, we suggest strategies to increase feminist theoretical dialogue and to further reduce the problem of language, power, and research interpretation.

WOMEN AND VALUE: AXIOMS FOR A SOCIOLOGY OF WOMEN

The central concept for our model of women's oppression is the notion of *value* as outlined by Benston (1969). Benston develops an initial concept of value and sets out two ideal types: *use value* and *exchange value*. She argues that all socially significant activity has use value; that is, it is useful to the individual actor or to others in some way. The other type of value is exchange value, which takes on meaning only in a market context. Both of these concepts have variability; the usefulness of a particular activity depends upon the audience or the individual actor as well as the time and place.

Variability in use value is essentially subjective and implies the first type of *verstehen* described by Weber: the subjective meaning of social action. The concept of exchange value has primary reference to the market, with information that can be gathered with both types of *verstehen:*

1. The rational relation of exchange within the market that can be verified to some extent independently of the respondent (What would this product or labor be worth if you sold it today?)
2. The subjective meaning of the market to the individual (Is it important what the market sets as the exchange value? To what extent is the individual woman aware of the exchange value and acting with that in mind?)

Benston argues from a materialist position that exchange value is determined within the confines of a capitalist system by the need for profit (capital) and the conflicting interests of the proletariat and the bourgeoisie. The workers seek to earn a living wage and to increase that wage as much as possible. Owners seek to increase their profits and, indeed, need to maintain profits in order to compete effectively in the marketplace. As we will see in the following chapters, the notion of use value and exchange value takes on special meaning for women's unpaid, but useful, contributions in reproduction, child care, household labor, care for the elderly, and emotional support within a family context.

We take the concept of value at a more abstract level than did Benston, however. Mainstream theorists refer to this abstract level of a concept as an *axiom*. We are using the concept in its societal market/nonmarket context, but we also include the definition of symbolic value, which is constructed by the individual in a social context.

At this more general level, a *value* is defined as something that has meaning to the individual or to groups. It can have positive or negative connotations, but our focus is on the greater or lesser meaning of material and nonmaterial aspects of culture. In most societies, important symbols of value are made available through verbal or nonverbal communication. Most of the important symbols are known within a given society, although access to control over those symbols (access to speaking, writing, or reading the symbols) may be restricted for certain groups or individuals.

Collins (1990) identifies just such a process operating in the colonized educational process that trains black feminist theorists in all disciplines. Access to positions in the academy, professional resources, and publication in journals has been restricted to those black scholars who have used the white masculinist language, theoretical models, and research techniques. Marginalized by their race or class background, as well as by gender, these scholars have been granted legitimacy only when their ideas fit within the existing knowledge base. Collins argues that the research symbols and processes of mainstream academia, by definition, distort the experiences of black women and men.

Some symbols are selected by an individual or group as an important basis for behavior or for constructing self-images. An example of symbolic value is the extent to which a certain visual presentation of the body is valued. This could involve clothing, coloring of the body (including cosmetic use), or even body size and shape. We can then observe the extent to which an individual or group in the society has the ability to control the definition of value (what makes a positively or negatively valued body type) and who has the resources to acquire that body type. In particular, we are interested in the patterns of institutionalized access to these resources and gender differences, in this case of the valuing and controlling of body types. Which groups influence media images of models, newscasters, and television stars? How do these images then influence the attitudes and behaviors of individuals with variable access to the consumer goods necessary to copy these images?

A value can be exhibited consciously or unconsciously by the individual or group. For example, changes in the valued body type may not be brought immediately to the attention of all members of the society but may be a result of gradual change. However, we can infer some of these changes from the actions or perceptions of groups and individuals. Chernin (1981) notes the shift of preferred female body type in the United States during the last century toward an ever-thinner form that values a childish female silhouette and can lead to a life-threatening array of consequences for women who starve themselves to achieve that form. We can also see its relation to other societal concepts, such as the value attached to the elderly compared with the young and the emphasis on the physical appearance of women in the workplace.

Societal *value* is more obviously set by a market economy where the process or product is assumed to be strictly evaluated by its exchange potential. However, exchange or economic value is influenced not only by supply and demand but also by cultural norms and beliefs. Economic rewards are also determined by those who have *power*. In the colonization model, this definition of group dominance is tied not to class per se, but to racial stratification patterns that influence the cultural norms of both dominant and subordinate groups.

The more generalizable question then becomes, Who has the power to control definitions of value? Using our example of body image, we see that economic rewards are associated with the valued body type. In advertising, there are certain prices paid at market values for certain body types. Some models are excluded on the basis of a gender or race "mismatch" with the product. Women may seek and maintain a valued body type; however, only certain individuals receive exchange value. Here, use value and exchange value are integrated and the powerful are those who determine when exchange value will be allocated, and for how long (note the relatively short career span of most models). The association of body type with class, race, and sex becomes a prism for analyzing these dimensions of power.

Propositions for a Sociology of Women

We next identify the relationships among important concepts in our model. What is the relationship of use value to exchange value in a given society? How does this relationship affect women in varying institutions such as the economy or the family? What are the relationships among patriarchy, colonialism, and capitalism in the construction of societal values? Given these relationships, what specific hypotheses might we generate about women's material and nonmaterial lives?

The first proposition for our model is that *in a capitalistic market economy, exchange value takes priority over use value.* We anticipate that if an activity has some relationship to market activity, the market value will influence its symbolic value in other dimensions as well. A contemporary example is the struggle over surrogate birthing. The contractual rights of birth mothers, genetic fathers (sperm donors), and genetic mothers (egg donors) are complicated by the economic and legal consequences of surrogate birth, especially when an attorney serves as the linkage between the parents and when the surrogate mother charges a fee for those services. Birthing takes on the same characteristics as other market transactions and generates profits for entrepreneurs in the field.

Under the colonization model, the control of value and of symbols is attached to race and cultural dominance through capitalism or other forms of economic oppression. The ethnocentrism of this system is developed and maintained through educational, political, and economic systems controlled by the dominant group. The colonization model frames the issue of reproductive choice and control for women in economically dependent situations. The surrogacy process requires a birth mother who is willing to undergo considerable risks to her own health and disruption to her personal and professional life in order to become pregnant in a contracted situation. This places poor and low-income women at considerable disadvantage, not only in the United States but throughout the world. Class relations and race relations will structure the patterns of *who* carries *what* types of children to reduce the health risks and increase the reproductive capacity of the dominant group.

Drawing on the radical-feminist theories, we also propose that *in a patriarchal system, men set the exchange value.* As Hartmann (1981b) and others have pointed out, capitalism goes hand in hand with patriarchy in most Western industrial nations. In the economic structure, men are able to control the definition of exchange value not only because they control profits but also because they control the bureaucratic administration of labor. With the surrogacy example, we find that judges, attorneys, and courts now determine the rights of contract parents and surrogate birth mothers. The patriarchal structure of the courts, and the paternalistic relationship of the state, may dictate the rights of the birth mother to future contact with the child. In these cases, the patriarchal rights of the sperm donor are not in question; it is the right of the mother that is disputed—as birth mother, genetic mother, or custodial mother.

Feminist theorists have argued persuasively that even the cultural notion of *female* is defined by men. De Beauvoir stated that men set the parameters for what is valued, and women are defined as "other," which contributes to their devaluation. In a market sense, much of what women "do" has been defined as useful by men, but the market value for this work has been set very low. We anticipate that when men "do" what women "do," these activities are more highly valued. In addition, when men have control of what women do, that behavior may take on (but need not necessarily do so) some type of exchange value. In a patriarchal system, men also control the use of symbols, especially in the public sphere. The exchange value set by men is reinforced in individual and group interaction through language and symbolic cues (Pearson, 1985).

In the next section, we illuminate the relationship of use value and exchange value under capitalism, colonization, and patriarchy in three areas: economics, sexuality, and self-esteem.

Economics and Value

We begin with an explanation of the classic Marxian model of economics as presented by Margaret Benston (1969). This model is expanded to show the interconnection of use value and exchange value in the patriarchal structure. The economic contributions of women are dichotomized by Benston into those which are associated with use value and exchange value. The contribution of feminist theory has been the recognition that throughout any period of economic history women have contributed in both types of labor, but patriarchal and ethnocentric theories and methodologies have omitted information about the latter.

Christine Bose (1987:268) tracks the public accounting of the value of labor through the history of census data omissions. Because the census defined work as "one's usual task," most married women's occupation was defined as housewife, even if they were temporarily working for pay. Home-based work was not officially recorded until 1940. Prior to that time, a significant number of women were taking in factory piecework or had boarders living in the home. A national study of urban workers in 1892 found that 27 percent of all married women took in boarders, and earned about 43 percent as much as their spouse's income (Jensen, 1980, as quoted in Bose, 1987).

In constructing the public discourse on exchange value, the focus of the media and of political discussion has been on white middle-class occupations and labor. Although the Census did record the occupations of slaves, no complete record of their roles has been preserved. Thus, the study of the lives of black women prior to the Emancipation Proclamation has been limited to a few diaries and to public records that define blacks as property. Immigrant women's and black women's work was not recorded separately from white women's work until the 1890s, and various Hispanic groups had been counted as white until the 1980 Census when significant Hispanic cultural groups such as Cubana, Chicana, and Puertoriquena were separated for research and policy discussion. Thus, school curricula, political history, and the economic process define white contributions to society as normative, given the scant information available about other groups.

In addition, the initial focus of white academic feminists was on the higher-status occupations (Seifer, 1976). Only recently have we included working-class women's lives and contributions in our studies. These new perspectives take into account the effects of international market economies, the economic depressions in the industrial northeastern United States, and the meaning of layoffs and unemployment for women in blue-collar occupations (Rosen, 1987). The use and exchange value of peasant workers in Third World nations can be assessed through dimensions of capitalism and colonization, as well as patriarchy (Mies, 1988).

These and other difficulties in recording women's contributions through a focus on empirical market or "exchange" data are presented in Chapter Four. In Chapter Five, we present information on the economic realities of women in the home and in the paid labor force.

Sexuality and Value

In the definition and everyday experience of sexuality, we should consider several frames of reference. The first is the family, as this is the major institution in which sexual behaviors, attitudes, and norms are structured. The other frames are the politics of motherhood and reproductive freedom and, finally, the public sexuality markets of prostitution and pornography. Each of these dimensions helps us to identify the integration and contradictions in the roles of heterosexual women predominately and the roles of all women in light of market and colonial factors.

Sex: In and around the family.   Women in the family, as children or as wives, exchange sexual fidelity for economic and social support or protection (Brownmiller, 1975; Dworkin, 1983). Indeed, Pateman (1988) argues that the original contract in human society is the sexual contract under patriarchy, with its social embodiment of women as sexual beings. Women without this contracted male protection are described in feminist literature as occupying the role of "open territory victims"—women who deserve their victimization according to society because they are not protected by men (indicating that they were in some way unwilling to enter into this exchange). This frame of victimization is focused on the concept of exchange and may extend to women who receive government support for dependent children, women who experience sexual or other physical assaults, and victims of spouse and child abuse (Russell, 1984).

This sexual exchange is recognized in many state laws regarding parental rights and marital responsibilities. Rights and obligations for sexual access are outlined without references to gender; however, until recently, state laws, often referred to as "marital rape exemptions," left sexual control to men. This meant that a husband could not be prosecuted for raping his wife. As cited by Diana Russell (1990), state laws as of 1989 showed that sixteen states had no exemptions, twenty-six states had some exemption, and eight states still had laws prohibiting the prosecution of a husband unless the couple were separated, living apart, or had filed for divorce.

As Rubin (1972) argues in her article "The Traffic in Women," the barter of wives and daughters in marriage is primarily an economic activity that takes on sexual meaning. Within this frame of reference, the use value of sexuality is predominately reproduction (ignoring here the developing surrogate-parent market) and recreation. Women who do not fit this family-centered framework (lesbians, nuns, spinsters, prostitutes, and women in the pornography industry) are thrust out of the normative definitions of sexuality. These groups are lumped together to highlight that their deviant status arises not from their illegality but because they are outside of the protection of men by choice or economic circumstances. What these definitions ignore is the reality that expectations for women's behavior and sexual norms have significant social interactions.

Sex as sex.   The notion of recreational, nonreproductive sex (the use value of sex) is a relatively modern phenomenon, particularly for married women (D'Emilio and Freedman, 1988). This new model of sexuality has generated an avalanche of media images, novels, advice books, and self-help groups to create norms for the practice and enjoyment of women's sexuality. Much of this recreational sexual identity has developed in interaction with historical and erroneous definitions supplied by men: the norm of the vaginal orgasm, definitions of the concept *sexually attractive,* and control of the verbal and nonverbal cues for sexual initiation (with sexual assault as the consequence of women who "ask for it") (Russell, 1984).

Even the use value of women's sexual behavior has been commercialized from the standpoint of men's definitions. Commercial images are generated in the core of the colonization institutions and are based on white middle-class norms of sexual behavior and attractiveness (Tuchman, 1978). However, these images are readily available to racial and ethnic minorities, not only in the United States but throughout the world, and generate a huge market in sexual objectification for all racial and ethnic groups of women.

Despite these profit-based distortions, the feminist reclamation of sex was a primary goal of the early 1970s women's liberation movement. "Clearly, women had been deprived, sexually stunted in service to the vaginal and phallocentric sex imposed by men" (Ehrenreich, Hess, and Jacobs, 1986:71). Ehrenreich et al. argue that women's sexual revolution has remained essentially unclaimed and unrecognized, despite a number of victories. Challenging old definitions of sex as a physical act and rejecting the version of male-oriented sex as narrow and unsatisfying, women expanded the notion of "normal sex." Beginning in the 1960s and throughout the 1970s and 1980s, women insisted on "a broader, more playful notion of sex, more compatible with women's broader erotic possibilities, more respectful of women's needs" (Ehrenreich et al., 1986:193).

Evidence that these reclamations occurred among women in the United States is documented in the history of sexuality traced by D'Emilio and Freedman (1988). Included in the changes they cite during these past three decades was the fact that across class lines, the frequency and variety of sexual practices among married couples increased. In addition, these men and women expressed considerable agreement about sexual satisfaction and frequency within marriage, and the responses of unmarried cohabiting couples provided roughly equivalent responses (D'Emilio and Freedman, 1988:338). They also cite changes in attitudes, particularly among younger heterosexuals, toward less traditional notions of gender roles and the abandonment of the double standard of behavior for men and women. These trends indicate a historic move toward sexual mutuality among heterosexual couples.

Espin (1984) focuses on the sexuality of Hispanic women, whose lives are closely tied to cultural images of female sexual purity and male codes of honor. She argues that Latinas, in general, face a unique combination of power and powerlessness. Latinas gain power from the strong female bonds encouraged within the culture, the support for discussion of personal problems, and the male code for defense of female honor. However, the double standard of sexual purity for females and sexual machismo for males (which she defines as including multiple, uncommitted sexual contacts) creates obvious contradictions for women. In addition, the adoption by women of new sexual behaviors may be associated with guilt and betrayal within the community, indicating Anglo influences. Espin is very careful to note that sexual machismo is "nothing but the Hispanic version of the myth of male superiority supported by most cultures" (Espin, 1984:156) and that many Hispanics do not subscribe to this perspective and may reject outright the strong connotations of social deviance attached by Anglo observers. Importantly for women, Espin argues that every culture allows women a different range of accepted sexual behavior, and Latinas vary significantly in their choices and expression, and display the full range of heterosexual and lesbian lifestyles.

There have been other changes that have enhanced women's sexual freedom, including improvements in accessibility and reliability of birth control (birth control should be safe, unobtrusive, and mutual); the drop in the birthrate among young women at the start of their education and career patterns; access to legal abortion (uncoupling sex from reproduction); the gay liberation movement (a renewed vision of sex); public discussion of lesbianism as a challenge to the "old medical notion of sex centered on heterosexual intercourse as the psychic and physiological means to fulfillment" (Ehrenreich et al., 1986:196); and the increase in the divorce rate, which released sexually experienced men and women back into the courtship arena. As important, women's growing economic independence from men, though not necessarily affluence, offered more sexual freedom than the affluence gained through the barter of marriage. This sexual independence has been reinforced in the last two decades by changes in patriarchal legal institutions that have provided some women with some levels of protection against domestic abuse, incest, sexual assault, and abusive divorce situations.

The sexual liberation movement also challenged the old social meanings of sex—especially the romantic, magical ideal of "eternal love, romance, and always, (women's) surrender" (Ehrenreich et al., 1986:195). The insistence that sex be pleasurable for women was an assertion of power that gave new social and individual meaning to sex. This challenge was not without its detractors, not only from the conservative religious right but also from within the feminist movement itself. The sexualization of society may have shifted the oppressive nature of sexual relations, but true "liberation" was questionable.

The concerns about the costs of this independence are not irrational, for if sex is disconnected from reproduction, it is also disconnected from marriage, childbearing, and family commitments. "Women stand to lose their traditional claims on male support" (Ehrenreich et al., 1986:199), and the concepts of exchange and use value in the realm of sexuality are considerably shifted. Sexual access to women no longer ties men to economic or parenting responsibilities with the same social and legal expectations. Male-controlled media have enhanced an environment in which to define women as sex objects (D'Emilio and Freedman, 1988). Women remain more vulnerable to the lags in sexual social change because we still bear the risks and costs of contraception, abortion, and support for children. Social norms continue to couple women's sexuality with youth, and with a consumer-oriented image that interacts with capitalist market development in pornography. Ehrenreich et al. argue for a feminist way out of these sexual ambivalences and choices. Feminism is a

> collective way of making sense of things as women . . . by asking what's good for women? Feminists will differ on some answers; but the feminist milieu of discussion, analysis, and respect for individual experience is still the only place in which we have to ask that question. (1986:202)

Sex, reproduction, and motherhood.   The ideology of motherhood and the politics of reproduction are closely intertwined in local and international politics and reveal many of the contradictions that still arise in sexuality, whether in contemporary "liberated" Western societies or in more traditional countries. Motherhood is a powerful issue for feminists because women are socialized to value motherhood, yet at the same time motherhood oppresses women. Michelle Hoffnung (1989) argues that motherhood limits women socially through the use value of the "motherhood mystique." This mystique incorporates societal beliefs that assume that women's ultimate achievement is in becoming a "good" mother, that is, one whose exclusive devotion is to mothering, with positive outcomes for home, children, and husband. Research cited by Hoffnung indicates that the prerequisites for effective, adequate mothering include mothers who are emotionally stable, educated, satisfactorily married, and in unstressed economic conditions. Such a combination of factors would allow few women globally or nationally to fulfill the motherhood mystique.

Kristin Luker's (1984) research on pro-choice and antiabortion activists also highlights the role of motherhood. She identifies a constellation of commitments that women make early in life that later affect their positions on abortion and women's reproduction. These commitments are either to motherhood and family or to education and career. The value orientations and social characteristics of anti-choice women, she argues, restrict their options in the public world of work (their exchange value) and increase their dependence on the motherhood role (their use value) and need for male support. The controversy over abortion and birth control is rooted in social norms about sexuality, politics, and women's status, and Luker argues, more specifically, it has become a "referendum on the place and meaning of motherhood" (1986:193).

The struggle for control over women's bodies has been a focal point for feminist theory and research in the last century. Linda Gordon (1974) outlines a general history of birth control that begins with nineteenth-century efforts by feminists toward "voluntary motherhood" in which choice, freedom, and autonomy for women was a central goal. These efforts arose during a time when patriarchal, medical, legal, and religious philosophies repressed female sexuality through an ideology that distorted women's sexuality and supported compulsory motherhood (Duggan and Hunter, 1995).

The early history of birth control and abortion is an oral history of inventions, not by scientists or physicians, but by women. The use of birth control and the birthing process itself were integral parts of society that were under the control of women. The technology practiced by midwives and wisewomen were a part of the folklore of nearly all societies and stretched over millennia, having been handed down from generation to generation (Gordon, 1974:26). Indeed, until the invention of the contraceptive pill in the 1960s, most practices of birth control (magical to herbal to barrier to interruption) had been available throughout history. Until the invention of the forceps as a birthing instrument and the development of "gynecology" as a surgical-medical specialty dominated by men, most birthing practices took place in a women-centered setting (Scully, 1980). Because of the different interests of men and women in the practice of birth control and the birthing process, these issues have social significance for feminists. Of particular importance have been the development of artificial/hormonal contraceptive pills in the 1960s and the legal restrictions on abortion that have led to social changes in sexuality and the struggles over women's reproductive rights throughout the world.

An assessment by the United Nations of levels and trends of contraceptive use worldwide in 1988 demonstrates the sex-biased results. Throughout the world, the most frequently used contraception is female sterilization (26 percent of all contraceptive interventions). Male sterilization is used in only 9.6 percent of interventions. The IUD, hormonal pills, and hormone injections for women account for another 35 percent of methods, while the use of a condom is claimed in only 9.6 percent of contraception methods. Vaginal barrier methods (e.g., cervical caps, diaphragms) account for 1.6 percent of methods. Finally, some 15 percent of contraception is rhythm or withdrawal, which requires mutuality between sexual partners.

In all, women carry the sole burden worldwide for birth control in 61 percent of contraceptive usage, and men account for 19 percent. The remaining percentages are either mutual contraceptive techniques or are unspecified (United Nations, 1989). In what the United Nations defines as "less developed regions" women carry a greater burden of contraception than do women in industrial nations. Through female sterilization, hormone injections, pills, and IUD use, these women are solely responsible for 71 percent of contraceptive methods (and only 8 percent are mutual withdrawal or rhythm methods), whereas women in industrialized nations carry 50 percent of the responsibility solely (with an additional 32 percent of mutual rhythm/withdrawal techniques). In either setting, men have sole responsibility through male sterilization or condom use in less than 20 percent of contraception.

A major theme of feminist critiques in women's reproductive rights has to do with the biases in research, family planning, and health outcomes for women (Gordon, 1974; Hartmann, 1987). Chief among these biases is the emphasis in research on modifying women's fertility, omitting men's fertility as a research target (only 7 percent of public health research dollars are spent on male reproductive technology innovation). From top to bottom, men dominate the reproductive research process and view birth control as primarily a woman's concern (Hartmann, 1987). The focus has also been on systemic (hormonal) and surgical (sterilization) control, as opposed to developing more effective and less invasive barrier methods (e.g., cervical caps).

These biases combine to generate a questionable reproductive technology, according to feminist analysts. Hormonal and invasive technologies result in negative side effects. IUDs and the Dalkon Shield operate on an "inflammation" model, with the fertilized egg unlikely to implant itself in a womb suffering a consistent low-grade infection. The Dalkon Shield proved highly virulent, and IUDs have been associated with deaths, leading to restricted sales in the United States. Hormonal manipulation, including estrogen replacement therapy, Depo-Provera shots, and the more common estrogen/progestin pills, have also led to maternal deaths from clotting, heart failure, high blood pressure, and other complications. Among the "milder" side effects are depression, nervousness, sleeplessness, depressed libido (sexual drive), and weight gain.

As Hartmann (1987) points out, the injected Depo-Provera has proved effective on both women and men in fertility control, but the possibility of depressed libido has caused this drug to be dropped from the contraceptive research program for men. For women, evidently, a depressed libido is less significant (to male researchers), and the use of Depo-Provera injections is on the increase in Third World countries as a "foolproof" contraceptive method. The use value of birth control as it is tied to sexual behavior is closely aligned with the double standards in societal norms. The patriarchal biases in research and practice in the United States have now filtered out to family planning programs on a global basis in colonized countries.

Birth control and colonization.   The dimensions of sexuality, birth control, and abortion overlap in important ways with the issues of colonization in feminist theory. Their role as cheap labor and the ethnocentrism of colonizing cultures have deprived poor women and women of color of adequate reproductive health care in contrast to more affluent and privileged women. Hartmann (1987) puts this inequity at the center of the issue of the "population-control" policies that have been structured in the United States and, consequently, in major health and family planning organizations throughout the world.

The core of these policies is the argument that much of the famine, crime, pollution, and lack of education in developing nations is the result of overpopulation, rather than the unwillingness of governments to invest necessary resources in adequate social programs. The targets of these family planning programs are the fertility rates of women in non-Western societies. Hartmann challenges the notion of overpopulation as the "cause" of global problems. Instead, she identifies the overlap of ethnocentric, racist, sexist, and capitalist interests as creating a widespread misapplication of contraceptive technology and coercive planning practices.

Taking as a given that a woman's right to control her own reproduction is a fundamental human right, along with access to health and social services, Hartmann (1987) then recounts numerous abuses of women in the global manipulation of reproduction. The dumping of contraceptives banned in the United States by the Federal Drug Administration is a process that is unregulated by most developing nations. As in the past, these colonized countries provide a market free of restrictions and a relief valve for large corporations with banned commodities. Often, too, countries such as China, India, and Kenya seek to resolve larger political and economic problems by focusing on population control—using inducements, financial incentives, or even legal sanctions to gain compliance in population control efforts.

Hartmann compares the family planning experiences of Indonesia and

Kenya with those of Cuba. In Kenya, where a woman today bears on average eight children, the failure of family planning is based on two factors. First, the subsistence economic structure causes both men and women to value larger numbers of children as an economic investment, a view that is strongly supported by cultural norms. Second, the national family planning program, designed by foreign advisors, ignored the cultural, health, and economic issues to focus on a media campaign for the IUD, based on a claim of urgent need to restrict population growth. Local communities reacted to the foreign advisors and the campaign with charges of a white plot of "genocide," and popular support was lost. In Indonesia, the focus has been on family planning as a health resource, for both mothers and children, emphasizing birth spacing (not sterilization) and education. However, Hartmann notes the problem of informal pressure and coercion set up through the use of community "target rates of contraceptive use" and incentives paid to (male) group leaders who may then unduly pressure women to enhance their own rewards in reaching these goals.

Finally, she cites the rapid decline in birthrates and increase in life expectancy rates in Cuba. A country with relatively low per capita income levels, Cuba achieved this goal through a comprehensive community-based health program, with freely available planning services. Though Hartmann notes the continuing sexism within the Cuban system, she also cites the economic and social reforms that accompanied this health program as a base for the significant demographic changes.

To bring this struggle closer to home, Hartmann and others note the coercive use of reproductive technology against women in the United States, particularly poor and racial/ethnic minority women. It was Puertoriquenas who were targeted as subjects for the first human tests of the contraceptive pill, with the negative, even lethal, health outcomes of those early high-dosage pills. Today, sterilization is the most widely used method of birth control in the United States (Hartmann, 1987), but that choice often takes on a coercive context. Compulsory sterilization of ethnic minorities was highlighted in the *Relf* federal court case, in which two young African American women were sterilized without their consent or knowledge. In 1976, the U.S. General Accounting Office cited the sterilization of 3,000 Native American women in a four-year period using improper consent forms. Today, over 50 percent of the adult female population in Puerto Rico has been permanently sterilized.

The introduction of competitive practices among family planning programs in reaching "targets" and the provision of health care and prenatal care with sterilization or contraception strings attached on a global basis are evidence that capitalism, patriarchy, and colonization have intersected in the struggle to maintain control over women and their reproductive activities and value. Patterns of racist and sexist family planning programs have been confronted by feminist political health and sexuality groups, including the Black Women's Health Network, the Committee for Abortion Rights and Against

Sterilization Abuse, and the National Abortion Rights Action League (Ferree and Hess, 1985).

Abortion and reproductive rights.   At the center of the struggle over reproductive rights is the issue of abortion. Mohr's (1978) history of abortion legislation and practices highlights the role of physicians in enacting antiabortion legislation in the United States during the 1860s–1880s, due to the high number of deaths from abortions performed by incompetent practitioners as well as strong moral arguments from religious and political leaders against reproductive control. These state laws established controls over the advertising of abortion services (cited as obscene), revoked common-law immunities for women, and dropped traditional rules that allowed abortions prior to quickening (the time in pregnancy when a fetus can be felt to move by the mother), all of which stayed in effect, unchanged, through the 1960s (Mohr, 1978:225).

During the period before *Roe* v. *Wade* (1973), estimates are that some 700,000 to 1 million illegal abortions per year were performed. In 1958, Kinsey estimated that one of every four women in the United States had experienced at least one induced abortion. These illegal abortions were associated with high rates of maternal mortality, sterilization, and debilitating social and economic consequences for many.

Rodman, Sarvis, and Bonar (1987) found that approximately 1.5 million women a year in the United States had an induced legal abortion, more than 90 percent of which occurred during the first trimester, with fewer health risks than would have occurred if the fetus had been carried to full term. These numbers do not represent real increases, because they are raw numbers and do not reflect the very large increase in women of fertility age (those born between 1945 and 1960) at the time that *Roe* v. *Wade* was decided. In fact, the number of abortions performed in the United States has remained constant since the late 1980s. In 1992, according to data from the Alan Guttmacher Institute (AGI), there were 1.529 million abortions in the United States, 89 percent of which occurred during the first trimester (Planned Parenthood of Idaho, 1997).

Those opposed to abortion, and opposed to contraception products and education, have sought restrictive laws, including constitutional amendments and state restrictions on *Roe* v. *Wade*. In many cities in the United States, antichoice or "pro-life" groups picket agencies providing fertility control information and services, block entrances to reproductive service clinics, harass women seeking those services, and in numerous instances, vandalize, set on fire, or bomb agencies providing abortion services (Rodman et al., 1987). In 1993, Dr. David Gunn was shot to death outside a Florida clinic by Michael Griffin (*Atlanta Constitution*, March 12, 1993). Paul Hill used a 12-gauge shotgun to kill Dr. John Bayard Britton and his escort, James Barrett, on July 29, 1994 (*USA Today*, December 7, 1994), and Rachelle Renee Shannon shot a Wichita, Kansas physician (*Los Angeles Times,* August 21, 1993). Between 1993 and 1995, six doctors, employees, and volunteers of abortion clinics were killed by violent protesters. During the first seven months of 1994, almost 50 percent of all clinics in the United States were targeted for violence (*USA Today,* January, 10, 1995). In order to protect their employees, volunteers, and patients from violent antiabortion protesters, some clinics have been forced to close (*Boston Globe,* January 9, 1995). In some ways, these antifeminist efforts target more than women's reproductive rights; they extend to an effort to preserve the patriarchal system of domination itself (Ferree and Hess, 1985).

Sex as market.   The third frame of reference for sexuality is in the economic activities of prostitution and pornography.[1] These sexual activities take place primarily outside the family institution and have many characteristics of a market activity. Prostitution and pornography follow many of the supply-and-demand characteristics of the larger economy, with the product being the sexual activity of women. In both instances, women are sexual objects, treated anonymously and without control over their own labor. The pornography and prostitution industries are controlled by males, whether as producers, pimps, or enforcers of the legal sanctions against these activities. When these sexual activities take place outside the family, they are nonlegitimate from the standpoint of significant cultural norms, and much of the economic activity must then be carried out in illegal markets.

Under colonized conditions, the pressures from war, economic upheaval, and geographic dispersal make women vulnerable to sexual exploitation. As Brownmiller notes (1975), colonizing wars have brought women into the prostitution trade as camp followers. Women of color come to symbolize the act of national conquest on an individual level. The atrocities of capitalism and imperialism are affected by stark combinations with patriarchy.

Self-Esteem and Value

The social-psychological construct of *self-concept* identifies important aspects of how society and the individual interact. Every social being has a self-concept. The self-evaluation of that identity provides the comparative concept that Weber stated we must come to understand. Use value, in this instance, would include both the individual self-evaluation that leads to personal well-being (Am I a good person? Do I have value?) and the social factors that influence the construction of that evaluation by which the self-concept becomes a resource or a liability in social settings.

---

[1]*Pornography* is defined here as reflecting the Greek root for the term "the graphic depiction of whores." As Dworkin (1981) asserts, feminists have made honorable attempts to distinguish erotica from pornography. However, in the male sexual lexicon, the distinction is in the marketing, not in the vocabulary of power. "In the male system, erotica is a subcategory of pornography" (Dworkin, 1981:ii).

Sandra Bem's (1976) classic work has demonstrated that the social interpretation of gender creates an evaluative system for individuals, including "expert" individuals such as counselors and therapists. These evaluations also have consequences for behaviors, with those who adhere to the more traditional dichotomies of self-concepts into masculine and feminine clusters having fewer behavioral options.

It is important to note that philosophically and socially, men and the institutions they maintain (mental health disciplines, media images, family, and church) control the discourse on "what is a woman?" This discourse poses a fundamental problem for women's self-esteem because their self-evaluation is always drawn from a social context that is controlled by more powerful "others." In patriarchy, men possess the power to define the generalized other—the basic standards and norms of the collectivity from which we draw our evaluation of self (Ferguson, 1980). In colonized cultures, one aspect of the triple oppression is the distortion of culturally unique symbols of women as vessels of purity or evil (Mirande and Enriquez, 1979). Thus, indigenous women struggle with images of their folklore as earth mothers or whores, which are then complicated by the sexism of the colonizing culture.

In a market context, self-esteem becomes both a resource and a liability. Much of the human capital required for employment is predicated on some self-resource: achievement in school; ability to persevere in the face of failure; and the presentation of a confident, skilled self. As a resource, we can build self-esteem through a range of self-help courses and books, but most psychological literature indicates that females, in general, will have access to lower levels of this resource than men. Thus, we have the proliferation of consumer products targeted toward women to "assert ourselves gently," or to "dress for success."

However, the basis of self-esteem and confidence is already set in those nonverbal skills that men demonstrate with more social approval than do women. The literature on nonverbal cues and speech patterns demonstrates that masculine behavioral traits are the medium of exchange in the market. Men use more expansive gestures, tower by stature over their subordinates, and assume the right to interrupt "others" in conversations (Pearson, 1985).

SYNTHESIZING THE MODEL

The concept of *value* provides us with a way to assess the structural effects of capitalism, patriarchy, and colonization on the diversity of women's lives. The socially constructed notion of use value, as it is perceived by individuals and groups, is influenced by the systems of dominance in a particular society. Structure and process are both present in the struggle by women to establish individual *value* within the construct of their market value or use value in the United States and throughout the world.

Feminist theorists have identified one or more areas of power locus, with socialist feminists bridging the twin systems of patriarchy and capitalism to assess women's oppression. We draw from the colonization model used in sociology and racial/ethnic studies to specify further the combined and unique effects of internal or external colonization and the effects on women of color. The inclusion of the colonization model highlights that capitalism is not the sole predictor of these colonized relationships but that indigenous systems of patriarchy and cultural colonization must also be addressed.

Chafetz's formal model suggests the range of structures and institutions where value is defined, ranging from family to religion to education, but with an emphasis on the work sphere. Social definitions arise out of and reinforce economic and other structural phenomena (Chafetz, 1988:138). The previous examples illustrate that definitions arise in the economic activities of women, not only in the labor market but also in the household and the community. Sexuality takes on meaning not only in the family but also in the market, especially when the mediating power of men is introduced. Self-esteem takes on its initial meanings in the family, school, and church, but then mediates social relations in other institutions. We extend Chafetz's model to deliberately include the activist, interactionist emphasis framed within women's studies paradigms proposed by Smith (1987) and Collins (1990). Chapter Four identifies the rationale, the historical antecedents, and the praxis of a sociology by, for, and about women.

This integrative model, with a focus on *value,* provides a framework for analyzing shifts in the consequences and dimensions of oppression for a wide range of women. In patriarchy, the meaning of sexuality and self-esteem is refocused depending on the location of family or economy within the definition. In a capitalist market economy, the value of sexuality and self-esteem is parallel to the economic exchange value that generates profits for a dominant class. Under colonized conditions, the norms of the dominant group manipulate the symbolic and material use of women in subordinated cultures during war and economic exploitation. In each of these arenas, the notion of use value as defined by women has been largely omitted from discussions of any major institutions.

In order for this integrative model to be effective, it must be applicable and challengeable through the use of feminist methodologies and praxis. In the next chapter, we outline feminist methodologies that tend to reduce or, if possible, eliminate the ethical and developmental problems of patriarchal research within sociology.

FOUR

Feminist Methodologies

The methods and practice of a sociology of women will inherently transform the discipline. Drawing from both women's studies and sociology, we identify those assumptions of social science research that have been embedded in the study of women and explore the alternative interpretations and methodologies proposed from a sociology of women.

Until very recently, almost all studies of women reflected the nature of the patriarchal structures of the society in which they took place. Whether it was the early philosophers or twentieth-century scientists, women were looked *at* primarily by men. Rarely did women do their own "looking" in the sense of having the privilege of observing, analyzing, and presenting their own observations. Moreover, looking *at* women generally meant subsuming women under *man* (i.e., assuming that when studying men we were also learning about women) or studying women separately and interpreting them as "other" than men, where men were used as the standard or norm. These biases created a distorted knowledge base with few theoretical or conceptual tools to confront it.

FEMINIST RESEARCH IN SOCIOLOGY

In recent years, there has been an increased commitment in research among sociologists interested in women and women's issues. Specifically, the recent focus in sociological literature on sex roles, the life course, social stratification, and occupation portrays a new commitment to women's lives (Lopata, 1976). The sociology of the family has taken a dramatic shift away from the traditional instrumental/expressive dichotomy of functional theory to look at both historical patterns and contemporary shifts with new alternative dynamic models (Thorne, 1982). The sociology of work has begun to analyze the research done in the stratification field illustrating the sex segregation and unequal reward systems. In addition, the sexist assumptions underlying "paid labor-force participation" are being questioned as women's work at home is being redefined and therefore made visible and each female-dominated job is no longer lumped together with other female occupations. The last two decades have also brought a dramatic change in research standards.

FEMINIST METHODOLOGY

Feminist research transcends the simple observation of women's lives; it also incorporates the dictates of a feminist methodology. A feminist methodology in sociology is informed by both the activist traditions of women's studies and the empirical background of sociology. It goes beyond the "add women and stir" tradition in sociology where traditional theories and research methods are applied to the population of women as research subjects.

Sandra Harding distinguishes among methodology, method, and epistemology. A *methodology* is "a theory and analysis of how research does or should proceed," whereas a *method* is "a technique for (or way of proceeding in) gathering evidence" (1987:2–3). *Epistemology* refers to

> a theory of knowledge. It answers questions about who can be a "knower" (can women?); what tests beliefs must pass in order to be legitimated as knowledge (only tests against men's experiences and observations?); what kinds of things can be known (can "subjective truths" count as knowledge?), and so forth. (Harding, 1987:3)

Epistemology plays a significant role in shaping a feminist methodology and raising questions about traditional methods. Sandra Harding outlines three characteristics of a feminist methodology or a feminist choice of method: First, it utilizes new empirical and theoretical resources that incorporate the full range of women's experiences, including those of women of different races, cultures, classes, and so on. Second, the research problem is seen as inseparable from the purpose of the research and analysis; researchers cannot remove themselves from the purpose and consequences of their research. Third, the researcher is seen in the same sphere as the research participant: "That is, the class, race, culture, and gender assumptions, beliefs, and behaviors of the researcher her/himself must be placed within the frame of the picture that she/he attempts to paint" (Harding, 1987:9). The empirical evidence itself includes the beliefs, attitudes, and behaviors of the researcher.

Feminist methodology is not an entity separate from other methodologies, but rather the application of feminist principles to the scientific enterprise. There is not a single methodological approach we can define as feminist. Reinharz and Davidman (1992) analyze *Feminist Methods in Social Science Research* "with an emphasis on the plural. It demonstrates the fact that feminists have used all existing methods and have invented some new ones as well. Instead of orthodoxy, feminist research practices must be recognized as a plurality" (1992:4). You may actually find a feminist quantitative experiment (Wallston, 1985) along with sexist qualitative research (Nebraska Sociological Feminist Collective, 1983). There are ways in which we alter the scientific enterprise, questioning the roots of scientism to develop a feminist methodology in the sociology of women.

Obstacles to Feminist Methodology

The selection of research questions and the formulation of research projects are affected by a number of factors, many related to power. A feminist research process is hindered by many things, including the political determination of who is to receive research funding, the tradition of gender-blind social theory, the omission of topics significant to women, the selective treatment of topics, the inadequate specification of research topics, and the trivialization of women through research language.

Research requires resources: money for salaries and equipment, access to information and research subjects, and the commitment of others (e.g., assistants, colleagues) to the research process undertaken.

The topics of research that can be funded are often politically determined. The allocation of funds for certain areas of research, often through "old boy" networks that favor the research of established/legitimate individuals and groups who have "track records," leaves women along with nonnetworked male researchers underfunded (Nebraska Sociological Feminist Collective, 1983). In addition, there is the general underrepresentation of women researchers, as well as the biases in past theory and research that omit, trivialize, or distort women's lives, as described throughout this text. What is evident is that the excellent feminist research that has begun to develop is most often the result of researchers who work without access to, and often in spite of, the research being conducted with mainstream resources.

Gender-blind social theory slows the feminist research process because past analyses have ignored women's conditions. In traditional research models, gender may be a significant factor in a setting, but the sex/gender system itself is not explored or incorporated into a theory, interpretation, or analysis. In a sociological analysis, context or situational factors are vital to understanding human behavior. When characteristics such as sex, class, or race are ignored, then the history of structural oppression is ignored, and contemporary explanations are incomplete.

The research on women's "fear of success" is one example. Early research concluded that women, particularly in business, had a motivational deficit that prevented them from succeeding (Horner, 1972). However, "women live in a society where they are punished for success in traditionally masculine areas; thus, what has been termed fear of success may instead be a realistic appraisal of the world" (Wallston, 1985:228).

Significant topics are ignored because they have no particular significance for male researchers or male-dominated funding agencies. One prime example is the insufficient research on the organization of housework and its economic and emotional impact upon women workers (both in and out of the paid labor force). The focus of most research on housework in the United States has been the amount of time spent (by both males and females), satisfaction rates, and efficiency of household division of labor (Berk and Berk, 1979). Ann Oakley's works, *The Sociology of Housework* (1974) and *Women's Work*, (1975), are notable exceptions: She incorporates a feminist qualitative methodology in her analysis of women's work. More recently, several socio-historical works have generated significant discussion, but few well-funded research activities are taking place in this area.[1] The focus has been on expected increases in the contributions of men to housework, rather than the meaning and costs of housework to those women who shoulder the burden on a day-to-day basis.

The selective treatment of topics once they are researched also contributes to an androcentric (male-centered) research process. Those research topics with special salience for men are defined as covering the entire topic, while aspects of special importance for women are underresearched. For example, the "acceptance" of women's work outside the home has focused almost exclusively on the reactions of the males (presumed to be heads of the households). The "acceptance" of women working outside the home by women is seen primarily as "relief from the boredom of housework" or an attempt to put aside some "pin money" for special expenses. The economic necessity of working for many women remains an unexamined social-psychological issue *in and of itself* with ramifications for women's preferences for their economic and household activities.

The inadequate specification of research topics reinforces the overt omission of women from research. Thus, when research on work excludes housework, no direct statement is made about this omission. Women's work, therefore, is unremarkable, unnoted, or perhaps only footnoted. Other aspects of this inadequate specification include the assumption that a research model, when specified for men only, has been adequately addressed. This has important policy consequences, as when Social Security payments were based on the employment patterns of male workers (see Chapter Five). As we shall see later, women's economic security in their later years is therefore left uncertain.

[1]Examples include Strasser's *Never Done* (1982); Lopata's *Occupation: Housewife* (1971); and Andre's *Homemakers: The Forgotten Workers* (1981).

The trivialization of women through research language includes the use of pejorative terms. In addition, studies of women in areas outside of their prescribed roles are often defined as the study of *deviant behavior* or problems; situations in which women conform to their prescribed roles are assumed to be nonproblematic.

FEMINIST CRITIQUES OF ANDROCENTRIC RESEARCH

In addition to these "in house" critiques of sexist biases, the women's movement has generated a critique of science generally and social sciences specifically that closely parallels that raised by black and other racial/ethnic groups in the early 1970s.

Feminist Critique of Science

As we saw in Chapter One, feminist theorists and researchers have criticized the strong androcentric bias embodied in science. Keller (1982) presents the critiques on a continuum from liberal to radical, with the liberal critique focusing on unfair employment practices within science occupations and a radical critique claiming that the androcentric bias is not only practiced in the "hard sciences"[2] but embodied in the structure of science itself. The radical critique challenges the very core of the scientific process by questioning the assumptions of objectivity and rationality (Keller, 1982). However, it is not simply the process of objectivity or the claim to rationality that feminists question: "The ideological ingredients of particular concern to feminists are found where objectivity is linked with autonomy and masculinity, and in turn, the goals of science with power and domination" (Keller, 1982:594).

Feminist researchers challenge claims to objectivity, rationality, and ethical neutrality on the basis that by using the traditional model of science, they will be neglecting the importance of subjective and ideological factors (Benston, 1982). Women's lives, experiences, and status become invisible in the objectification process either by omission or commission.

> Women and gender are either routinely ignored, yielding dimensionably unbalanced conclusions, or that, when they are taken as a direct object of inquiry the results are deeply flawed and transparently reflect sexist affirmation of popular (pre)conceptions about the superiority of men and the inevitability of women's subordination. (Wylie et. al., 1989:379)

Feminist critiques, as well as class- and race-based critiques, of sociology and the other social sciences have been made at many points in time. However,

---

[2]Pauline Bart (1971) discusses the phallocentric terms of *hard* and *soft* science with the obvious connection between more masculine sciences and the *hard* sciences.

the structure of the political movements of the 1960s gave coherence and impetus to these critiques.

> The result is . . . configuration that should be analyzed from the view of the oppressed—not the oppressor. Such an analysis is Black sociology. If white sociology is the science of oppression, Black sociology must be the science of liberation. (Staples, 1973:162)

The Myth of a Value-Free Sociology

For a variety of historical reasons, sociology as a discipline adheres to several assumptions that are not challenged by the reformist views just presented. These revolve around the issue of objectivity. We assume that it is impossible to be value-free in one's research. "Feminists, then, argue for bringing values to consciousness and developing a value-sensitive science" (Wallston, 1985:227). According to Francine Blau (Blau and Jusenius, 1976), there are three areas where researchers will be influenced by values: first, in selecting the problems to be studied; second, in making decisions on how the research is to be carried out; and third, in interpreting the findings. Facts rarely speak for themselves in the social sciences and must be interpreted; therefore, it is not only important but vital that the role of values in research be legitimated and recognized in the process.

Quantitative Versus Qualitative

The issue of objectivity and subjectivity in research often leads to a debate over quantitative versus qualitative research techniques. Quantitative research, sometimes referred to as "hard" methods, implies the use of survey techniques and data analysis; in sum, the quantifying of human behavior. Qualitative research involves a more subjective approach, utilizing such techniques as ethnographies, extensive interviewing, and observational studies. It has been argued that feminist research can only be conducted using qualitative methods. The sexism of research methods can be not only in the method but also in the researcher. Therefore, we leave open the possibility of quantitative feminist research.

THE DANGER OF A UNIDIMENSIONAL
FEMINIST METHODOLOGY

It is vital to the development of a feminist methodology that the focus on women's lives include all women and not simply those most accessible (i.e., white, middle-class, ablebodied, heterosexual, educated women). The necessity to develop a sociology of women does not imply that gender issues should be analyzed at the exclusion of race and class issues. Women's lives are not so unidimensional. However, a model that simply applies the traditional scientific techniques to women's lives will inevitably lead to this form of exclusionary practice. Zinn et al., in their article on the costs of exclusionary practices in women's studies, illustrated the trend toward this practice.

> Scholarship that overlooks the diversity of women's experience cannot reveal the magnitude, complexity, or the interdependence of systems of oppression. Such work underestimates the obstacles to be confronted and helps little in developing practical strategies to overcome the sexist barriers that even privileged women inevitably confront. (1986:299)

The authors highlighted the academic and financial problems that women of color and working-class women face in higher education, especially the limited resources available throughout the education process and also in public institutions where many women hold positions. Elitism of private universities makes the inequities between private and public institutions more dramatic.

In addition, Zinn et al. critique feminist theory, claiming that it has failed in its attempt to explore the intersections of race, class, and gender. They recommend three courses of action: First, feminists should fight for heterogeneous college faculties that include minority and working-class women and men. We would extend this to include lesbians, elderly women, and the physically challenged. Second, feminists should develop links among various types of institutions, thereby rejecting elitism. Third, feminists need to move beyond tokenism for minorities and working-class women (Zinn et al., 1986).

There are many difficulties inherent in the attempt to develop research methods that are not exclusionary and hold the potential for illustrating the diversity of women, as well as empowering them. However, if these difficulties are not confronted, feminist methodology runs the risk of repeating the same mistakes made by traditional patriarchal research.

Bonnie Thorton Dill (1983) illustrates that it is possible to analyze the intersection of race, class, and gender. She argues that in order to truly understand black women's lives, we must investigate not only the social-structural components that affect their lives but also the relationship between these components and the self-perception of black women themselves:

> For Black women and other women of color an examination of the ways in which racial oppression, class exploitation, and patriarchy intersect their lives must be studied in relation to their perceptions of the impact these structures have upon them. (Dill, 1983:138)

By incorporating the social-structural analysis with the diversity of individual perceptions, we can begin to weave together the varied components of women's lives.

THE RESEARCH PROCESS

In all research processes, guidelines exist for the development of hypotheses, choosing the research method, selecting the sample, and so on. These traditional techniques for data collection are analyzed in terms of the omission or trivialization of women's roles in human behavior. We now examine four of these processes: the review of the literature, the selection of the population and sample, validity issues, and the interpretation of research results.

Review of Previous Research

One principle of sociological research is to build upon the observations and interpretations of past work in the field. In sociology, researchers often fail to mention that samples (subjects) are single-sex or have highly imbalanced sex ratios. The results of past studies are cited without reference to the general focus on males and attention to male samples. This reinforces the general problems of omission and distortion.

Methodological weaknesses of past research are often ignored. Prime among these are the conclusions of past researchers that cast women in an inferior light, or that trivialize their experiences. Past studies suffer from serious bias and methodological weaknesses, but the reviewer fails to warn the reader about these problems and how they may invalidate previous conclusions and interpretations.

Selection of Population and Sample

Women are often arbitrarily excluded from a sample, and we are thereby denied knowledge and information about women. For example, most studies of the military had very little information on the small number of women who participated during peacetime and the larger numbers who participated in wartime conflict. Thus, as the armed forces turned to a volunteer army and drew women as part of a reserve labor force of military recruits, we had little or no information on these women, though they have always been a part of the armed forces.

Often the exclusion of women comes from arbitrary decisions involving costs for the research, or researchers are unfamiliar with women's lives and assume that the topic is only relevant for men, or the reverse, only relevant for women.

Another difficulty is the focus on white middle-class employed women. It ignores the diversity of poor or working-class women's experiences, or employment discrimination against lesbians, or the professional contributions of black, Hispanic, and Asian women (Rosen, 1987).

Validity Issues

Validity refers to the ability of any researcher to assure that he or she study a social situation in an optimal fashion, without bias, and with methods that will yield reasonably accurate information for making interpretations. Major obstacles that invalidate research include the following:

1. *Biased questions in surveys:* For example, a person is asked to indicate who the *male* head of household is, which will yield only one conclusion, that the individual named is the only and the most powerful head of household. The U.S. Census did this until 1980.

2. *Scales validated on the basis of a single sex and then applied to both sexes:* A scale is validated, for example, on a sample of men but then is applied to samples of both men and women. An example of this is the research on work satisfaction. Research findings have been contradictory concerning why women generate positive feeling about their nonwage labor roles but relatively low satisfaction with their actual work tasks. Oakley's (1974) in-depth interview techniques reveal that women value the role of "housewife" but find the work itself to be degrading and uninteresting, which is why men avoid it.

3. *Cross-sex interviewing (e.g., men questioning women), particularly on highly sensitive, gender-related questions:* Efforts need to be instituted to use interviewers who will yield the least bias in eliciting responses. This is especially true in being able to reach women of diverse racial and ethnic backgrounds and also to discuss emotionally charged issues, such as marital rape (Russell, 1982).

Interpretation of Research Results

Given the general problems of sampling, bias in questions, and the paucity of information on women by women, it is not surprising that the American Sociological Association Committee on the Status of Women concluded that many inferences drawn from data are unwarranted. In addition, the direct bias built into a researcher's expectations for women lead to overgeneralization of studies and improper reference (such as that to "society" when we really only have information about men) and conclusions that have adverse implications for women.

ETHICS OF RESEARCH IN A SOCIOLOGY OF WOMEN

Because of the subjective, interpersonal, and often political nature of research that impacts women's lives, ethics are an integral component of the feminist research enterprise. A traditional research ethic differs from a feminist research ethic. A traditional ethic is concerned with protecting the anonymity and confidentiality of the respondents as well as avoiding undue harm to subjects as a result of the research enterprise. The focus is on minimizing costs only in relation to achieving the traditional goals of research, which include the advancement and enlightenment of the discipline. Traditionalist researchers see themselves as accountable only to the profession.

Feminist ethics, on the other hand, analyzes social oppression in order to empower women and minorities. Feminist researchers are accountable to their peers, the women's movement, and feminists, as well as to their own research participants (Nebraska Sociological Feminist Collective, 1988).

The Nebraska Sociological Feminist Collective (1983) focused on four key issues for developing feminist ethics in the social sciences. The first issue addresses women's objectification as research objects in a process that defines males as the objective experts on women's lives. The second focuses on research that has neglected to involve women throughout the research process. Third, they confront sexist language and its use throughout sociological research. Finally, they address the gatekeeping process, which has effectively kept feminist research marginal.

Objectification of Women as Research Objects

The objectification of women as research objects defines males as objective/known and dichotomizes women to other/unknown. There is power inherent in the research process (e.g., use of the term *experimenter*), and by definition a lack of power is implied in the use of the term *subject* (Wallston, 1985). Feminism calls for a redistribution of power and for empowering women both as research participants and as researchers. The Collective recommends three steps for researchers to use to minimize the objectification of the research participant (1983):

1. Learn, accept, and use qualitative, historical, and other methodologies that highlight women's oppressions.
2. Learn, critique, and use new research techniques, even those that have only been used in the patriarchal enterprise.
3. Institutionalize reflexiveness, self-criticism, and accountability into the research process. Reflexiveness involves the participant/subject's account of the research process.

Clearly, we must incorporate methodological pluralism into our research designs.

Research by, for, and About Women

As the cultural feminists indicated, it is necessary to focus on analyzing women's everyday reality. The Collective (1983) recommends the following:

1. Conduct research that enables women to speak about their own lives and in their own words.
2. Analyze the conditions of women in all areas of sociological specializations such

as sociology of law, race and ethnicity, stratification, and not simply look at women in relation to marriage and the family or sex roles.

Male scientists should not be unquestioned experts in knowing women's lives.

Language as Used and Abused in Sociology

Patriarchal and classist language is an integral component of the sociological enterprise. This excludes and trivializes women. Exclusiveness of the sociological jargon prevents research subjects from learning about their own lives and reaffirms that social scientists can become experts in knowing women's lives. The Collective (1983) recommends the following:

1. Publicly critique patriarchal language, theory, and concepts and then use only language that is nonexclusive, accessible, and demystified.
2. Eliminate the exclusive use of English by incorporating bilingualism in journals, abstracts, course syllabi, and so forth.
3. Stress the active voice instead of the passive voice.

The Gatekeeping Process

The gatekeeping process in employment, funding, and research reinforces the traditional and marginalizes the new and different. The Collective (1983) recommends the following:

1. Empower feminist ethics and feminist accountability in the development of new journals (such as *Gender and Society*) as well as incorporating them in the current sociological journals.
2. Create shared decision-making processes that involve boards and editors with more input from readers, research subjects, and the general public.
3. Improve access to sociology and feminist conferences, meetings, and presentations through sliding fees, accessible language, and recruitment of community participants.
4. Improve access to journals in the same way by recruiting nonacademic search reviews, particularly by groups who have become the "objects" of the research.

SUMMARY: A FEMINIST METHODOLOGY

In analyzing women's lives, traditional patriarchal sociology reinforced biased views of women and distorted the knowledge base. We define a feminist methodology as the application of feminist principles to the scientific enterprise. It is inherently transformist to the discipline and transcends simple observations of women's lives.

In developing a feminist research process, many issues need to be addressed and continually reexamined. We need to challenge many of the traditional academic processes, including the political nature of research funding; the selection of topics that either ignore or trivialize issues important to women; and the use of patriarchal, demeaning language. Instead, we need to use empowering language, develop a value-sensitive science, and strive to capture the diversity of women's lives.

Use of a feminist ethic is an integral component of the feminist research process. It is different from traditional social science ethics in that it analyzes social oppression in order to empower women and minorities.

FIVE

Women and Work

Women's work takes on different meanings in different societies. As the United States moved from being a rural agricultural society to an industrial and now postindustrial multinational economic system, women's work has changed in some ways and remained the same in others. The decades before and after World War II have shown significant changes in the types of jobs, amount of pay, working conditions, and social attitudes about women as workers and employers. So, too, have factors changed that push or pull women into wage labor, including family responsibilities, consumption patterns, educational preparation, legal rights, and work opportunities.

It is also illuminating to contrast the economic conditions of diverse groups of women. While women in management struggle with barriers to promotion, their situations are different from women struggling with part-time jobs in the service sector. As daughters of poverty, or as young AFDC mothers, some women share conditions similar to older women whose retirement or displacement from families reflects a history of discrimination in wages, marital laws, benefits, and social attitudes toward women and poverty. Among women of color, economic conditions vary as well. The lives of African American women should be contrasted to those of Asian women or Chicanas in the United States, whether in their professional work as lawyers or nurses, or in their struggle with poverty at various stages of the life cycle. The status of new immigrant women in the United States—Vietnamese, Cambodian, and Haitian—reminds us that our international connections to women are vital to our understanding of and search for solutions to women's economic issues.

While the overall proportion of women with wage-earning jobs has remained fairly stable throughout the world for the past few decades, new patterns in economic participation of women have emerged (Blau and Ferber, 1986). The participation rates are steadily increasing and some have predicted that women's labor force participation rates in industrialized societies will approximate those of men by the year 2000. Throughout the world women have been entering the paid labor market in increasing numbers, and they are taking up an increasing share of the paid labor force worldwide, except in sub-Saharan Africa and Central Asia (see Table 5-1).

The graph in Figure 5-1 illustrates that while the economic activity of women is on the rise, there is an overall decline in the economic activity of men. In the industrialized countries, women now make up almost one-half of the labor force, and in 1996 women made up 31 percent of the labor force in developing countries. Increases in women's participation rates have been especially dramatic over the past twenty years. For example, in Portugal the female labor-force participation rate grew from 21.3 percent in 1970 to 43.7 percent in 1990 (United Nations Blue Book Series, 1996).

TABLE 5-1   Economic Activity Rates, by Sex, 1970–1990 (percentages)

	1970		1980		1990[a]	
	Women	*Men*	*Women*	*Men*	*Women*	*Men*
Developed Regions						
Eastern Europe[b]	56	79	56	77	58	74
Western Europe[b]	37	78	42	75	51	72
Other developed	40	81	46	78	54	75
Africa						
Northern Africa	8	82	12	79	21	75
Sub-Saharan Africa	57	90	54	89	53	83
Latin America and Caribbean						
Latin America	22	85	25	82	34	82
Caribbean	38	81	42	77	49	72
Asia and the Pacific						
Eastern Asia	57	86	58	83	56	80
Southeastern Asia	49	87	51	85	54	81
Southern Asia	25	88	24	85	44	78
Central Asia	55	76	56	77	58	79
Western Asia	22	83	26	81	30	77
Oceania	47	88	46	86	48	76

[a] Based on national population census and survey data as reported by countries and not adjusted for comparability to internationally recommended definitions. Covers fewer countries than the ILO estimates.
[b] Figures for 1970 and 1980 include ILO estimates for states succeeding the former USSR.

Source: United Nations. 1995. *The World's Women, 1995: Trends and Statistics.* Social Statistics and Indicators, Series K 12 (Sales No. E.95.XVII.2). New York: United Nations Publications, chart 5.4B, p. 110.

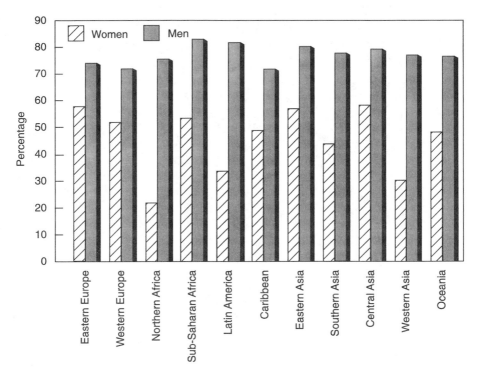

FIGURE 5-1   Economic Activity Rates by Sex, 1990
Source: Based on *The World's Women, 1995: Trends and Statistics.* United Nations publication, Series K 12 (Sales No. E.95.XVII.2), chart 5.4B:110.

Although women's labor-force participation rates have increased worldwide, their rates of unemployment have also increased. In fact, as illustrated in Table 5-2, their share of the unemployment rate often exceeds their share in the paid labor force in many developing countries and in some industrial countries.

In addition to unemployment rates, women often are underemployed. The International Labour Organization (ILO) defines the underemployed as "those who would like additional work, who work for low wages or whose skills are underutilized" (United Nations Blue Book Series, 1996:625). Given this definition, many women in industrialized countries are underemployed because women who seek full-time paid work end up in part-time employment.

Throughout the decades of change, women have always worked, but they have not always been paid equitably, or paid at all, for their labor. To fully understand women's work, we must include an analysis of women's unpaid labor in the home (housework, child care, care to disabled or elderly family members) and in the community as volunteers. This nonwage labor is rarely treated as significant by economists or social scientists because much of what we value

TABLE 5-2 Female Share in the Unemployed and Economically Active Populations: Selected Countries or Territories, 1975–1995 (percentage)

Selected Countries	1975		1985		1995	
	Unemployed	Economically Active	Unemployed	Economically Active	Unemployed	Economically Active
Developing Countries						
Barbados	57.1	43.3	59.4	47.2	57.6	49.4
Brazil	28.3	24.2	33.8	27.2	—	39.4
Chile	35.2	24.8	30.8	28.0	36.2	32.4
Costa Rica	38.3	19.7	30.1	21.6	38.4	—
Ghana	21.5	41.9	30.7	40.6	—	—
Jamaica	67.2	44.6	66.2	45.8	—	47.4
Panama	45.6	25.8	47.1	26.7	49.4	34.3
Puerto Rico	25.5	28.3	26.1	29.4	31.2	39.6
Republic of Korea	22.5	33.3	22.8	34.0	33.2	40.2
Syrian Arab Republic	9.2	13.2	25.5	16.0	—	—
Thailand	38.5	47.1	60.8	45.9	—	—
Trinidad and Tobago	37.5	27.8	36.3	29.7	44.6	37.2
Venezuela	22.1	23.3	25.0	26.7	41.8	33.6

Industrialized Countries

Austria	54.1	39.6	39.6	40.2	44.4[a]	42.8
Belgium	54.1	32.2	55.9	33.8	54.1	—
Denmark	31.9	40.0	55.6	44.2	56.2	45.3
Finland	34.8	45.0	46.6	46.6	46.1	47.0
France	56.6	37.7	53.8	39.6	53.4	45.2
Germany	42.0	37.2	44.1	37.7	50.7	42.8
Greece	34.6	25.9	42.5	26.4	58.5	38.1
Italy	54.6	30.1	57.4	31.7	—	—
Netherlands	21.7	28.6	34.6	31.0	51.2	41.5
Norway	47.5	35.0	54.9	40.5	43.0	45.7
Portugal	44.8	30.9	56.9	24.1	—	44.6
Switzerland	23.3	35.3	45.9	36.7	51.2	43.2
Turkey	11.4	36.5	16.4	34.0	30.9	30.4
United Kingdom	18.7	37.1	31.2	38.7	34.9	—
United States	44.0	39.1	45.6	41.5	46.2	46.1

— Data not recorded.

[a]All industrialized countries use the labour force survey for total unemployed with the exception of France, which is an official estimate.

Source: United Nations Blue Book Series. 1996. *The United Nations and the Advancement of Women, 1945–1996* (Vol. VI, Sales No.E.96.I.9). New York: United Nations Publications, Table 2. p. 626 (1975 and 1985 data). International Labour Office. 1996. *Year Book of Labour Statistics, 1996* (55th Issue). Geneva, Switzerland: International Labour Organization Publications, Table 1A and Table 3A (1995 data). Copyright © International Labour Organization 1996.

as a society is indicated by its price tag. In the case of women's work, its devaluation due to the lack of a wage is compounded by the fact that much of the actual labor is in service to the relatively powerless—children, the infirm elderly, the poor, and the sick. In the economic world, the classic definitions of *use value* and *exchange value* have powerful connotations.

The advertisement that women "have come a long way, baby" is based on a distorted view of women's objective economic conditions of low wages, restricted job patterns, and unrecognized volunteer labor. In the next section, we provide a profile of women workers in the 1980s and 1990s, contrasting their position to that of women workers during the economic and civil rights expansion period of the 1970s. We then introduce several theoretical explanations for these patterns and highlight frameworks for a theory of work within the sociology of women. The baseline economic information is also used to examine the range of options and resources women have in addressing other key issues, including some discussed at length in this book: crime, legal discrimination, victimization, aging, health care, sexuality, and education.

SEX SEGREGATION AND THE LABOR MARKET

As seen in Table 5-3, women and men work in the United States in very different sectors of the labor market. Although women make up close to one-half of all professional workers, it is clear that *within* the professions women are constrained to a small range of professions that form what some call the *semiprofessions* (Etzioni, 1969). These semiprofessions include jobs that are identified as having less autonomy, lower wages, and lower prestige than the *true professions*. Among these are nursing, teaching, social work, and library work. The largest category of employment for women remains in clerical, or administrative support, work. Note that while women dominate the routine, semiskilled tasks of office work, men are overrepresented in the supervisory, authority positions when compared with their general participation in the clerical category.

These data also indicate that some sectors of the labor market, particularly skilled crafts, remain resistant to entry by women. In 1970, women made up fewer than 6 percent of the skilled labor force, and by 1986, after more than fifteen years of nontraditional programs and training efforts, participation rose to only 9 percent and remained constant into the 1990s. Generally, women are confined to the bottom of the occupational hierarchy, in service and clerical work, or even to the lower-prestige professions. Fully one out of every three working women is involved in clerical work. The service sector of the labor market has become feminized, having predominately female employees in a particular occupation with corresponding lower wages, in most countries throughout the world. Women tend to be concentrated in public service occupations, teaching, administrative and commercial enterprises, and domestic services. Women often account for 90 percent of employees in those occupations

TABLE 5-3   Sex Segregation of Workers, 1983–1995

Occupation	Males (%) 1983	Males (%) 1995	Females (%) 1983	Females (%) 1995
Managerial and Professional Specialty	*59.1*	*52.0*	*40.9*	*48.0*
Executive, administrative, and managerial	67.6	57.3	32.4	42.7
Professional specialty	51.9	47.1	48.1	52.9
Architects	87.3	80.2	12.7	19.8
Engineers	94.2	91.6	5.8	8.4
Physicians	84.2	75.6	15.8	24.4
Registered nurses	4.2	6.9	95.8	93.1
Teachers, college and university	63.7	54.8	36.3	45.2
Teachers, except college and university	29.1	25.3	70.9	74.7
Technical, Sales, and Administrative Support	*35.4*	*35.6*	*64.6*	*64.4*
Sales occupations	52.5	50.5	47.5	49.5
Sales workers, retail and personal services	30.3	34.4	69.7	65.6
Administrative support, including clerical	20.1	20.5	79.9	79.5
Supervisors	46.6	40.0	53.4	60.0
Secretaries	1.0	1.5	99.0	98.5
Bank tellers	9.0	9.9	91.0	90.1
Service Occupations	*39.9*	*40.0*	*60.1*	*60.0*
Private household	3.9	4.5	96.1	95.5
Child care workers	3.1	3.2	96.9	96.8
Protective service	87.2	84.1	12.8	15.9
Precision Production, Craft, and Repair	*91.9*	*91.1*	*8.1*	*8.9*
Mechanics and repairers	97.0	96.1	3.0	3.9
Operators, Fabricators, and Laborers	*73.4*	*75.7*	*26.6*	*24.3*
Machine operators, assemblers, and inspectors	57.9	62.7	42.1	37.3
Textile sewing machine operator	6.0	14.3	94.0	85.7
Truck drivers	96.9	95.5	3.1	4.5
Laborers, except construction	80.6	79.4	19.4	20.6
Farming, Forestry, and Fishing	*84.0*	*80.1*	*16.0*	*19.9*
Farm operators and managers	87.9	74.7	12.1	25.3
Forestry and logging occupations	98.6	96.4	1.4	3.6

Source: U.S. Bureau of the Census. 1996. *Statistical Abstract of the United States 1996* (116th ed.). Washington, DC: U.S. Government Printing Office, Table 637.

(United Nations Blue Book Series, 1996). The prospects for women employees in the future will probably remain the same since of the twenty occupations that are predicted to have the largest growth by the year 2005, the vast majority are in services.

In 1994, 58 percent of women in the United States participated in the paid labor force. Historically, black women have participated at higher rates than white women, often concentrated in low-paying occupations. However,

TABLE 5-4   Occupation by Sex and Race: March 1994

	Black		White	
	Male	*Female*	*Male*	*Female*
Number employed 16 years and older in thousands	5,836	6,487	55,786	47,094
Percent employed in				
Management and professional specialty	14.7	20.1	27.5	29.9
Technical, sales, and administrative support	17.6	39.4	20.6	43.2
Service	20.0	26.9	9.8	16.8
Farming, forestry, and fishing	2.0	0.2	4.3	1.2
Precision production, craft, and repair	15.0	2.5	18.5	2.1
Operators, fabricators, and laborers	30.7	10.8	19.3	6.8

Source: Bennett, C., U.S. Bureau of the Census. 1995. *The Black Population in the United States: March 1994 and 1993.* Current Population Reports, P20-480. Washington, DC: U.S. Government Printing Office, Table 2.

the participation rates have become more similar in recent years primarily due to increases in delayed marriage and childbearing and divorce rates among white women. Although the participation rates are similar, unemployment rates are still more than twice as high for black women compared with white non-Hispanic women (12 percent compared with 5 percent, respectively).

Table 5-4 illustrates the percentage of men and women in standard occupation categories by race. Forty-three percent of white women were employed in technical sales and administrative support jobs in 1994 compared with 39 percent of black women. Black women were more likely to be employed in service occupations (Bennett, 1995).

It is clear that the U.S. labor force continues to be sharply segregated by sex. Only a small number of women hold high-paying jobs, and other types of work are almost exclusively held by women. As Table 5.3 illustrates, 90 percent of all receptionists, child-care workers, bank tellers, nurses, secretaries, bookkeepers, private household workers, and typists are women.

Since the 1980s, women have increasingly joined the ranks of managers and professionals. However, they remain concentrated in the professional fields of nursing and teaching, two of the lowest-paid professional categories (Taeuber, 1996).

The Market for Women

This job segregation can account for some of the wage differentials experienced by women and women of color compared with minority and non-minority men. Women's work is compartmentalized into what economists refer to as the *secondary labor market,* with low wages, high job instability, and few benefits (Treiman and Hartmann, 1981).

A more detailed summary of race and gender segregation of workers is provided in Table 5-5. The categories of professional, skilled crafts, and service workers are highlighted, with the latter a predominately female sector. Within skilled crafts, women are overrepresented as telephone installers, but people of color are represented more evenly across the spectrum.

Among service workers, both African Americans and Hispanics predominate in categories of servants and cleaners, kitchen workers, cooks, and janitors. Note the high participation of African Americans in welfare services and nursing assistance. Women as a group are substantially less likely to be em-

TABLE 5-5 Employed Persons by Sex, Race, and Occupation, 1995

Occupation	Female (%)	Black (%)	Hispanic (%)
Professional			
Architects	19.8	2.5	5.8
Engineers, mechanical	4.6	3.8	3.0
Physicians	24.4	4.9	4.3
Dentists	13.4	1.9	2.6
Registered nurses	93.1	8.4	2.6
Counselors, educational	68.3	14.2	7.2
Librarians	83.9	7.6	1.3
Psychologists	59.2	10.2	8.4
Social workers	67.9	23.7	7.8
Lawyers	26.4	3.6	3.2
Service			
Child-care workers	96.8	9.6	19.3
Servants, cleaners	94.6	20.0	28.0
Bartenders	53.5	2.0	5.9
Waitery	77.7	4.5	9.7
Cooks	44.5	17.6	18.1
Kitchen workers	70.7	10.7	10.4
Dental assistants	98.5	3.6	12.3
Nurse aides, orderlies	89.4	30.4	8.4
Janitors	35.0	20.1	19.1
Barbers	16.3	29.0	7.0
Hairdressers, cosmetology	92.0	9.9	9.4
Protective Services			
Firefighting and fire prevention	2.7	15.1	5.1
Police	10.4	11.2	8.7
Correctional institution officers	17.8	28.2	6.4
Welfare service aides	85.1	29.4	11.8
Skilled Crafts			
Automobile mechanics	0.6	7.8	11.2
Telephone installers	16.0	6.2	6.0
Construction	2.3	7.6	12.2
Carpenters	0.8	5.7	9.4

Source: U.S. Bureau of the Census. 1996. *Statistical Abstract of the United States 1996* (116th ed.). Washington DC: U.S. Government Printing Office, Table 637.

ployed as protective service workers or as cleaners of public places (janitors). However, within the private sphere, women provide cleaning services, and child-care and nursing services in both public and private settings. The intersection of sex and race dimensions in the work world is exemplified in the segmentation of women-of-color workers into low-wage occupations.

Among the professional categories, both women and racial minorities are overrepresented in the semiprofessions. Education, social work, librarianship, and nursing are the dominant categories for these workers, in contrast to the higher-paying professional categories of lawyers, doctors, and architects.

Note in Table 5-6 the relatively low wages for women compared with men across the sectors in which women are highly represented. The disproportionate number of women working in hourly-wage sales positions, compared with males in higher-earning commissioned sales positions (see Table 5-3), accounts for some of the overall differences in economic resources for women and men. However, even in clerical work, men make significantly higher wages than do women, whether they are secretaries or supervisors.

Though the majority of workers find high wages, stable jobs, and greater benefits in the primary market of large corporations, women and minorities are again internally stratified. They occupy a disproportionate number of positions in the data entry room and few, if any, positions in the corporate board room. Blum and Smith (1988) review the data on women's mobility in corpo-

TABLE 5-6   Median Income, Year-Round Full-Time Workers, 1994

Occupation	Males	Females	Female % of Male Wages	Proportion of all Women Workers
Total[a]	30,854	22,205	71.9	
Executive, administrators, and managerial	45,944	30,299	65.9	(16.6)
Professional specialty	46,488	32,321	69.5	(16.8)
Technical and related support	35,235	27,202	77.2	(4.2)
Sales	32,850	18,986	57.8	(10.4)
Admin. support, include clerical	26,874	20,942	77.9	(27.4)
Precision production, craft, and repair	29,527	21,637	73.3	(2.4)
Machine operators, assemblers, and inspectors	24,173	16,359	67.7	(6.0)
Transportation and material moving	26,036	23,249	89.3	(0.7)
Handlers, equipment cleaners, helpers, and laborers	18,239	14,800	81.1	(1.4)
Service workers	20,996	13,518	64.4	(13.1)
Farming, forestry, and fishing	16,261	10,685	65.7	(0.7)

[a] Includes persons whose longest job was in the Armed Forces

Source: U.S. Bureau of the Census. 1996. *Statistical Abstract of the United States* (116th ed.). Washington, DC: U.S. Government Printing Office, Table 665.

rations and note that women have substantially increased their participation in managerial positions. However, those positions that are labeled "management" span a wide range of jobs throughout organizational hierarchies. Generally, they conclude that women are concentrated in the lower levels, with lower pay and few promotional opportunities. In March 1995, the Federal Glass Ceiling Commission found that women made up only 5 percent of senior managers at Fortune 1000 companies. Other research in Fortune 500 service companies and Fortune 1000 industrials have estimated that women occupy between 7 and 9 percent of senior management positions (Post and Lynch, 1996). Some have argued that this is a reflection of the limits of a qualified labor pool—typically an MBA and twenty-five years work experience—and that women, by choice, are opting out of the rigorous work schedules demanded to gain this experience (Post and Lynch, 1996). However, intraoccupational sex segregation is pervasive in economic organizations, and the gains that women have made in management are often in positions that have become deskilled or "clericalized," such as administrative assistant.

Referring once again to Table 5-6, we find that women in management and the professions are receiving far fewer rewards than are men in the same general categories. Some researchers have argued that this is due to the relative influx of women into low-level professional and managerial positions, and they believe that pay inequities in these areas will level out over time. Myra Strober's (1982) research indicated that even among relatively new business-school graduates from Stanford, men had a 20 percent salary advantage over their female counterparts after only four years in the job market. Bielby and Baron (1987) found that large organizations often resegregate formerly "male-dominated" jobs into "women's jobs," which become attached to lower salaries and are perceived as inappropriate for men. This reinforces the identification of sex-segregated processes in other institutions, such as educational and vocational training.

The Wage Gap

The wage gap between women and men as measured in the ratio of median women's earnings to the median men's earnings had remained virtually constant from 1955 through the 1970s, averaging about 60 cents to the male dollar. In the 1980s the gap started to decrease and it reached a low of 72.0 in 1994 (see Table 5-7).

For women's wages to catch up to men's, their real wages must rise faster than men's, or men's real wages must fall. The recent reduction in the wage gap, while indicating some progress in the labor-market position for women, also represents a decline in the real earnings (i.e., controlled for inflation) of men. If men's annual earnings had remained at their 1979 levels in real terms, the female-male ratio would have risen to only 64.2 percent, almost exactly where it was in 1955 (see Table 5-8).

TABLE 5-7   Women's Earnings as a Percentage of Men's Among Full-Time Workers, 1955–1995

Year	Median Annual Earnings Ratio	Year	Median Annual Earnings Ratio
1955	63.9	1988	66.0
1960	60.7	1989	68.7
1965	59.9	1990	71.1
1970	59.4	1991	69.9
1975	58.8	1992	70.6
1980	60.2	1993	71.5
1985	64.6	1994	72.0
1986	64.3	1995	71.4
1987	65.2		

Note: The median annual ratio of women's to men's earnings represents workers 15 years and older.

Source: Institute for Women's Policy Research. 1997. *The Wage Gap: Women's and Men's Earnings,* p. 3, Table 1. www.iwpr.org/wagegap.htm

Although we have witnessed some progress for women's equity in earnings in the United States, Table 5-9 illustrates that earnings for young women worldwide are closer to parity with men only in industrialized nations; they continue to fall far short of men's earnings in most of the developing world. "The wage differential is particularly significant in the developing countries and in those industrializing countries where labor standards were allowed to deteriorate under the pressure to compete successfully in the world market for man-

TABLE 5-8   Median Annual Earnings of Women and Men in Current and Constant Dollars

Year	Current Dollars			Constant Dollars[a]		
	Women	Men	Ratio	Women	Men	Ratio[b]
1979	10,151	17,014	59.7	20,204	33,864	62.0
1985	15,624	24,195	64.6	20,982	32,491	63.1
1990	19,816	27,866	71.1	21,908	30,808	64.7
1991	20,553	29,421	69.9	21,805	31,214	64.4
1992	21,440	30,358	70.6	22,082	31,267	65.2
1993	21,747	30,407	71.5	21,747	30,407	64.2
1994	22,205	30,854	72.0	19,583	27,211	63.9
1995	22,497	31,496	71.4	19,294	27,011	63.0

[a]CPI adjusted.
[b]Hypothetical ratio calculated with men's real wages in 1979 as base.

Source: Institute for Women's Policy Research. 1997. *The Wage Gap: Women's and Men's Earnings,* p. 3, Table 2. www.iwpr.org/wagegap.htm

TABLE 5-9 Women's Wages as a Percentage of Men's Wages by Region, 1970–1990

	Agriculture			Nonagriculture			Manufacturing		
	1970	1980	1990	1970	1980	1990	1970	1980	1990
Africa									
Mean	70.0	58.41	69.21	61.46	81.79	89.43	63.50	60.00	73.25
Maximum	75.00	67.52	83.63	61.46	114.00	113.50	63.50	62.00	97.00
Minimum	65.00	49.00	55.00	61.46	64.30	73.00	63.50	55.00	49.00
Latin America and the Caribbean									
Mean	77.00	67.55	87.58	—	74.52	68.86	82.00	70.25	74.75
Maximum	83.00	78.11	98.21	—	81.24	75.97	82.00	81.00	94.00
Minimum	70.00	52.16	74.81	—	69.97	64.62	82.00	51.00	65.00
Western Europe and Other States									
Mean	81.70	80.31	85.17	68.84	77.16	78.35	66.04	75.00	74.64
Maximum	111.00	98.00	98.55	86.93	87.43	90.80	80.00	90.00	89.00
Minimum	56.00	63.12	64.45	57.53	64.69	65.15	55.00	61.00	59.00
Asia and the Pacific									
Mean	74.00	78.57	79.31	91.51	69.78	68.22	60.00	44.00	41.00
Maximum	90.00	91.55	92.20	91.51	101.53	89.90	84.00	86.00	97.00
Minimum	48.00	57.15	60.76	91.51	44.40	49.61	60.00	44.00	41.00
Eastern Europe									
Mean	73.00	—	74.00	69.18	70.40	75.39	68.80	69.67	72.75
Maximum	73.00	—	74.00	69.18	72.39	82.00	69.60	73.00	78.00
Minimum	73.00	—	74.00	69.18	68.41	71.00	68.00	68.00	68.00

Source: United Nations Blue Book Series. 1996. *The United Nations and the Advancement of Women, 1945–1996.* (Vol. VI, Sales No. E.96.I.9). New York: United Nations Publications, Table 4, p. 628.

TABLE 5-10   Median Annual Earnings of Women and Men by Race and Ethnicity, 1995

	Women	Men	Ratio
All races	$22,497	$31,496	71.4
White	$22,911	$32,172	71.2[a]
African American	$20,665		64.2[a]
		$23,019	74.0[a]
Hispanic[b]	$17,178		53.4[a]
		$20,379	63.3[a]

[a]The basis for this ratio is the earnings of white men.
[b]Persons of Hispanic origin may be of any race.

Source: Institute for Women's Policy Research. 1997. *The Wage Gap: Women's and Men's Earnings*, p. 3, Table 3, www.iwpr.org/wagegap.htm

ufactured goods and to attract foreign investment" (United Nations Blue Book Series, 1996:625).

Race and ethnicity differences as seen in Table 5-10 illustrate that all women earn less than white men, and African Americans and Hispanic workers of both sexes continue to earn significantly less than white men (Institute for Women's Policy Research, 1997).

THEORIES OF WOMEN'S WORK

These economic patterns indicate that women and men, and minorities and whites, form different pools within the labor market. Several theories reviewed in earlier chapters suggest what might have caused these differential pools and what maintains them in the face of educational and legal changes. These range from the functionalist models, which emphasize the integrated stability of economic and educational institutions, to the conflict models, which pose a dynamic model of struggle between competing interest groups, including women and men.

Functionalist Models of Inequality in Exchange

Beginning with the functionalist model, sociologists have focused on the human capital (skills) that men and women bring to the marketplace. Human-capital theorists argue that wages are indicators of the productive contributions (or exchange value) of individuals or groups. "Women thus lose out in competition with men . . . [because] gender-differentiated socialization functions to reproduce inequality by failing to arm females with the personal characteristics needed to successfully compete with men in the labor market" (Chafetz, 1988:100). These theorists and economists agree to consider a range of factors prior to concluding that unequal wages adequately represent the differential value of one group's or individual's work. These factors might include education and training, experience on the job, supervisory responsibility, the risk to employers of losing investment in employee training (especially through high turnover), and work conditions.

The data in Chapter Six indicate that most ethnic groups of women in the United States receive similar amounts of education compared with men in terms of years completed. But for all women, and especially for some groups of women of color, the translation of these years of educational investment into economic rewards is not on an equal footing with men. Table 5-11 demonstrates that for all women, their achievement of human capital at the level of a college degree is rewarded less than the human capital of a white male who achieves a high school degree. It is true that both women and men increase their earning potential with increased educational attainments. However, the return from further education is not parallel. This is true for women of color and men of color. The intersection of race, gender, and social class is patterned economically, with Hispanic and black men earning less than their equally educated Anglo/white male peers. In each instance, women of color earn less than all other groups, including Anglo/white women. This hierarchy of economic privilege contradicts the human-capital equation.

If the amount of education is not a factor in explaining these income inequities, could it be that on-the-job characteristics or any other human-capital factors, such as turnover rates, willingness to take supervisory responsibilities, and so forth, make women a poor investment for employers?

Women as employees. Several studies suggest that these are not plausible explanations. Janet Chafetz found in her 1976 national study of employers, and of women and men employees, that turnover rates for women and men in similar occupations were equivalent. What distinguishes the two groups is the

TABLE 5-11 Average Annual Income by Education, Ethnicity, and Sex, 1993

Education	Anglo	Black	Hispanic	Male	Female
Not a high school graduate	$11,412	$8,556	$9,432	$14,532	$7,452
High school graduate	17,064	12,852	13,272	21,744	12,096
Some college	19,788	14,664	14,868	24,540	13,668
Vocational	21,216	17,136	15,948	27,816	16,476
Associate degree	24,252	20,952	24,828	30,732	18,528
Bachelor degree	32,184	27,996	26,232	41,160	21,708
M.A. degree	41,736	34,008	31,260	51,576	30,060
Ph.D. degree	53,388	45,336	32,124	53,052	48,240
Professional degree	67,080	41,340	27,804	75,744	42,360

Source: U.S. Bureau of the Census. 1996. *Statistical Abstract of the United States 1996* (116th ed.). Washington, DC: U.S. Government Printing Office, Table 244.

purpose of the turnover. Men leave their jobs to move to different jobs that provide greater promotional opportunities. Women are more likely to leave the market entirely to fulfill childbearing and childrearing responsibilities. The results for employers are the same; they lose their investment in training the worker. The results for workers are quite different. Men make occupational moves that enhance their promotional opportunities and take advantage of their seniority; women leave the market and lose seniority, disrupting promotion lines, to return at a later date when their skills may be obsolete.

A second factor in turnover rates is that more women are remaining in the labor market as their economic options are reduced or their need for retaining seniority has increased. In the 1970s, several Supreme Court decisions concluded that (1) an employer cannot refuse to hire a woman because she is a mother (*Phillips* v. *Martin Marietta*, 1971); (2) compulsory maternity leave is illegal (*Cleveland Board of Education* v. *LaFleur*, 1974); and (3) seniority cannot be removed while on leave to give birth (*Nashville Gas Co.* v. *Satty*, 1977). By 1986, women with children under the age of six had the same labor-force participation rate as women in general. However, unlike most Western European nations, the United States had no national policy guaranteeing a woman maternity leave without the possibility of losing her job until the Family and Medical Leave Act signed by President Clinton in 1993. This act applies to workers with companies of fifty or more employees and provides job protection and twelve weeks of unpaid leave with a twelve-month period to care for newborns or adopted children, or to cope with a serious family illness. We are the only major industrialized nation without a national insurance plan covering medical costs for childbirth and compensation for lost benefits.

Pay equity studies. The economic factors of supervisory responsibility, work conditions, and seniority have also been the object of pay equity studies, in a series of states, since the early 1980s. As a result of political and legal action on the part of underpaid women workers (and men workers who labor in female-dominated jobs), the state of Minnesota hired a consultant firm, Robert Hay and Associates, to assess the state personnel structure. The consultants developed the Hay Point Scale, which rated positions in the state on the basis of job descriptions, including information on education requirements, supervisory responsibilities, work conditions (including mental and physical effort, hazards, and surroundings), and the effect of the work on a final product or organizational goal. They then rated each of the state personnel positions on a scale from 1 to 500, with 500 the highest score. Higher scores were equated with higher salaries in general. However, when they examined the positions by the proportion of women and men employed, and then compared the extent of underpayment or overpayment, the results were significant.

For example, the Hay Point Scale for Clerk Stenographer 2 position was set at the same level as General Repair Worker (134 Hay points), yet the difference in monthly salary indicated that women workers were underpaid by approximately $4,700 per year. Overall, several characteristics of this compensation and classification system identified a sex-segmented labor market.

Originally it was determined in the Minnesota study that female jobs were consistently paid less than male jobs of the same point value. There were substantially more male classes than female classes—209 male classes and 70 female classes. In several instances, male classes had only one incumbent—job description and salaries were assigned on an idiosyncratic basis. The largest female classes were concentrated at the low end of the point scale and were relatively low paid, whereas the largest male classes were relatively high paid.

This illustration of underpayment suggested that the issue of women's wages could not be addressed solely by changing the discriminatory attitudes of employers, or the human capital of workers. Most personnel pay scales are entrenched in a history that reflects an economy segregated not only by sex but also by race and age. As noted by the U.S. Commission on Civil Rights (1985:31), a "degree of subjectivity is inherent in all these systems," and in the private sector, it is highly probable that the majority of firms do not use job evaluation systems such as the Hay Point Scale.

However, since the 1980s many state and local governments have adopted the Hay Point Scale or a comparable point system in an attempt to bring equity into their pay scales. Table 5-12 illustrates the Hay points and pay scale used by one state government and how these points correspond to some of the top-ten most female- and male-dominated occupations according to the 1996 census. The point system has been effective at standardizing pay scales, yet there are still subjective definitions that determine the awarding of the Hay points.

The following factors are used in determining the Hay classification points: (1) know-how, including depth and breadth of specialized knowledge, know-how of harmonizing and integrating, and human relations skills; (2) problem solving, including thinking environment and thinking challenge; and (3) accountability, including freedom to act, job impact of end results, and magnitude. In addition, physical effort, environment, hazards, and sensory attention are included as additional compensable elements.

Liberal feminists have taken the issue of pay equity to dozens of state legislatures, seeking revisions of state personnel structures and state laws encouraging comparable-worth guidelines. They have been successful in states such as Washington and Minnesota. But in the restricted state budget era of the 1980s, the dilemma was whether to bring women's (and some men's) pay up to equitable levels while holding other salaries level. This would mean that a disproportionate number of men would receive little or no salary increase over a period of time. The other options were to lower the inflated wages of men (not likely to be supported by union lobbyists or legislators) or to find the money to bring women's wages into equity while continuing to increase male salaries. In 1982, the state of Minnesota enacted a comparable-worth law covering all state employees, with an estimated overall payroll increase of 4 percent. Dr. Daniel Glasner of the Hay Associates estimated that reducing the 80

TABLE 5-12   Top Female- and Male-Dominated Jobs: 1996 and Their Corresponding Hay Points

Percent Female	Job Class/Title	Hay Points	Policy Pay/Hr
99.4	Dental hygienist	342	$16.79
97.9	Family child-care providers	130	$8.12
97.8	Secretaries, stenographers, typists		
	Secretary	177	$10.06
	Word processing generalist (typist)	125	$8.12
96.5	Receptionist	125	$8.12
95.4	Licensed practical nurse	219	$12.65
92.4	Financial records processor	226	$12.65
92.0	Hairdressers and cosmetologists	226	$12.65
2.8	Transportation occupations, except motor vehicles	199	$11.31
2.3	Firefighting occupations		
	Fire area manager	496	$21.97
	Fire and fuels specialist	479	$19.98
	Fire warden	436	$19.98
2.3	Construction trades		
	Construction supervisor	416	$18.27
	Construction foreman	321	$15.48
	Construction manager	571	$23.22
	Electrician	230	$12.65
	Plumber	226	$12.65
	Painter	168	$10.06
1.7	Aircraft engine mechanics	296	$15.48
0.8	Carpenters	191	$11.31
0.7	Vehicle and mobile equipment mechanics/repairers	166	$10.06
0.6	Automobile mechanics	230	$12.65

Sources: U.S. Bureau of the Census. 1996. *Statistical Abstract of the United States* (116th ed.), Table 637. 1997 Hourly State Compensation Schedule.

percent pay gap would result in a 320-billion-dollar increase in wages and benefits for women. This would add nearly 10 percent to the existing inflation rate (U.S. Commission on Civil Rights, 1985:38).

The assessment of many, including the U.S. Civil Rights Commission, is that if comparable worth were implemented, it would disrupt the labor relations system of the country. "It is an ill-defined concept which means many things to many people. . . . The first thing I tell my students is that there is no such thing as a fair wage. It's only a matter of opinion" (Professor Northrup, testimony, as cited in U.S. Commission on Civil Rights, 1985:39). It is not unusual to hear state legislators and private employers state that it is simply not feasible to pay women what they are worth.

The wage differential was first addressed by the Equal Pay Act of 1963, which prohibits employers from paying employees of opposite sexes different rates for jobs that are equivalent in terms of skills. It explicitly restricts employers from lowering the wages of any one group in order to comply (Lindgren and Taub, 1988). This prohibition against unequal pay has been interpreted by the courts to include jobs in distinct classifications where the work performed by women workers is substantially equal to that performed by better-paid men.

Unlike the U.S. Civil Rights Commission, Treiman and Hartmann (1981) conclude that there is substantial discrimination in pay. These discriminatory effects are difficult to document because of the widespread concentration of women and minorities into low-wage jobs. They argue, however, that once an evaluation system is established, the use of one evaluation plan that covers all jobs within a firm would be necessary in order to compare wages of women, minority men, and nonminority men.

The Conflict Model: Wages and Work

The conflict theorists have suggested a range of possible explanations for the origin and maintenance of economic inequality for women. Important frameworks are offered by the Marxist and socialist feminists. The original Marxian hypothesis of the division of society into the major social classes of the bourgeoisie and the proletariat provides an interesting baseline for assessing this inequality. Women are potential members of either the ruling or working class by means of birth, marriage, or individual effort. Socialist feminists have revised some of the early models proposed by Marx and Engels to include the effects of patriarchy and to account for more contemporary structures of the labor market.

In classical Marxian thought, the industrial worker's family consisted of a woman who labored at home, doing reproductive and service work, while the man labored for a wage. Within this model, the primary benefactor of all work, both wage and nonwage, must be the bourgeoisie. Owners no longer provided room and board for the workers, as they did in the early days of industry. The sleeping quarters and meals (both on and off the job) are arranged, purchased, and prepared by the homeworker. The clothing of the worker is usually purchased and laundered by the homeworker.

According to Margaret Benston (1969), these activities form a "hidden tax" on the worker. "His" wages, in the classical worker family, do not reflect these purchases and do not provide a living wage for the worker family. The need for profit and competition among owners drives those wages even lower, as owners simultaneously raise prices on consumer goods.

Several other "functions" are performed by the woman homeworker. She has the time and opportunity to shop—to be the consumer cog in the wheel of capitalism. Only in a few advanced industrial nations has shopping become a recreational activity for women. Presumably, workers with long hours and restricted activities would have little time to creatively consume the goods cranked out by industrial capitalism. Women also reproduce and socialize a new generation of workers, who are trained by their mothers (with some help from the schools) to be docile and punctual and to have some basic skills. Thus, the owners have a family unit that replenishes the worker's needs on a daily basis, and meets their need for workers of the future.

Benston's model of women's use value.   Women also form a reserve pool of potential workers that can be manipulated by the owners. Because women obviously do work for lower wages than men, they can be brought in as cheap, flexible laborers when necessary. Historical examples include the recruitment of women into expanding secretarial work as offices and paperwork grew in size with industrialization (Davies, 1975), and the pull of women into the war economy during World War II with their encouragement to return home immediately afterward. This role as a reserve pool of labor has also been noted for racial and ethnic minority groups. When labor unions excluded blacks and other minorities, the use of blacks as strikebreakers during union struggles benefited the white employers (Reich, 1981). As a result of this reserve-pool status, black and white racial antagonisms maintain an enmity that keeps workers at odds and reduces the identification of their common exploitation by white owners.

Recent research and theory have encouraged a reanalysis of women's work from a more global perspective as well. Kathryn Ward (1990) identifies the restructuring of a "global assembly line" such that many women in Latin America, Asia, and the United States perform work in low-wage peripheral manufacturing jobs, as well as "informal work" in the home. This informal homework is often subcontracted piecework or peddling of goods. Peripheral manufacturing shifts low-wage work onto developing countries, retaining the high-wage management tasks and accumulation of capital in the United States and other core countries. Ward points out that this restructuring is built on the increasing use of female industrial workers and the growth of export industries such as electronics and garment manufacturing.

Bernard (1987) identifies this restructuring as the incorporation of women everywhere into a system regulated by the market norms of the Western male world, particularly the World Bank and International Monetary Fund, as well as individual multinational corporations. The net effect was to place "women in Korea in competition with women in New Jersey" (Bernard, 1987:202). However, as Ward (1990) notes, this regulation by multinationals does not include benefits to pay and working conditions, or the monitoring that accompanies labor legislation. Much of the expanded peripheral and informal subcontracted labor of women is unregulated by laws to guarantee fair treatment, healthy work conditions, or job security.

Informal sector, subcontracted work creates a "third shift" for women workers, adding piecework at home to their formal wage labor and unpaid domestic labor. Coping with the demands of this triple burden can overwhelm the waking hours of many women. Hadjicostandi (1990) describes women of

Kavala, Greece, who participated in unregulated subcontracted garment homework. Ninety percent of the women owned their own machinery, purchased after long hours of work. The majority worked nineteen hours per day, came from working-class families, and desired the flexibility to stay at home and supervise children or take care of elderly relatives. Hadjicostandi concludes that the two most important problems facing homeworkers were the long, irregular hours and the need to acquire their own means of production (a machine). In contrast, the major problem facing women who worked in formal industrial jobs in the same city was child care.

Ward summarizes the situation for women involved in the informal sector of an internationalized economy. This work "subsidizes (other) worker's wages, lowers the risks of capitalists, and together with housework stabilizes or maintains the class positions of households" (Ward, 1990:8). The importance of these informal wages to the subsistence of families is illustrated by the rate at which women have moved into both the informal and periphery manufacturing jobs throughout the world.

Finally, the worker family serves as a conservative force, keeping male workers from going on strike as often. It is not just the worker who suffers, but "his" dependents as well. These factors suggest to the Marxist analyst that women's nonwage labor functions to maintain capitalism.

We need to ask who benefits from women's work in its traditional, nonwage sense. The burden of full-time housework continues for women, and it is modified only slightly when they work part-time or full-time for a wage (Berk, 1988). In the case of work in the home, the child-care, buying, feeding, and cleaning functions seem to directly benefit the family. Thus, some have argued that men benefit directly from this structure of paid and unpaid work, as a function of their privilege within patriarchy (Sokoloff, 1980). As a direct result of this radical analysis, many feminists have encouraged the increased participation of men within domestic and parenting work. This theme has been well received by liberal feminists, also, who seek to share equally the opportunities of child care and homework with their partners. Others have argued that the productive results of women's unpaid work in the home as outlined by Benston should be compensated by wages for housework (Sokoloff, 1980).

Mies (1988) argues that the definition of work must be expanded from the capitalist productive focus (including only predominately male labor) to incorporate the work of women in what she calls "life work and subsistence work." Added to the exploitation of formal labor in the capitalist system is the nonwage labor of women, which parallels the exploitation of colonized, peripheral nations and people of color.

Splitting and feminizing the labor market.   The Marxist position presented by Benston has been questioned by others, as well. If capitalists could gain so much profit by hiring women and minorities at lower wages, why, then, do they not fill their factories and offices with cheaper labor? Several theorists have addressed this dilemma to suggest that the labor market has become split between high-priced (mostly white and male) and cheap wage labor (mostly minority and female) (Bonacich, 1972; Blau and Jusenius, 1976; Reich, 1981). The primary and secondary labor markets described earlier in this chapter provide structural restraints on workers, regardless of their individual characteristics. Thus, we can look for historical evidence of white male resistance to the entry of women or minorities into high-wage, high-skilled jobs in the primary market.

A number of researchers have found such evidence, with examples ranging from the restriction of women from entry into male unions to the protection of women's working hours and conditions, which made them more "expensive" workers (Lindgren and Taub, 1988), to the segregation of women within occupations to low-wage classifications. However, within the primary market, a type of internal segregation takes place, so that women working in the large corporate industrial world are likely to find themselves structurally limited in terms of pay and promotion (Blau and Jusenius, 1976).

Davies (1975) provides an excellent historical example of the "feminization" of clerical work in the early part of this century. Prior to the 1900s, office work was a predominately male job, held often by sons of small-business owners. The office was usually small, with one or two "clerks," with minimal paperwork. Men were 97.5 percent of the clerical labor force at this time. These clerks were engaged in accounting or sales work, and this was a good starting place for sons who were being trained in the family business.

However, major external changes in society began to influence this job. Industrialization enlarged the work setting and increased the complexity of the production process. Business communication expanded as the distribution of goods flowed with new railroads and roadways. As the industrial process was itself based on an elaborate division of labor, so too did the work of the office become divided and hierarchically arranged. Menial tasks such as filing and sorting were separated from the tasks of office management, supervision, and sales. As technology provided the first typewriter, and later the computer, the processing of letters and numbers was assigned to typists and keypunch operators.

Crucial to the employment of women in these new office tasks were two other social factors. Women were a large pool of relatively untapped, but educated, labor that could be drawn in throughout the periods during and after the U.S. Civil War and World War I when men were less available. Second, the social attitudes toward employment of women shifted. Where at first there were concerns about the effects of long hours and tedious tasks on the moral and reproductive safety of women, these attitudes changed. By the 1920s, William Henry Leffingwell concluded in his guide, *Office Management: Principles and Practices,* that

> a woman is to be preferred for the secretarial position, for she is not averse to doing minor tasks, work involving the handling of petty details, which would irk and

irritate ambitious young men, who usually feel that the work they are doing is of
no importance if it can be performed by someone with a lower salary. (as cited
in Davies, 1975:293)

Not surprisingly, by the 1920s, women made up over 90 percent of the typists
and stenographers in the United States. Davies concludes that this sexual division of labor in the office is reinforced by the positions that women and men
hold outside the office.

Davies and others argue that clerical work, teaching, and a number of
other predominately female jobs underwent a process of "feminization." Routine tasks were assigned to the newest entrants in the labor market. As these
clerical positions and others were filled with women, wages were held at a low
level, while other positions in the office (management, sales, and supervision)
were taken by men who demanded and were given higher wages. Thus, a complex set of historical and technological changes identified clerical work as
"women's work" in the modern era. A feminized job, then, is one in which
workers become predominately more female in proportion, and wages remain
low, while other (men's) wages inflate at a higher rate.

Feminizing the global assembly line.   As noted by Mies (1988) and others, the shifting of low-wage industrial labor to women in developing, peripheral nations has not brought incremental modernization or economic benefits
to their families and communities. Mies outlines the connections between
women's subordination under both patriarchy and capitalism to identify historical connections between the subordination of women and of colonized
peoples in general. The expansion of capital into peripheral nations was accompanied by the "civilizing" process, which brought colonized peoples under
the control of monopoly capital.

Susan Tiana (1990) illustrates the material outcomes of this global assembly line in her analysis of the "maquiladores" (those who work the assembly plants) along the northern Mexican border. She cites data indicating that
over one-half of all imports from less-developed nations comes from this region, which is the second most important source of Mexican foreign exchange.
Most of this work is done by women and does little to reduce the high unemployment rates for men in the region. Primary industries in this area include
sophisticated electronic assembly plants and low-investment apparel assembly
subcontracted through small local shops. She notes that the differences in
these two major industries leads to intense competition for the higher-paying
electronics jobs; apparel assemblers, with lower wages and more insecure jobs,
draw from the women who are less-educated, single heads of households with
children. She also concludes that the employment of young, single, relatively
well-ed   ted women in the electronics industry will do little to relieve the effects of male unemployment and female underemployment in working-class
households that require two adult earners. Within one generation, the export-

processing labor force has created a female workforce that is highly segmented and poorly compensated in India, Greece, Mexico, and throughout the world.

The theories of women's work just presented suggest that we examine the structural characteristics of employment for patterns that situate women at the bottom of the economic hierarchy. From a socialist-feminist perspective, these structures are linked both to capitalism and to the drive for increased profits, as well as to the patriarchal authority system in national and international settings. Others, particularly conservatives and liberal feminists, argue that some constellation of human capital (education, skills, experience) and attitudes combine to place women at a disadvantage in the labor force. In the next section, we look at an underlying theme of women's work—caretaking—to untangle some issues of attitudes, skills, and structural effects of the labor market.

CARETAKING AND WOMEN'S WORK

The caretaking roles of women overlap dimensions of both paid and unpaid labor. As nurses, nurses' aides, social workers, early childhood teachers and child-care workers, as mothers and as daughters, women carry the responsibility for the emotional and physical care of others. Qualitative researchers have commented on the "seamlessness" of women's lives as they move from caretaking in their homes to caretaking in the labor force or in volunteer work. "Their lives are not composed of easily discernible, discrete compartments," but rather of interwoven, interdependent activities (Statham, Miller, and Mauksch, 1988).

Etzioni (1969) suggests that teaching, nursing, librarianship, and social work are not true professions, but constitute semiprofessions. These semiprofessions are defined by Etzioni as having lower pay, less authority, and a different relationship between client and practitioner than other professions. In essence, these jobs constitute semiprofessions because they are linked to the female gender—through feminized wages, lack of patriarchal authority structures, and attachment to the caretaking role.

Corley and Mauksch examine the status and roles of registered nurses and conclude that the "social presence of nurse is pervasively linked to the female gender" (1988:135). They link nursing to female stereotypes of a high commitment to service and care for patients, accompanied by low career commitments. They examine the notion of commitment among registered nurses and find that as the commitment level of nurses increases, the responsibility of others, including doctors, administrators, and so on, is reduced. Commitment for nurses is a romanticized notion that releases others from guilt—guilt over low wages (women do this because they want to do it, or are naturally good at it) or guilt over treatment of clients (it is the nurses' responsibility to care for emotional and social aspects of health care or nurses can take up the slack in nurse-patient or physician-patient ratios).

This ethic of care or commitment among nurses generates several con-tradictions. Nurses had many additional nonnursing tasks "dumped" on them, which they (for the most part) took on due to their loyalty to patient care and physician authority. A conflict then developed between spending time with "hands on" care versus the paperwork of documentation demanded by the business of health care. In general, these nurses felt a strong need to mediate the organization's ability to provide good, safe, adequate care for patients. Overall, the authors conclude that the nurses' commitment to the organiza-tion (e.g., hospital, nursing home) is contingent on the perceived commitment of the organization to the patient (Corley and Mauksch, 1988:146).

Double Jeopardy and Caretaking

Timothy Diamond (1988) provides a critical ethnography of nursing as-sistants in a nursing home that contrasts with the profession of nursing. Some important structural factors should be noted. First, wages for nursing assistants are far lower than for nurses. In addition, the majority of the nursing assistants interviewed by Diamond were nonwhite. Finally, nursing homes are not eco-nomically stable places for clients or workers. Clients can be moved to public-aid wings as their individual resources run out. In addition, the wages of work-ers are dependent upon a health care industry that is tied to government aid and policy. Thus, the workers are in a secondary labor market, with high turnover, the possibility of layoffs, and few benefits due to part-time job structures.

But Diamond's focus is on the workers and their experience of caretak-ing. These workers have even less autonomy than the nurses: "We learned not to ask questions, but to do as we were told" even when patients' health care was at stake. This lack of autonomy and voice reinforced the double jeopardy of minority and female statuses. As one black Jamaican woman joked: "I can't fig-ure out whether they're trying to teach us to be nurses' aides or black women" (Diamond, 1988:40).

An important dimension of the caretaking work done by nurses' aides is its invisibility. Their physical tasks such as showering, feeding, and talking to patients are not chargeable items in the medical environments. They have no exchange value: "If it's not charted . . . it didn't happen." The social interac-tion that accompanies the unskilled labor done by nurses' aides is transformed by defining people as bodies, as "market phenomena," whose assistance is writ-ten up on medical charts as business entries. Thus, "the social relations in-volved in holding someone as they gasp for breath" (Diamond, 1988:48) is omitted from the business of nursing homes and the job descriptions of nurses' aides. However, as do the nurses in Corley and Mauksch's (1988) research, these aides articulate an ethic of care that blurs the boundaries between the semiprofessions and unskilled labor. The attachment of both of these occupa-tions to the traditional feminine role of caretaking contributes to restricted rewards and autonomy, but also creates contradictions in the meaning of work in everyday construction.

WOMEN'S UNPAID LABOR

In the United States and throughout the world, the notion of *women's work* raises connotations of low-wage or no-wage "dirty work" associated with washing diapers, scrubbing toilets, and cleaning up after others. There are also the day-to-day functions surrounding food and feeding: breastfeeding babies, caring for crops and domesticated animals, cooking, and washing dishes. Gender roles throughout the world assign to women the mothering, nurturing, caretaking roles of society, linking female stereotypes to various tasks and family statuses. A vast portion of this work is unpaid labor in the fields, in the home, and in communities.

Unpaid Labor in Agriculture

Women have always known "who weeds the sorghum, transplants the rice seedlings, picks the beans and tends the chickens. But it has taken a long time for the rest of the world to discover the facts" (Taylor, 1985:16). Much of women's agricultural work in the United States and throughout the world tends to be overlooked because it is unpaid. Moreover, liberal feminist theorists have largely ignored the role of women outside of major industrial nations. However, these agricultural roles demonstrate important dimensions of the critical economic theories.

Feminist analysts have argued that women are the invisible farmers, yet their labor produces half of the world's food. In Africa, three-quarters of the agricultural work is done by women, and in Asia women constitute one-half of the agricultural labor force. Even in countries such as Egypt, where the official census lists only 3.6 percent of women involved in agriculture, local surveys reveal that 35 to 40 percent of women in some regions are involved in planting, tilling, and harvesting.

Deere and de Leal (1981) provided a detailed assessment of women's agricultural labor in the Andes. They considered the sexual division of agricultural labor and its relation to material conditions of development. Women accounted for 25 percent of family agricultural labor, yet they made up only 10 percent of agricultural wage labor. Deere and de Leal paid attention to the qualitative aspects of this sexual division, as well, noting that "both men and women consider the tasks carried out by women to be much less important" (1981:349). Women were generally excluded from those tasks that involve tools and were more likely to be involved in animal care, agricultural processing, and support services (cooking for field hands). Overall, however, they concluded that the sexual division of labor in agriculture was influenced by the economic structure of the district. In highly capitalized sectors, women were less likely to engage in actual field work and marketing activities and were more likely to be involved in service, processing, or animal care. In noncapitalist, smallholder agricultural sectors, where independent peasants produce most of the agricultural goods, women were more involved in marketing and field work.

In highly industrialized nations such as the United States, the role of women farmers is also undercounted and unanalyzed. Rachel Rosenfeld's (1985) work on farm women reveals that 60 percent of women living on farms describe their occupation as "wife, mother, housewife or homemaker," only 5 percent say farm wife, and less than 4 percent claim the occupational title of farmer, rancher, or producer. This theme of not identifying as farmers runs counter to the finding that 83 percent of women are regularly involved in direct agricultural tasks. Most frequently, women reported regularly taking care of a vegetable garden (74 percent) or animals (37 percent) for the family's food, doing the bookkeeping (61 percent), and running farm errands. Only small percentages reported doing machine-assisted field work (17 percent), plowing or cultivating (11 percent), or applying herbicides or pesticides (5 percent) on a regular basis. As in the capitalized farming practices of Andean women, only a small percentage of U.S. farm women report making major purchases for the farm operation (14 percent) or marketing the farm products (15 percent).

Interestingly, fully one-third of the farm women report working in a family or in-home business other than farm or ranch work on a regular basis. This may reflect the increasing participation of farm women in off-farm employment as well. Ollenburger, Grana, and Moore (1989) found that Nebraska farm women increased their paid labor-force participation at a rate equal to that of rural nonfarm women during the farm crisis years of the 1980s. This may well be due to the changing production and consumption roles of women in rural families. Rosenfeld (1985) notes that women on farms today produce far fewer consumer goods than in the past and that farm family consumption patterns now mirror the patterns of urban families. The result is that farm women's work is less involved in producing goods for the family during times of economic crisis. Thus, in the farm crises of the 1890s and 1930s, farm women were able to increase their production on farms to stabilize family economies. In the 1980s, this was less true, with more women turning to part-time and full-time wage labor.

The analysis of farm women sits at the intersection of paid and unpaid labor, of pre- and postindustrial wage-labor roles for women, and provides a number of insights. First, the labor of farm women is often invisible, not only to theorists but to economists and policymakers as well. Second, the issues of child care, unpaid housework, and lack of benefits that affect all women workers are exacerbated for women in rural areas of industrial countries or in nations that are still predominately agricultural, due to the inaccessibility of resources such as day-care centers, health care facilities, and political organizations.

Finally, the capitalization of work in non-Western nations and the concentration of agriculture in the United States onto large corporate farms has made women's farm labor problematic. Both economic trends ignore the contributions of women in the past and narrow the range of potential work for women in the future. These women and their nonwage labor represent an intersection of patriarchal privilege and capitalist exploitation that has consequences for the social, political, and economic resources and everyday lives of a majority of women in the world. Access to industrialized, capitalized labor will dislodge large numbers of people from rural agricultural labor and drive them to unskilled, low-wage jobs in urban areas that lack adequate housing or relocation services. When not in the fields (those owned by either their families or large corporations), these women continue to labor, along with their industrial wage-earning sisters, on the schedule of the "double day." They are likely to be thrown into wage-earning jobs without adequate preparation, with few options for employment, and with continued expectations for fulfilling their reproductive and productive work within the family.

Housework and Its Discontents

The addition of housework to wage or agricultural labor has been identified as a double burden for women. Houseworkers[1] are predominately women, whether in the paid labor force or in the home. The total time spent by women on unpaid household labor is high, with some estimates ranging from 30 to 60 hours per week, and others as high as 99 hours per week, when child care is included (Oakley, 1974; Berk, 1985, 1988). Close to half of all adult women claim housewife as their major occupation.

With married couples, the vast majority of time spent on housework is spent by the wife, about 70 percent on average, with the husband and children combined providing the remaining labor (Walker and Woods, 1976). The time devoted to housework has changed little over the past century. "Labor saving" devices have reduced some types of work (e.g., dishwashing), but changing standards (e.g., shiny floors) and increased emphasis on leisure time and consumer patterns in the home (e.g., food processors for caesar salads) have maintained these intensive activity rates (Oakley, 1974).

Heidi Hartmann (1981b) argues that the tasks performed by husbands and wives illuminate the burden of housework for women. In the United States, men perform a small, selective amount of housework—most likely cooking,

---

[1]Helena Lopata defines a *housewife* as "a woman responsible for running her home, whether she performs the tasks or hires people to do them. . . . A man or girl can behave like a housewife . . . but they are usually recognized as substitutes, assistants, or deviants" (Lopata, 1971:3). Lopata, then, uses the term *housewife* to denote a position and a social role. Her definition is powerful in revealing the association of housework with women, but we are interested in those who actually *perform* this unpaid labor, not merely those who organize or benefit from the work of others: thus, the term *houseworker.*

rather than cleaning or tasks such as laundry and ironing. Among those tasks most disliked among British women were laundry, dishes, cleaning the bathroom, shopping, and cooking. Those tasks were described by the women as monotonous, boring, isolating, and repetitive (Oakley, 1974). Hartmann concludes that the benefits to men under this system are significant, both in the loss of leisure time for women compared with men and in the relative burden on wage-earning women in the labor force compared with men.

In her work on the "second shift," Arlie Hochschild (1989) notes that women with paid jobs work an "extra month of twenty-four hour days a year," which accumulates over a dozen years into an extra year of work. She focuses on the social and economic consequences for heterosexual couples, examining the "leisure gap" in addition to the wage gap for women and men, and highlights the various coping mechanisms of both women and men for accommodating the second shift. Her interviews demonstrated that women perform distinct household work that includes a "speed up" factor that even men who share housework equally do not share. This speed up occurs as women expand paid labor hours, but have the same domestic responsibilities. Because women do more child care and more daily tasks (cooking, cleaning up), their work schedules are more rigid and less autonomous. "A child needs to be tended daily, while the repair of household appliances can often wait . . . dinner needs to be prepared every evening around six o'clock whereas the car oil needs to be changed every six months, any day around that time, any time that day" (Hochschild, 1989:8). She concludes that the second shift becomes a prism through which each person's ideas about gender and marriage become focused, along with the emotional meanings behind those ideas. She also highlights the important class differences, noting that the second shift in working-class households is affected by the absence of money to pay for services they need, poor day care, economic insecurity, and the lack of autonomy in each partner's "first shift" jobs to accommodate home tasks (e.g., time to run errands during a flexible lunch hour). She also concludes that men and women experience negative effects of the second shift, though these are shared differently. Women may feel guilty for not meeting their traditional domestic responsibilities, and men may feel inadequate because their spouses must work for a wage.

Other factors that frame housework, according to Oakley (1974), are the social status and material conditions of being a houseworker. The prestige level accorded to housekeepers, child-care workers, and those who perform typical household labor in a paid job (e.g., fast-food worker) is typically very low. These rankings included 26 points for baby-sitter/preschool teacher, 51 points for bookkeeper, and 15 points for cook. When all the jobs that constitute the major tasks of housework are averaged together on the Duncan Socioeconomic Index of Occupations, they come to 35 points. Nilson (1981) and others have found that the role of housewife itself is accorded a much higher prestige rating (average scores range from 58 to 70), though men score the position significantly higher than do women. When given varying descriptions of family background factors (including husband's socioeconomic status [SES]) the status of the housewife varies significantly as well (Nilson, 1981), with higher SES families assigning a higher prestige rating to their housewives. Oakley (1984), too, found that women's responses to the position of housewife reflect the dichotomy of "woman of the house" as compared with her actual tasks. While most women are satisfied with the occupation, housewife, most are dissatisfied with the major tasks associated with it (over 70 percent of houseworkers).

Volunteer Work

Little research has been conducted on women's volunteer work outside the home. However, most of this volunteer work takes place in the public sphere and thus has more visibility than the housework just described. It is estimated that volunteer work contributes many billions of dollars per year in monetary worth. In 1965, the estimate was over 14 billion dollars; in 1983, that figure had risen to over 60 billion dollars (Gold, 1971; Berk, 1988).

However, we do know some things about the profile of volunteer workers. First, women are more likely to volunteer than are men. "The average volunteer is a woman who is married, middle aged, not employed, college educated and who lives in an upper-income midwestern urban household" (Berk, 1988). Most volunteer work takes place in the churches (19 percent), followed by health care facilities (12 percent) and schools (12 percent). Informal volunteering outside of traditional organizations accounts for approximately 23 percent of this use-value labor. These figures can be misleading and may omit information about the work of women of color, single women, older and younger women, and poor women who work within their communities to assist people or organizations outside of their own families.

Doris Gold (1971) provides a critical feminist analysis of volunteer work. She assesses the conscious and unconscious motives of women for participation in such activities that come from social conditioning, structural discrimination, and women's long history of serving within the church and the family with no economic reward or authority.

First among these motives is the "caretaking" or "helpmate" roles assigned to women, along with the added opportunity to get outside of isolated household tasks. While men "go out with the boys" for rather ambiguous activities (for a drink, to a game, to fish or hunt), women are more traditionally circumscribed to appear in appropriate public places. If not a place of employment, then a church or community organization such as a YWCA or women's league becomes a suitable site for women's activities. Gold notes that many of these organizations become part of the paternalistic institutional life of hospitals, schools, and organizations providing paternalistic programs (e.g., "preventing pregnancy" programs targeted at young women). Berk (1988) notes that women may choose to participate in volunteer work in order to increase their human capital for future employment opportunities. This may be true for those women whose family's economic resources are such that they do not need to be employed for periods of time.

Gold (1971) also argued that "meaningful" part-time work for well-educated, economically privileged women was relatively unavailable prior to World War II, given traditional employer stereotypes and the sex segregation of the marketplace. Thus, these women took on part of the "white woman's burden" for those less fortunate, while maintaining a high level of autonomy. This makes volunteerism a class issue. In a classist or racist welfare model, white middle-class women have the authority to define the problems and the solutions that they are willing to support with their time and contributions.

Historically, the wives and daughters of wealthy businessmen volunteered to provide schooling and religion classes for immigrant children. Their goals were to remove the negative effects of their students' home lives and to train docile, punctual workers (Katz, 1975). By the beginning of the twentieth century, social work as a profession had developed from the early activities of women volunteers. Thus, a dual system of public and private welfare was developed, rooted in the economic interests of noblesse oblige among the wealthy classes and in patriarchy.

The relationship of class to social welfare in the private sector was never broken. Note that middle- and upper-class volunteers can take a tax write-off for their volunteer expenses. Poor and low-income women have no such opportunity to reimburse their expenses from state and federal tax resources because, although they may pay taxes, they do not have the property resources to itemize deductions. The volunteer efforts of poor women are made more invisible. Overall, Gold concludes that the volunteer workforce reinforces the paternalism of the general welfare state. As we see in the next section, women and their children are also the prime targets of the system of poverty in the United States and throughout the world.

In sum, the caregiving roles of women, which span both paid and unpaid labor, are not integrated into the economic and social policies of most nations. Hochschild (1988) argues that we should analyze the gender strategies of individuals and households (as in the division of second-shift work) but also the gender strategies of governments. She highlights the contradictions in former President Reagan's policies and states that he confused "profamily" with being against women's work outside the home. The Reagan Administration's Panel on the Family offered a "profamily package" that included measures against crime, drugs, and welfare. "In 'protecting' the family, the Republicans proposed to legalize school prayer and eliminate family planning services. They did nothing to help parents integrate work and family life" (Hochschild, 1988:267). She argues that an honest pro-family policy in the United States would look to other progressive countries that address the caregiving status of all citizens through comprehensive maternity and child-care policies, tax breaks to companies that encourage "family leave," job sharing, part-time work (with dignity and benefits), and flex time. She notes that these programs would save on long-range costs due to reductions in work disruptions, and would reduce worker stress and the need for income-support programs for unemployed mothers.

THE FEMINIZATION OF POVERTY

The *feminization of poverty* is a phrase that describes the specific economic vulnerability of women who are the sole support of themselves and/or their children (Scott, 1984). It also describes the subordinate economic position of women in general that rebounds throughout the life cycle: teenage unemployment, nonwage household labor, unpaid child care, lack of benefits for part-time employment, loss of economic support when divorced or widowed, and poverty among elderly women with sporadic or low-wage earning histories. The international scope of this feminization of poverty is evident from the statistic that women comprise 50 percent of the world's population, provide 70 percent of the labor (paid and unpaid), earn 10 percent of the wages, and own less than 1 percent of the property.

Poverty has a range of economic definitions, as well as a variety of social and political meanings for women in the United States and throughout the world. Several different objective measures are used by the U.S. government to set limits for poverty assistance. Essentially, what is meant by *poverty* is the absence of enough economic resources to secure life's necessities, including food, shelter, and clothing. We know that these standards vary across time and from one culture to another, but in the United States, most government programs follow the Social Security Administration's definition of a family budget. According to the U.S. Census Bureau, in 1994, an average family of four was considered to be under the poverty level if their combined wages and income were $15,141 or less. Therefore, a family of four supported by one full-time minimum-wage job will remain more than $5,000 below the poverty line. The poverty amount increases or decreases depending upon the number of persons in the household and whether they live in urban or rural residences, as well as with changes in the consumer price index set by the U.S. Census Bureau (see Table 5-13).

In 1995, 36.4 million people in the United States (13.8 percent) lived below the poverty line. The 1994 poverty rate for black families was almost four times as high as for white non-Hispanic families, 27.3 percent compared with 7.2 percent). Given the disproportionate effects of adult poverty on childhood poverty, estimates are that one-half of black and Hispanic children are being raised in families below the poverty line (Kozol, 1988). In fact, 49 percent of the poor in the United States in 1995 were either under 18 years of age or 65 and over. There were 14.7 million children (20.8 percent) living in poverty. Between 1992 and 1993, children made up almost half (48 percent) of the chron-

TABLE 5-13   Poverty Line and Household Size, 1994

Number of People in Household	Poverty Line
1	$7,547
2	9,661
3	11,821
4	15,141
5	17,900
6	20,235
7	22,923
8	25,427
9 or more persons	30,300

Source: U.S. Bureau of the Census. 1996. *Statistical Abstract of the United States 1996* (116th ed.). Washington, DC: U.S. Government Printing Office, Table 732.

ically poor, a situation in which families stayed below the poverty cutoff every month during 1992 and 1993 (U.S. Bureau of the Census, 1996b).

Almost ten million adult women of all racial and ethnic backgrounds live in poverty in the United States, comprising 52.4 percent of all poor adults. In 1995, the annual median income for all adult women working full-time was $22,497 as compared with $31,496 for adult men. The reasons for this poverty include low wages, discrimination in pensions and benefits, unpaid labor for women, and divorce, desertion, separation, widowhood, and motherhood without an economic partner.

The Material Conditions of Poverty

The consequences of this poverty, the material conditions of poverty, cannot be captured in government statistics. As Smith (1987) reminds us, the everyday life of women highlights the problematic definition of poverty in the discussion of a sociology of women. Those who claim that life on the welfare roles is a "free ride" ignore the experiences of women in poverty. Daily life for women on and off Aid to Families with Dependent Children (AFDC) was examined in a University of Michigan study of 300 women whose AFDC grants had been cut in 1983 (Sarri, 1983). Nearly half of those interviewed said they had completely run out of food in recent months; 89 percent said they had run out of money. Sixteen percent had experienced utility cutoffs, and 11 percent did not have telephone service. Sarri (1983) points out that nearly half of these families were able to obtain food by culling old produce from grocery stores, and over two-thirds sought used clothing for themselves and their children. About one-third bartered services and resources with neighbors, and one-fifth earned money by collecting bottles and cans for refunds.

Birch (1985) focuses on the unsheltered (homeless or substandard housing) woman, particularly female heads of households who have children under the age of eighteen or who are themselves elderly. These two types of family structures represent 15 percent of all housing units, with 25 percent of all family units experiencing housing problems. These problems include lack of plumbing in multiple-dwelling units; overcrowded rooms, especially from "doubling up" families in public and private rooms; and a housing-cost burden that exceeds 30 percent of their monthly economic resources.

In New York City, the focus of research by both Birch and Kozol (1988), found that 40 percent of all households are headed by women. These households include 308,000 women and their children, 312,000 elderly women, and 282,000 single women. These women face active discrimination in the rental market, especially if they receive supplemental aid from the city or the state. One significant result: homelessness.

The government estimates of homelessness are as suspect as their definition of poverty. Officials in the U.S. Department of Housing and Urban Development (HUD) suggested a reliable estimate of 12,000 persons in New York City on a given night, yet over 16,000 were recorded in city shelters the same date. This latter number does not include the large number of people living on streets or in cars who receive no shelter (Kozol, 1988). Nationally, the Coalition for the Homeless estimates some 3 to 4 million homeless people.

In New York City, estimates are that 4,962 families were homeless in June 1987. These families included over 11,000 children, with 70 percent of these children having only one parent (Kozol, 1988:210). Homelessness is a ubiquitous condition of women heads of household and their children. They are placed in emergency shelters in one of several settings: congregate shelters (barracks), short-term hotels, or long-term hotels. Approximately 3,400 families were placed in sixty long-term hotels in the New York City area in a single year. The larger of these hotels house 300 to 450 families for an average of thirteen to sixteen months, although some hotels house them for as long as four years. Permanent public housing in New York City has a waiting list of over 200,000 families, with an estimated waiting period of eighteen years.

Women and Family Poverty

Families maintained by single women are one of the fastest-growing economic units in America, and in 1995, 32.4 percent of individuals in those families were in poverty. This compares with fewer than 5.6 percent in poverty for those families that have two heads of household and 10 percent for those that are male-headed.

In 1940, mothers of 1 out of 10 children were in the paid labor force; by 1990, 6 out of 10 children had working mothers. Most married mothers with children work, about 18 million women representing three-fourths of married mothers. Two-thirds of mothers with children under six worked in the paid labor force at some time in 1992. The average cost for paid child care in 1991 was $63 a week, or 7 percent of family income. Among poor women who must pay for child care these costs on average consumed 27 percent of their family budget (Taeuber, 1996).

Women who are single heads of households face the most serious economic difficulties. In 1993, there were 12 million women-headed families in the United States. The median income for black single-female-headed families was $10,380 and for white women, $16,020 (see Table 5-14). This compares with a median income of $36,660 for black married-couple-headed households and $46,380 for white couples. Female single heads of households have actually witnessed a decrease in median income (based on 1993 dollars) since 1979.

Clearly, the single woman with children is vulnerable to poverty in the United States. In 1970, 5.6 million families were maintained in the United States by women with no husband present. This number increased to 12.2 million single-female-headed households by 1995 (U.S. Census Bureau, 1995). As can be seen in Table 5-15, in 1995, single-female-headed households averaged $12,186 less than single-male-headed households and $25,781 less than families headed by a married couple. Although the average median incomes increased across all family types between 1994 and 1995, female-headed household incomes did not increase as dramatically as male-headed households. In addition, black households averaged $14,785 less than white, non-Hispanic households, and across all race and Hispanic-origin categories only Asians and Pacific Islanders and householders of Hispanic origin realized decreases in median income between 1994 and 1995.

As Lenore Weitzman (1981) points out, women who are divorced and maintain responsibility for their children do so at considerable economic risk. Using 1991 Census data, Table 5-16 indicates that 56 percent of divorced cus-

TABLE 5-14   Median Income of Families with Children, by Type of Family and Race of Householder, 1979 and 1993 (in 1993 dollars)

	1979	*1993*
Married couple		
Black	$33,920	$36,660
White	$44,350	$46,380
Female householder, no spouse present		
Black	$12,820	$10,380
White	$17,690	$16,020

Source: Bennett, C., U.S. Bureau of the Census. 1995. *The Black Population in the United States: March 1994 and 1993.* Current Population Reports, Series P20-480. Washington, DC: U.S. Government Printing Office, Figure 10.

TABLE 5-15   Comparison of Income by Household Type and Race, 1994 and 1995[a]

	1995		1994		
	Number (thousands)	Median Income	Number (thousands)	Median Income (in 1995 dollars)	Percent Change in Real Income
All households	99,627	34,076	98,990	33,178	2.7
Household Type					
Family	69,594	41,224	69,305	40,506	1.8
Married-couple families	53,567	47,129	53,858	46,317	1.8
Female householder[b]	12,514	21,348	12,220	20,435	4.5
Male householder[b]	3,513	33,534	3,226	31,336	7.0
Nonfamily	30,033	19,929	29,686	19,484	2.3
Female householder	16,685	15,892	16,496	15,372	3.4
Male householder	13,348	26,023	13,190	25,290	2.9
Race and Hispanic Origin of Householder					
White	84,511	35,766	83,737	34,992	2.2
White, not Hispanic	76,932	37,178	77,004	36,121	2.9
Black	11,577	22,393	11,655	21,623	3.6
Asian and Pacific Islander	2,777	40,614	2,040	41,629	−2.4
Hispanic origin	7,939	22,860	7,735	24,085	−5.1
Age of Householder					
15–24	5,282	20,979	5,444	19,888	5.5
25–34	19,225	34,701	19,453	34,090	1.8
35–44	23,226	43,465	22,914	42,848	1.4
45–54	18,008	48,058	17,590	48,600	−1.1
55–64	12,401	38,077	12,224	36,230	5.1
65 and over	21,486	19,096	21,365	18,608	2.6

[a]As of March 1996.
[b]No spouse present.

Source: U.S. Bureau of the Census. 1995. *Money Income in the United States, 1995* (based on March 1996 Supplement). Washington, DC: U.S. Government Printing Office, Table A.

todial mothers were awarded child support in 1991, and of those only 52 percent received the full amount that was due. Almost one-quarter (24 percent) of the custodial mothers awarded child support in 1991 received no payments. In 1981 Weitzman reported that when women and children experienced a family disruption through divorce, research indicated that their economic resources decreased to some 24 percent of their former level, whereas divorced men's economic situation remained at 87 percent of the family's total resources (Weitzman, 1981:47). There is little indication that this has improved in the 1990s.

Table 5-17 illustrates the overall percentage of children who lived in poverty between 1960 and 1994 compared with the percent of children in

TABLE 5-16   Child Support-Award and Recipiency Status of Custodial Parents, 1991 (number in thousands)

	Custodial Parents (n)	%	Custodial Mothers (n)	%	Custodial Fathers (n)	%
All custodial parents total	11,502		9,918		1,584	
With child support agreement or award	6,190		5,542		648	
Supposed to receive payments in 1991	5,326	100.0	4,883	100.0	443	100.0
Actually received payments in 1991	4,006	75.2	3,728	76.3	278	62.8
Received the full amount due	2,742	51.5	2,552	52.3	189	42.7
Received partial payments	1,265	23.8	1,176	24.1	89	20.1
Received no payments in 1991	1,320	24.8	1,156	23.7	164	37.0

Source: U.S. Bureau of the Census. 1996. *Statistical Abstract of the United States,* 1996 (116th ed.). Washington, DC: U.S. Government Printing Office, Table 604.

poverty who lived in a single-female–headed household. Although the proportion of children who lived in families with incomes below the poverty level decreased substantially during the 1960s to 15 percent in 1970, the rate increased to 22 percent in 1993 and 21.2 percent in 1994. In 1994, both black and Hispanic children were more than twice as likely as white children to live in

TABLE 5-17   Percentage of Children (Under 18) Who Live in Families with Incomes Below the Poverty Level, 1960–1994

Year	Percent of Children Who Live in Poverty				Percent of Children in Poverty Who Live with a Female Householder			
	Total	White	Black	Hispanic[a]	Total	White	Black	Hispanic
1960[b]	26.5	20.0	65.6	—	23.8	21.0	29.4	—
1970	14.9	10.5	41.5	—	45.8	36.6	60.8	—
1980	17.9	13.4	42.1	33.0	52.8	41.3	75.4	47.1
1985	20.1	15.6	43.1	39.6	53.8	43.0	78.4	49.6
1990	19.9	15.1	44.2	37.7	57.9	46.9	80.3	47.8
1994	21.2	16.3	43.3	41.1	57.7	46.4	82.2	45.6

— Not available.
[a] Hispanics may be of any race.
[b] Data presented for 1960 include 1959 data for blacks and 1960 data for whites and total.

Sources: U.S. Bureau of the Census. 1996. *Income, Poverty, and Valuation of Non-Cash Benefits: 1994.* Current Population Reports, Series P60-189, and U.S. Department of Education, Office of Educational Research and Improvement. 1996. "Climate, classrooms, and diversity in educational institutions." *The Condition of Education 1996,* p. 142.

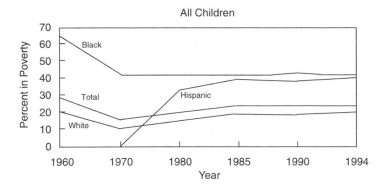

FIGURE 5-2
Source: U.S. Department of Commerce, Bureau of the Census. *Income, Poverty, and Valuation of Non-Cash Benefits: 1994.* Current Population Reports, Series P-60-189.

poverty. Since 1975, at least half the children in poverty lived in female-headed households. In 1994, 57.7 percent of all children in female-headed households lived in poverty, while 82 percent of black children and 46 percent of Hispanic children in female-headed households lived in poverty. Although the overall percentage of children living in poverty has remained fairly constant, since 1980, the percentage of children from female-headed households living in poverty has steadily increased (U.S. Bureau of the Census, 1996b).

Older Women and Poverty

Older women have contributed to society in many ways—including their nonwage household and childrearing activities, volunteer work, and labor-

FIGURE 5-3
Source: U.S. Department of Commerce, Bureau of the Census. *Income, Poverty, and Valuation of Non-Cash Benefits: 1994.* Current Population Reports, Series P-60-189.

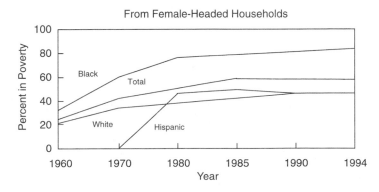

force participation. Yet, they receive little economic payoff for this labor. Low-paying "women's work," time spent in nonwage labor, and intermittent work-force participation keep women on the edge of poverty, especially during their "golden years."

Median income of householders 65 and older in 1995 was $19,096, up 2.6 percent from 1994. The wage gap between women's and men's earnings is smallest at younger ages and increases with age. Men's earnings rise substantially until the men are in their fifties, while women's earnings show little growth over the life cycle. As shown in Table 5-18, after their late fifties, men's wages begin to fall, which narrows the gap slightly for the 55 and older age group.

According to the Survey of Income and Program Participation (SIPP), which analyzes 20,000 households monthly, about 5 percent of the elderly population (persons 65 and over) were chronically poor. This accounts for 11 percent of the chronically poor in the United States. Chronic or long-term poverty refers to the situation where families stayed below the poverty cutoff every month during 1992 and 1993 (Eller and Short, 1996).

Substantial numbers of older women are forced into the labor market by divorce, widowhood, or separation. These "displaced homemakers" face limited employment opportunities due to age and gender discrimination and dated technological skills. In 1992, the median annual income for women 65 and over, from all sources, including pensions and Social Security, was only $8,189 compared with $14,548 for men (see Table 5-19). Elderly black women had median incomes of $6,220 at the same time period. Most elderly women have to support themselves on these low incomes because of their isolated living situations. Forty-three percent of older women live alone or with unrelated adults (Hobbs and Damon, 1996).

Social Security is a program of support for the elderly that was developed on a model of male career patterns to provide economic resource after retirement or removal from the workforce due to disability. Thus, the intermittent and low-wage work conditions for many women, and their nonwage household and childrearing activities, are largely uncompensated by this system. In 1993, the average monthly Social Security benefit for a woman worker was $549.30.

TABLE 5-18   Median Income of Year-Round Full-Time Workers by Age and Sex, 1994

Age Group	Women	Men	Ratio
25–34	$22,426	$26,572	84.4
35–44	25,744	35,586	72.3
45–54	25,911	40,367	64.2
55–64	22,875	37,799	60.5

Source: U.S. Bureau of the Census. 1996. *Statistical Abstract of the United States 1996* (116th ed.). Washington, DC: U.S. Government Printing Office, Table 725.

TABLE 5-19   Median Income of Persons 65 Years
and Over by Sex and Race, 1992
(in dollars)

	Male	Female
Total	$14,548	$8,189
White	15,276	8,579
Black	8,031	6,220
Hispanic[a]	9,253	5,968

[a]Hispanic origin may be of any race

Source: U.S. Bureau of the Census.1993. *Money Income of Households, Families, and Persons in the United States: 1992.* Current Population Reports, Series P-60-184. Washington, DC: U.S. Government Printing Office, pp. 100–107, Table 26.

The overall monthly average benefit for black women was $475.70 compared with $558.50 for white women (see Table 5-20). For women who are 62 or older and are wives of retired or disabled workers the benefits average only $281.50 for black women and $354.60 for white women.

A divorced homemaker whose marriage lasted less than ten years does not qualify for any benefits as a dependent spouse. If the marriage lasts more than ten years, she can receive no more than 50 percent of her former husband's Social Security benefits. No matter what her age, a divorced wife receives no benefits until her former husband either chooses to retire, dies, or becomes disabled. If widowed, a woman can receive 100 percent of her husband's Social Security when she is 65. Prior to that, she can only receive benefits if she has a child in her care, is disabled, or elects early benefit after age 62 at a reduced level of support.

Women's economic security is dependent on her life chances to participate in the labor force where she can earn adequate wages as opposed to performing nonwage labor and low-wage labor. It is also tied to her family status and her chances of being divorced, widowed, or separated during her child-rearing years. The Women's Equity Action League (WEAL) concludes:

> It is not surprising that women are the majority of the poor. After all, many women are "groomed" for poverty. They face a lifetime of limited educational and employment opportunities coupled with childrearing responsibilities. This leaves women, and especially minority women, with . . . more roadblocks than resources. (WEAL Agenda for Women's Economic Equity, 1985–1986)

The Social Functions of Poverty

Herbert Gans (1972) noted at the end of the 1960s civil rights decade that poverty has unintended consequences for society that benefit certain groups. He cites a number of these latent functions of poverty that are fulfilled by the

TABLE 5-20 Average Monthly Benefit for Women Beneficiaries of the Old Age Security and Disability Insurance (ASSDI) Program, by Type of Benefit and Race, December 1993

	Total	White	Black	Other
Total	$549.30	$558.50	$475.70	$453.30
Workers	574.40	582.70	507.60	506.90
Retired	580.70	588.60	508.50	511.30
Full benefit	737.10	753.20	811.40	642.60
Reduced benefit (claimed before age 65)	521.50	528.10	457.00	458.00
Disabled	516.40	520.20	504.20	481.30
Wives of retired and disabled workers	333.70	341.10	248.80	251.20
Entitlement based on care of children	165.00	171.70	143.40	130.90
Husband retired	235.40	247.80	200.60	168.00
Husband disabled	137.30	141.90	122.40	106.90
Entitlement based on age (62 or older)	349.60	354.60	281.50	278.10
Husband retired	351.90	356.90	284.00	279.10
Full benefit	441.50	453.00	328.30	318.70
Reduced benefit	332.10	336.30	270.10	266.90
Husband disabled	229.40	231.90	208.30	208.70
Widows	618.00	634.90	480.30	487.00
Entitlement based on care of children	455.10	484.40	374.90	366.90
Nondisabled, aged 60 or older	632.10	645.90	501.40	516.70
Disabled, aged 50-64	437.50	454.50	380.60	396.20
Mothers of deceased workers	556.10	586.00	484.40	517.80
Special age 72 beneficiaries	183.30	183.40	183.40	183.40

Source: Social Security Administration. 1994. *Social Security Bulletin,* 1994 Annual Statistical Supplement. Washington, DC: U.S. Government Printing Office, Table 5.A.7.

poor and that raise important questions as to the benefits that accrue to the nonpoor as well as to men through the poverty status of women.

Gans speaks first of the creation of a group of workers who will perform tasks that others do not want to perform. His major examples are of people involved in the making of clothing, cooking, cleaning, and other dirty, menial, low-wage or nonwage jobs. Thus, the persistence of high rates of poverty and economic dependence among women may help to ensure that many women have so few options that they will fill positions no one else wants.

Second, poverty benefits the nonpoor by keeping prices down. The consumption patterns of the more affluent are subsidized because the existence of the poor keeps government involved in price supports for basic necessities, such as food and clothing. Third, poverty benefits the nonpoor by creating jobs and income for persons who can regulate, supervise, or serve those who become economically dependent on the state or other social services. This includes not only social service workers, administrators, and clerks in the welfare business but also academicians and teachers who study the poor or who train those who will serve the poor. As Jonathan Kozol points out, the poor also fill the welfare hotels, operated as private businesses but contracted to provide housing in large cities (Kozol, 1988). Evidence presented in the *New York Times* and cited by Kozol indicates that these one-room, substandard housing services charged New York City $1,200 per month. In one instance, a hotel now in the hands of private investors was originally owned by the city, sold in the early 1980s, and by 1986 was charging the city over $1 million a year for rent (Kozol, 1988).

Beeghley (1989) notes an additional function of the poor: to absorb the costs of social and economic change in a society. As we have changed policies in education, employment, support of the military, and so on, the poor have been in the least powerful position to assure that those changes benefit them as a group. For example, as more women entered the labor force to help families keep ahead of inflation (and above the poverty level), these women workers were coerced by social attitudes, norms, and lack of resources to shoulder the time and emotional burdens of child care and the double day. "Put bluntly, this means that the existence of mass poverty provides a class of people who can be exploited by the rest of the population—at least so long as they do not protest in some way" (Beeghley, 1989:111). The cry for welfare reform has traditionally come from affluent people interested in protecting their interests against higher taxes, not as a powerful political force from grass-roots poor women. In 1997, welfare reform legislation was passed limiting recipients to two years of services. In addition, the legislation requires recipients to participate in job training or educational/vocational programs. The movement to limit taxes was the primary impetus in gaining passage of this legislation.

The Social Stigma of Poverty

A final latent function of poverty ties together the triangle of poor women, the reproduction of the labor force, and the family ethic. Mimi Abramovitz (1988) argued that the social welfare policy was embedded in a conservative ideology of women's roles. This ideology placed women in the private sphere, as the reproducers and socializers of new generations of contributing citizens (that is, hard-working, docile wage earners). Thus, the establishment of "mother's pensions" and eventually "Aid to Dependent Children" programs by Congress reflected negative attitudes about specifically husbandless mothers and their fitness to reproduce the labor force. AFDC was designed to release women from wage earning under the condition that they give their children the guidance to make them contributing citizens (Abramovitz, 1988:315). AFDC legitimated the state's role of subsidizing the reproduction of the labor force and the maintenance of the non-wage-earning female family head. The receipt of these grants became highly conditional upon compliance with the family ethic. Thus, the terms "suitable home" and "fit parent" became part of the AFDC provisions.

According to Abramovitz, this *family ethic* was a constellation of women's roles that reinforced traditional white middle-class family patterns, including norms for marriage; wage earning by the male head of household; subordination of women and children within the family; and reproduction, child care, and socialization as women's responsibilities. Patriarchal control in the family and the market became aligned with capitalism and its interest in the maintenance of the labor force (including women as a reserve pool of low-wage labor). For poor women, women of color, and immigrant women, the separation of the public and private spheres of family and economics was problematic. Social welfare policies, explanations for poverty, and levels of support did not take into account women's experiences of low-wage labor, the disjuncture of family life by the welfare policies, and the economic structures of slave and immigrant labor histories.

In *Rachel and Her Children* (1988), Kozol described the double bind of this family ideology for poor women. A scenario repeated on a daily basis in the United States is the homeless family that applies for AFDC. The social worker determines that the children are endangered by their lack of shelter, and the children are placed in foster care. The parents are no longer eligible for AFDC because they no longer have dependent children. "So the family *as a family* receives nothing. The children have been institutionalized. The family, as such, no longer exists" (Kozol, 1988:49).

Added to the family ethic is the *work ethic,* which holds in contempt those individuals who "do not work for their keep." The prevailing political opinion among people in the United States is that poverty is generated by individual deviations from the work ethic: lack of thrift, lack of effort, lack of ability, loose morals, and sickness (Feagin et al., 1972; Nilson, 1981). The poor, however, are less likely to accept this definition and are more likely to cite structural factors such as lack of opportunity, inability to earn good wages, and the inheritance of poverty.

Perhaps these differences have to do with the demographics of poverty. Over half of all the poor are elderly, disabled, or children who are unable to work. Another significant proportion are the working poor, whose incomes place them below the poverty level. For example, more than one-third of all single-women householders in 1993 lived on incomes below the poverty level. In 1993, approximately 33 percent of blacks and 31 percent of Hispanics lived in poverty in the United States. The rate for Anglos was 12 percent (U.S. Bureau of the Census, 1995). Women supporting their families alone and elderly women living alone are the most likely individuals to be poor in the United States. The 1997 welfare reform legislation will likley have little influence on these demographics.

WORK AND VALUE

These functions of poverty as outlined by sociologists and socialist feminists highlight the ongoing importance of assessing use value and exchange value in the work of women. Whether it is nonwage housework or the low-wage caretaking positions of women in the labor force, the historical and contemporary structure of women's work demonstrates that as a class or group, the exchange resources for women are restricted. They have been restricted by the structural forces that "feminize" useful occupations such as nursing, teaching, and clerical work and degrade their wages and social prestige. Current employment patterns indicate that sex segregation is pervasive and that racial/ethnic segregation further compounds the wage inequalities for women of color.

Throughout the individual life cycle, these restrictions influence family and individual choices as to who labors in the home, for how long, and under what conditions. Housework and child care, exalted in their symbolic dimensions in many cultures, are taken for granted by houseworkers, family members, employers, and the government.

The role of the state also reflects the family context of use value and the market exchange value of women's work in social welfare and Social Security programs, as well as in social services for women. Whether they are children, elderly, single heads of household, or homeless, women's place in the social welfare system is tied to their usefulness (past, present, or potential) in a narrowly defined family structure. Fiscal conservatives in government argue for the replacement of federally funded social services with volunteer efforts. As we have seen, women provide much of that direct-service volunteer work. Substituting federal exchange value (grants to states and cities for social service provision) with the use value of women's caretaking work recycles the sex stratification of inequality back to women's disadvantage. Note that the elimination of social service jobs would have a tremendous effect on employment for women and people of color.

The treatment of women's issues (homeless children, child care, early childhood education) by political policies of volunteer effort has a parallel dimension in exchange value. The payment of wages for child care in the marketplace is often an exchange among women. Employed women with low wages pay child-care workers (predominately women) minimum wages. This is a circulation of poverty-level exchange value among women, which guarantees the entrenchment of economic dependence on the state or on a higher-wage male earner.

On the international scale, the wage and nonwage labor of women workers takes on new dimensions of dependency and structural restrictions. International dependency relations are created by the capitalization of industry and farming. The shift of many of the traditional operative jobs of "highly paid" U.S. workers to women in Southeast Asia, Mexico, and elsewhere has threatened the economic security of all women (Rosen, 1987).

The agricultural roles of women throughout the world are influenced now by economic factors, chemical fertilizers, and trade agreements that are enacted with little or no input from these producers. Across cultures, women's work in the field is discounted, uncounted, and devalued. As unpaid family workers, or as low-wage agricultural workers, these women struggle with the

layers of use value and exchange value that have been attached to the sex stratification of the economic sphere.

Worker Resistance

The image of women passively accepting the material conditions of their
working lives must be corrected. Historically, women have been involved in successful unionization struggles and strikes, ranging from the all-female garment
factory strikes in Dover, New Hampshire (1828), and Lowell, Massachusetts
(1830s), to the current unionization efforts of nursing, teaching, and clerical
workers (Kessler-Harris, 1981).

Hossfeld's (1990) in-depth analysis of immigrant women of color working the shop floors in the Silicon Valley, California, electronics industry demonstrates two aspects of resistance. First, the new immigrant workforce is kept "in
line" through management manipulation of race, class, and gender ideologies.
"Management taps both traditional popular stereotypes about the presumed
lack of status and limited abilities of women, minorities, and immigrants and
the worker's own fears, concerns, and sense of priorities as immigrant women"
(Hossfeld, 1990:156). Thus, there is little challenge of the low-wage and in-
flexible shop conditions through formal channels, including complaints about
unequal treatment or militant unionization efforts.

Second, Hossfeld reports that immigrant women do respond to the gender
strategies of shop managers in kind, to manipulate their work environment in-
formally. "Just as employers harness racist, sexist, and class-based logic to manipulate and control workers, so too workers use this logic against management"
(1990:169). Among the examples Hossfeld gives are those of a Filipina who
turned the boss's argument that women are "too weak" to do the (higher-paying)
men's work into a refusal to carry heavy boxes of circuit boards to her work station and a Haitian woman who took a lot of "kidding" from her employer about
voodoo and black magic, insisting that she could not work the night shift because
of evil spirits. When Hossfeld tried to establish her actual belief in spirits, the response was "Does it matter? The result is the same: I can be at home at night with
my kids" (1990:174). Hossfeld concludes that these struggles are not merely ideological and do result in concrete changes in working conditions. However, they
are couched not in labor or class terms but in ethnic and gender terms.

A GLOBAL AGENDA FOR ECONOMIC ACTION

Out of the United Nations Decade for Women (1975–1985) came a series of
recommendations, which are discussed here. These recommendations need attention at national and local levels, as well as in the arrangements of individuals and families in their working lives. Thus, political, educational, and religious changes are necessary to the accomplishment of these goals. However,

we address only the economic changes and include issues of economic equality and development, economic security programs and welfare, and child-care and family strategies.

Economic Equality and Development

Women's greatest need is not just for political equality but for economic equality as well. To prohibit discrimination in their jobs and their ability to obtain credit and benefits, women must be in the economic (and political) position to make decisions. The development of hiring policies and training programs, and the reform of government and private corporate policies related to benefits must be reconceptualized and implemented with women's perspectives as to who should get what in the economic system.

These changes must not only include attitudinal and behavioral changes for individuals and organizations. They must also incorporate economic development in the United States and globally. Women's present contributions to work need to be equitably rewarded in the waged economy through the implementation of pay equity programs at all organization sizes and levels. This means eliminating the exploitation of women, immigrants, and people of color and their subsidy of high-wage earners in the primary labor market. This wage equalization process is critical when we look at the expansion of low-wage clerical (secretarial, clerk) and service jobs (food service, janitors, keypunch operators) that will absorb the rising proportions of women moving into the economy in the future. Women also need more and better training programs to take their place in the array of technical jobs (computer operators, electrical engineering, medical assistants) that are also increasing in number.

Economic Security and Welfare

The huge expenditures of national and international budgets on defense programs are being questioned during this period of changing international relations. What is needed is a shift of major resources toward economic security that takes into account the health care, family leave, and unemployment and retirement patterns of women throughout the world. Women must clarify and reformulate the policies that separate the "deserving" from the "undeserving" in terms of benefits. The nonwage contributions of women in housework, reproduction, and child care are systematically ignored in most economic security policies. Women who are denied unemployment benefits because they resign for "family" reasons are unjustly punished. Poor women who need both health care and economic support face a widely fluctuating state-to-state set of regulations and benefits. Nowhere have these programs provided the housing, child care, and educational training necessary to provide women with the resources to recover from divorce, widowhood, or the burden of dependent children. Nowhere are politicians considering how to generate an economic system that can survive without the poor.

Striking Out on Their Own: Women-Owned Businesses

One of the responses to the glass ceiling in traditional businesses has been for women to establish and run their own businesses. Women with business training and skills have been establishing their own businesses in the United States at record numbers. This is not surprising given that 45.8 percent of B.A.s in business management in 1990–1991 went to women and 72.2 percent of vocational students in business are women.

One factor that certainly helped this trend was the 1977 federal public works law passed by Congress that set aside a minimum percentage of government work for "disadvantaged business enterprises." In addition, during the 1980s many of the city and county governments throughout the United States established "minority enterprise" laws that helped to ensure that small businesses owned by women and minorities would get a certain share of public contracts. However, these laws have been challenged, and recently the Supreme Court has upheld a 1995 ruling that struck down Philadelphia's "set aside" program, claiming it was based on racial and gender politics rather than remedying any specific form of discrimination. Even though the 1990s has seen an eroding of the "set aside" laws, women have continued to make significant strides in women-owned businesses.

The rate of employment growth for women-owned businesses was 118 percent between 1991 and 1994 (Post and Lynch, 1996). Women-owned businesses in 1995 contributed more than $2.38 trillion in revenues to the economy (U.S. Small Business Association, 1996). Census data from 1992 indicated that women owned 6.4 million businesses, and the U.S. Small Business Association estimated that women in 1996 owned almost 8 million firms. Employment by women-owned firms rose by more than 100 percent between 1987 and 1992 while at the same time there was only a 38 percent increase in employment by all firms. Employment increased by 158 percent for women-owned companies with 100 or more workers. One of every five U.S. workers, approximately 18.5 million employees, works for a woman-owned business.

In 1996, the top-growth industries for women-owned businesses were

- Construction
- Wholesale trade
- Transportation
- Communications
- Agribusiness
- Manufacturing

Further, women are entering the global marketplace at the same rate as all U.S. business owners. In 1992, 13 percent were involved in international trade. Also, women-owned businesses are more likely to remain in business than the average U.S. firm. Nearly three-fourths of women-owned businesses in 1991 were still in business three years later, compared with two-thirds of all U.S. firms (U.S. Small Business Association, 1996).

Clearly, the data illustrate the strength of leadership and management skills women bring to the business world. Rather than trying to break through the glass ceiling in traditional, and often patriarchal, corporations, women are establishing their own footing in the business world and are now competing with the more traditional companies.

Child-Care and Family Strategies

Without a national comprehensive child-care and family health care policy, employers have left families, particularly women, to sort out the responsibilities of life. By ignoring women's nonwage contributions, we have an economic system that falsely omits a sizable productive dimension, and an economic balance sheet that benefits from women's caretaking and volunteer work. We can implement family-leave policies that assume that both women and men can absorb family responsibilities; child-care programs that are safe, reliable, and accessible; and family health care programs that cooperate with families to provide long-term care for the elderly or the dependent in more humane, family-oriented settings.

Certainly attitudes must change, and this requires education and socialization practices in the future that highlight these issues as global, not just as "women's issues." But women must have equal political and economic influence to transform those changes in attitudes into behavioral outcomes that benefit families and societies. It is clear that profit-driven child care, economic development, benefit packages, and health care will only serve to widen the gap between the haves and the have-nots, including men and women, who struggle over a "piece of the pie" that is baked in a male perspective of work and its rewards.

SIX

Women and Schooling

Education structures the patterns of women's lives. How much education and the type of education we receive influence the work and economic rewards available to us. We spend an average of 1,000 hours per year in the classroom between the ages of five and sixteen, reading texts, interacting with teachers, and socializing with other students. Our sense of who we are and who we might be is shaped by the role models, reading materials, skills, and friends that we acquire in school.

Sociologists also agree that schools organize and provide for the larger society a number of *manifest* or intended social functions, including certifying skills, transmitting culture, and implementing social change. The type of skills, the content of that culture, and the social changes sought through "schooling" are gendered in significant ways that we analyze in this chapter. Being male or female is reflected in the context of roles, texts, and process of education. In addition to the formal curricula, schools provide an arena for passing ideas, values, and beliefs through informal interaction with teachers, administrators, and student peers. These ideas, values, and beliefs are called the "hidden curriculum," the *latent* (unintended), but powerful, consequences of attending schools that reinforce larger social patterns. Among those we consider in this chapter are norms for the hierarchical arrangement of gender, male authority patterns, "women's spheres" in majors, cultural resources of women of color, and the dominance of heterosexual norms. Schools, then, are another social institution that can be analyzed from conflict and functionalist perspectives in sociology, as well as through feminist analyses of institutionalized sexism, classism, and racism.

Economics and sociology are not the only, or even the main, culprits in this attempt to keep women off the record, and practitioners of education have been busy promoting and substantiating the belief that men are more important, their behaviour more significant, and their education more crucial. (Spender, 1982:28)

FUNCTIONALIST THEORISTS: HUMAN CAPITAL AND WOMEN'S EDUCATION

As we would anticipate, functionalist theorists assert that education and training enhance individual *human capital,* the individual skills and abilities we acquire. Economists argue that investment in education and training is much the same as investment in capital goods. These theorists focus on the rate of return of time or money invested in gaining skills critical to the functioning of the society. Education is assumed to bring a substantial return to the individual through income enhancement and to the society through the training of an adequate supply of skilled workers.

The social connection made by functionalist theorists such as Talcott Parsons (1959) is among higher educational levels, increased worker skills, and increased income for individuals. In the classroom, students are taught skills and evaluated on their abilities in "the cognitive or technical component and the moral or social component" (Parsons, 1959:302). Students are evaluated on their capacity to act in accord with these values and "this differentiation underlies the processes of selection for levels of status and role in adult society" (ibid.). Functionalists conclude that if a group suffers inequality in the economic sector, the solution is to increase the human capital of group members through increased educational achievements.

As we saw in the chapter on economics and work, women who have skills and abilities that are certified by schools do not necessarily receive the same rewards as do men with similar certification. On the average, a woman with a college degree will earn less than a man with an eighth-grade education. This economic inequality is also evident for minority women and men, with Hispanic, black, and Native American women earning considerably less than their male peers or white women. The functionalist model of equal reward for equal skills cannot explain these unequal outcomes.

Furthermore, critics of the human-capital theory have argued that employers actually have little empirical evidence on which to base their preference for higher education credentials. In fact, they are accused of overinflating their job requirements because of the enlarged pool of high school and college graduates available (Berg, 1971). Thus, many women and men work in jobs for which they are educationally overqualified. Some 12.6 percent of women doing clerical work hold a bachelor's degree or above but are unable to find jobs that are commensurate with their training (Glenn and Feldberg, 1989). But the failure of the "education = skill = income" equation is only one criticism made of education on behalf of women and other groups.

CONFLICT THEORISTS: CULTURE AND CONFLICT
IN THE SCHOOLS

Schooling is a term coined by the theorists Samuel Bowles and Herbert Gintis to describe the complex educational process that includes both the manifest and latent outcomes of education—that is, both the intended and unintended consequences. Bowles and Gintis (1976) argue that schooling has important dimensions that go beyond publicly stated, manifest goals of technical training, job preparation, and individual achievement. Students also learn verbal and nonverbal cues through the authority relationships of teachers and students, habits such as punctuality and following directions, and expectations for educational and occupational achievements. These latent consequences are no less real than the mastery of subject matter for which certificates or diplomas are granted. Bowles and Gintis further question the widely held belief that increased education is good in and of itself and provide a conflict analysis of education that highlights schooling as a scarce resource. Schooling becomes an economic resource that subtly tracks people into acceptable modes of belief, behavior, and skills that may support inequality in the larger society. These authors focused primarily on issues of race and class, identifying the formal classroom tracking of students in schools based on intelligence tests and achievement measures.

Rosemary Deem (1978) extended their argument to include the domestic and service skills emphasized for women in education, particularly for working-class girls in the public schools. In her assessment of British schooling, she found that young girls are taught the formal skills attached to "women's place" in society: domestic, caretaking, and social skills. The informal norms of the school reinforce the dichotomy of public/private lives, emphasizing the centrality of the private and marginalizing the public: "Home life becomes central for adolescent girls and wage labor secondary" in the United States as well (Weis, 1988:183). Given the reality of generations of working-class women laboring in the public sphere, this dichotomy has serious implications for the double bind of employed working-class women who struggle to uphold the "Domestic Code," or expectations for women's unpaid work in the home and in child care.

Conflict theorists question the content of the educational curriculum. They argue that it reflects strong cultural biases derived from the dominant Anglo-Saxon Protestant norms. Thus, they suggest that the children who are most likely to achieve well within schools will be those children who arrive at the school door with early training in the language, customs, institutions, and norms of the dominant culture. They argue that these skills become a type of *cultural capital* that is exchanged easily for additional information and rewards from teachers who have the same exchange capital.

Bourdieu and Passeron (1977) argue that for those students who arrive with a different language or set of customs or beliefs, the exchange will be more difficult. The schools will make few, if any, modifications to meet the needs of cultural minorities. Thus, in the conflict model, the advantages of the dominant group, which begin with language, customs, and beliefs that are shared with the schools, are reinforced by their achievements within the schools. These inequalities in educational achievement are then used as a rationale for later economic inequalities, based on the functionalist model that school credentials actually measure ability.

This notion of cultural capital is perhaps most obvious in language skills. Students who do not speak English as a native language are at a disadvantage; they will need to "catch up" in the basic exchange system of symbols in order to understand all of the other educational lessons. The resistance of the dominant group to any change in this advantage for English-speaking students is exemplified in a number of ways—from the "English as the official language" movements, which have led to such legislation being passed in some states, to the designation of English as a Second Language (ESL) curricula as programs to move non-English speakers toward English, rather than moving English-speaking children toward bilingualism.

Cultural capital also includes gendered biases such as those outlined by Deem (1978) and Weis (1988). In addition to an emphasis on the Domestic Code, information about the norms, beliefs, and contributions of women have often been omitted from the curriculum. Instead, by describing the political, military, and social activities of "our forefathers," students presumably learn about the parallel (or subsumed) experiences of women. Feminist scholars are rapidly demonstrating that male-defined histories and lists of "Who's Who" in most subject areas consistently exclude and distort women and the dimensions of life important to women.

This book is part of a growing tradition of educational works designed not only to add information to the curricula in the schools but also to reanalyze and reinterpret the meaning of women's lives in the framework of the larger society. Later in this chapter we discuss not only the sexist structure of the schools and their curricula but also the importance of heterosexist bias to our understanding of the education of lesbian students and the intersection of gender, race, and class in the education of Chicanos and Chicanas.

SCHOOLING: A GENDERED HISTORY

Schooling is a significant issue for women today because they are increasingly involved at a number of levels and in a variety of settings, from preschool and kindergarten to elementary, secondary, and perhaps college education, moving through the same structure as male students. In each of these schooling situations, women and men students are exposed to textbooks, materials, and teacher attitudes that will subtly affect their thinking about themselves and their society. But schools separate women into particular patterns, similar to those described in the chapter on work. Women participate in different areas of studies (for example, more women than men major in the humanities and home economics, as opposed to the physical sciences) and even different types of schools (women's colleges in the United States, or sex-segregated schools in Islamic countries such as Saudi Arabia). Thus, Florence Howe (1987) and others argue that we have developed a myth of coeducation in the United States that does not stand up to feminist analysis and a standard for educational training that is inapplicable in other cultures.

As educators, women also take a variety of roles as administrators and teachers that reflect feminization patterns similar to those in the larger labor market. Women administrators are disproportionately represented at the bottom of the educational hierarchy and remain relatively small in number. Women teachers are segregated by disciplines, with limited areas in which they teach or do research, and women educators in general are paid feminized salaries.

All of these factors occur as subtle or overt forms of sexism in an institution that is touted as the gateway to opportunity for immigrants, minorities, and women. Historically, schooling was made compulsory at the elementary and secondary level to ensure an informed voting public and a skilled workforce. Higher education was made more accessible through open admissions policies in community and four-year colleges, the removal of gender restrictions on admission to professional schools, and the promise of affirmative action. In the next section, we look at the effects of these institutional changes on educational attainments for women and men.

How Much Schooling?

It is difficult to estimate the early educational patterns of women and men in the United States because colonial society depended upon tutoring for the wealthy classes and charity or church schools for the poor, with few publicly supported schools for the working classes. It seems, however, that formal education for women was restricted by law and custom through most of the early history of the United States. The laws indicated that basic literacy for women was to be encouraged so that mothers could teach their own children to read and cipher, but sustained higher education was to be discouraged. Town-supported grammar schools in the North sometimes admitted girls but often held separate sessions for girls and younger children in the summer months, when adolescent males were needed to work in the fields (Kerber, 1983:5).

After the Revolutionary War, the push for public education grew. By the 1830s, Horace Mann became a spokesperson for a national reform movement demanding free, tax-supported schools. The growth of democratic elementary education promised social mobility for working people and a docile, trained workforce for industrial capitalists. From 1840 to 1860, the number of males and females in common schools rose from 38 percent to 59 percent of the white population (Kerber, 1983). For females, the emphasis continued on education that would create more useful wives and mothers, since "our ladies should be qualified to a certain degree by a peculiar and suitable education, to concur in instructing their sons in the principles of liberty and government" (Benjamin Rush, 1798, as cited in Kerber, 1983).

Access to higher education was more stringently restricted for women in the early years. The establishment of Harvard (1636) and William and Mary (1693) as the first universities in the United States reflected a "male only" policy that continued for two hundred years. In 1821, Emma Willard opened the Troy Female Seminary in New York State with a curriculum parallel to that offered by men's colleges. Her goal was to educate "good" American mothers and teachers. In the next three decades, higher educational opportunities for white women in America began to expand. Oberlin College opened its doors to women and to blacks in 1832, and Lawrence College followed by admitting women students in 1847. By 1872, there were approximately one hundred women's coeducational colleges. The first women's college, Wheaton, opened in 1834, followed by Mount Holyoke in 1837. The New England and Philadelphia Female Medical Colleges opened in 1848 and 1851, respectively.

Only a tiny proportion of women attended these colleges, almost all of them from white middle- and upper-class families. The number of women who earned college and graduate degrees began to rise by the 1890s, with women earning close to one-fifth of all B.A. and M.A. degrees, though fewer than 1 percent of the Ph.D.s. Often, graduate work at the doctoral level was explicitly denied to women applicants on the basis of sex. For women of color, explicit racial entrance barriers were in place in medical and law schools up through the late 1940s. But a steadily increasing number of women gained entry to colleges, completed their undergraduate degrees, and indeed went on for the M.A. or Ph.D. in their chosen fields.

Today's Profile

The expansion of educational opportunities for women since the 1860s has been uneven. The proportions of white women who were trained in the expanding public elementary and secondary schools increased steadily, but they lagged slightly behind white men in completion rates until the 1970s. Today among whites, men and women complete high school at relatively even rates. In 1991, 79.9 percent of white women and 79.8 percent of white men had received a high school diploma (see Table 6-1). High school completion rates for blacks and Hispanics, particularly Puerto Rican and Mexican American groups, have lagged behind whites. This educational lag is a consequence of complex factors, including language and cultural biases in curriculum, lack of economic resources to support sustained educational participation, and the economic reality that many jobs in the labor force do not require or reward advanced education.

The proportion of women earning higher education degrees also increased from the 1850s until post–World War II, when massive numbers of mates returning from war activities flooded the college campuses. While the number of women remained steady, the postwar expansion of higher education primar-

**TABLE 6-1   Education Completed by Persons Age 25
and Over by Race/Ethnicity, 1991**

	8 Years	High School	College Degree
White			
Female	95.0	79.9	19.3
Male	94.3	79.8	25.4
Black			
Female	89.2	66.7	11.6
Male	88.5	66.7	11.4
Hispanic			
Female	72.3	51.2	9.4
Male	72.9	51.4	10.0
Asian–Pacific Islander			
Female	n/a	80.0	35.5
Male	n/a	83.8	43.2

Source: U.S. Bureau of the Census. 1993. Current Population Reports, P20-426. Washington, DC: U.S. Government Printing Office.

ily benefited men until the late 1970s, when the proportions of women began to rise again. Today, white women and men 25–34 years old are close to parity in the number of B.A. and M.A. degrees awarded, but women still lag far behind at the Ph.D. level or in professional degrees. In 1990 women earned 53.2 percent of all bachelor's degrees and 52.6 percent of master's degrees, but only 36.3 percent of Ph.D. degrees (U.S. Bureau of the Census, 1993a). Among blacks and Hispanics, college completion rates are significantly lower, but for Asians they are as high or higher. For example, in 1992, Asians earned 3.9 percent of all doctorate degrees, though they represent less than 2 percent of the population. American Indians earned 0.3 percent of doctorate degrees, though they represent more than 1 percent of the population. For blacks, the rates are 3.1 percent of Ph.D.s (12 percent of the population) and for Hispanics, 2.0 percent of Ph.D.s (9 percent of the population). Note, however, that black women and men are completing college degrees at similar rates, which may reflect strong cultural expectations for education of women and men in the African American community (Jones, 1985). The most disturbing trend in higher education is the decreased enrollment and completion rates of minority men and women in undergraduate and graduate education since the late 1970s. Between 1979 and 1986, the proportion of new black Ph.D.s dropped by 22 percent, such that African Americans earned only 3.8 percent of all Ph.D.s in 1986. By 1992, this percentage dropped to 3.1. (National Center for Education Statistics, 1994). It is quite likely that this trend is due to restrictions in funds at the federal level for advanced education, as well as the process and content of higher education.

The percentage of women receiving bachelor's degrees has increased significantly since 1971 in agriculture, business and management, engineering, and law (see Table 6-2). More than 50 percent of the following master's

TABLE 6-2 Percent Female of Earned Degrees Conferred by Field of Study and Level of Degree, 1971–1993

Field of Study	Bachelor's		Master's		Doctorate's	
	1971	1993	1971	1993	1971	1993
Total	43.4	54.3	40.1	54.2	14.3	38.1
Agriculture and natural resources	4.2	34.0	5.9	37.5	2.9	25.1
Architecture and environmental design	11.9	35.2	13.8	37.6	8.3	29.1
Area and ethnic studies	52.4	63.9	38.3	51.9	16.7	49.4
Biological/life sciences	29.1	51.4	33.6	50.7	16.3	39.9
Business and management	9.1	47.2	3.9	35.7	2.8	28.0
Communications[a]	35.3	59.7	34.6	62.0	13.1	51.5
Computer and information sciences	13.6	28.1	10.3	27.1	2.3	14.4
Education	74.5	78.4	56.2	76.9	21.0	59.2
Engineering[a]	0.8	14.4	1.1	14.9	0.6	9.6
English language and literature/letters	65.6	65.7	60.6	65.8	28.8	59.0
Foreign languages	74.0	71.1	64.2	66.8	34.6	57.2
Health sciences	77.1	83.1	55.3	79.7	16.5	57.4
Home economics	97.3	89.2	93.9	83.0	61.0	71.9
Law	5.0	67.6	4.8	32.6	—	24.4

Liberal/general studies	33.6	60.3	44.6	65.2	31.3	53.1
Library and archival science	92.0	89.2	81.3	80.3	28.2	66.2
Mathematics	37.9	47.2	27.1	39.6	7.6	23.8
Military technologies	0.3	(Z)	—	7.4	—	—
Multi/interdisiplinary studies	22.8	62.8	25.0	51.1	6.8	41.3
Parks and recreation	34.7	50.5	29.8	50.2	50.0	30.6
Philosophy, religion, and theology	25.5	31.1	27.1	38.0	5.8	17.3
Physical sciences	13.8	32.6	13.3	29.0	5.6	21.9
Protective services	9.2	37.7	10.3	38.3	—	28.1
Psychology	44.4	73.2	40.6	72.4	24.0	61.2
Public affairs	68.4	77.3	50.0	70.4	24.1	53.2
Social sciences[b]	36.8	45.8	28.5	43.1	13.9	36.3
Visual and performing arts	59.7	61.0	47.4	56.6	22.2	45.8
Other and unclassified	0.9	35.9	—	30.3	—	16.2

(Z) Less than .01 percent
— Represents zero
[a]Includes Technologies (for BA)
[b]Includes History

Source: U.S. Bureau of the Census. 1996. *Statistical Abstract of the United States 1996* (116th ed.). Washington, DC: U.S. Government Printing Office, Table 302 and 303.

TABLE 6-3   Highest and Lowest Earnings by Undergraduate Major, by Sex in 1993

Women		*Men*	
Top 5			
Pharmacy	$47,567	Engineering	$52,998
Engineering	46,389	Mathematics	52,316
Computer and information sciences	41,559	Physics	51,819
Physical therapy and related	40,491	Pharmacy	50,805
services		Economics	50,360
Nursing	40,096		
Bottom 5			
Education, including physical	28,696	Education, including physical	35,216
education		education	
Theology, philosophy, and religion	28,375	Visual and performing arts	33,571
Agriculture	28,178	Foreign languages and linguistics	32,346
Social work	27,619	Social work	31,507
Home economics	27,496	Theology, philosophy, and religion	29,966

Source: Bureau of Labor Statistics. Summer 1996. "Earnings and Major Field of Study of College Graduates." *Occupational Outlook Quarterly,* 40(2). Washington, DC: Office of Employment Projections, Table 1.

degrees were awarded to women in 1993: area and ethnic studies, communications, biological/life sciences, education, English language and literature/letters, foreign languages, health sciences, home economics, liberal and general studies, library and archival sciences, multi/interdisciplinary studies, parks and recreation, psychology, public affairs, and visual and performing arts. Also, there are consistently more women receiving doctorates in 1993 as compared with 1971.

In terms of annual earnings by college undergraduate majors, the highest-paid majors for men include engineering, mathematics, physics, pharmacy, and economics. For women, the highest-paid majors include pharmacy, engineering, computer science, physical therapy, and nursing (see Table 6-3).

There have been dramatic increases in the number of women receiving first-professional[1] degrees over the past three decades—dentistry, medicine, and law have all witnessed a larger percentage of degrees being awarded to women. As illustrated in Table 6-4, only .4 percent of dentistry degrees (D.D.S. or D.M.D.) were awarded to women in 1963–1964, but by 1993–1994 more than one-third of dentistry degrees went to women. Only 1 in 20 M.D.s were awarded to women in 1953–1954, but by 1994, 61 percent of degrees in medicine were awarded to women. There were also large percentage increases for women's professional degrees in law. Only 3 percent of L.L.B.s and J.D.s went to women in 1963–1964, but by 1994, 43 percent of law degrees were awarded to women.

---

[1]First-professional degrees are degrees beyond the bachelor's in a specialized field such as law (J.D.) or medicine (M.D.).

TABLE 6-4　Percent Female by First-Professional Degrees in Dentistry, Medicine, and Law, 1953–1954 to 1993–1994

	Dentistry (D.D.S. or D.M.D.)	Medicine (M.D.)	Law (L.L.B. or J.D.)
1953–1954	1.3	5.0	([a])
1963–1964	0.4	5.8	2.9
1973–1974	1.9	11.1	11.4
1983–1984	19.6	28.2	36.8
1993–1994	38.5	61.0	43.0

[a]Data prior to 1955–1956 are not shown because they lack comparability with the figures for subsequent years.

Source: U.S. Department of Education, National Center for Education Statistics. 1996. *Digest of Education Statistics 1996* (NCES 96–133). Washington, DC: U.S. Government Printing Office, Table 254.

WHAT KIND OF SCHOOLING?

Public education in the United States today is essentially a coeducational process. As we have seen, the gap between female and male educational rates is shrinking, although that is most true for Asians and Anglos/whites. Other areas in which we can analyze the differential experiences of women and men in education include the curriculum, teacher interaction, sexual harassment, and the hierarchy of educational authority.

Because students spend approximately 1,000 hours per year in a classroom setting, we should analyze the structure and content of the classroom itself. What are the images of women presented in school materials and textbooks? Do these reinforce limiting sex-role stereotypes? What kinds of educational programs do women participate in? What are the outcomes for these students compared with male students of similar education?

Reinforcing Limited Sex Roles: Sex Bias in Texts

As early as 1946, researchers were examining the issue of stereotyping in elementary school textbooks, based on the notion that children are positively and negatively reinforced as they read: "[I]n reading a story a child goes through symbolically, or rehearses for himself [sic], the episode that is described" (Child, Potter, and Levine, 1946:84). These early researchers found striking differences in gender roles in the printed stories. Males were more often provided information or demonstrated activity, aggression, and achievement to gain recognition. Females were in general omitted from these stories altogether: Seventy-three percent of the main characters were male, only 27 percent female. Graebner's (1972) study of 554 stories found no changes in these depictions in the decade from 1963 to 1973.

In 1975, a comprehensive study by the U.S. Department of Health, Education and Welfare (HEW) surveyed 134 texts and readers. Researchers conducted content analyses of pictures, story themes, and the language descriptors used for male and female characters. Overall, male figures were more often presented as central figures in stories, or as notable Americans. These textbooks carried a total of 88 different biographies of men; only 17 women were represented in biographical accounts.

This omission of women's lives and activities is compounded by the portrayal of women in narrow, gendered roles. Women are rarely shown in paid labor-force positions; they were mostly confined to the home. DeCrow (1972) found no women portrayed in textbooks as working outside the home with the exception of teachers or nurses during a time period when women's actual labor-force participation was rising significantly. In the HEW textbook study, men were portrayed in 147 different types of jobs, while women were in 26. All of these 26 jobs were traditional female activities such as cafeteria workers, secretaries, nurses, and teachers.

The HEW study found that even when controlling for the differences in the proportions of portrayals, males were four times as likely to be described as ingenious, creative, brave, persevering, achieving, adventurous, autonomous, and self-respecting. These active/mastery themes were in direct contrast to passive themes assigned to females. Women were six to ten times as likely to be described as dependent, as domestic (a helper in cooking and cleaning), as victims, or as females who can be humiliated because of their gender.

In 1972, Scott, Foresman and Company, a major textbook publisher, published *Guidelines for Improving the Image of Women in Textbooks*. By 1978, the National Education Association reported that all of the major publishing houses had such guidelines. More recent analyses indicate that the omission of female characters in new texts and readers has been partially addressed. Grauerholz and Pescosolido (1989) analyzed 2,216 picture books published throughout the twentieth century. During the 1980s, the overall ratio of males to females as central characters was still 2 to 1; adult male characters outnumbered females 3 to 1. However, the mere depiction of females in illustrations or as characters is not sufficient. The content of the stories and the meaning they give to the female role is crucial (Best, 1983).

Weitzman et al. (1972) conducted a content analysis of those picture books honored by a Caldecott Award from 1967 to 1971. These are among the most influential of children's picture books selected in school and family libraries. This research has been updated twice, the most recent for the 1981 to 1985 Caldecott Award winners (Williams et al., 1987). These researchers found that females are now visible, but the nature of that visibility shows continued gender biases. The most frequent behaviors for females were passivity and submission; the most frequent for males were activity, independence, and persistence. The researchers conclude that traditional gender roles are the norm for these award-winning books:

Not only does Jane express no career goals, but there is no model to provide any ambition. One woman in the entire twenty books has an occupation outside the home and she works at Blue Tile Diner. How can we expect Dick to express tender emotions without shame when only two adult males in this collection have anything resembling tender emotions and one of them is a mouse? (Williams et al., 1987)

The *Digest of Education Statistics* (U.S. Department of Education, 1989:30) shows that eighth-grade students report occupational expectations (for themselves at age 30) in continued gender-segmented patterns. Males were twice as likely as females to report science, engineering, and technical careers as goals and seven times as likely to report a skilled craft occupation. Females, in contrast, were three times as likely to report service work, homework, or sales/clerical jobs as expectations. Females did report professional occupations at a greater rate than males (38 percent to 20 percent, respectively). However, these categories were not further broken down by specialty, and the infrequent selection of science and engineering choices by females suggests these professional expectations follow traditional gendered patterns. Clearly, textbooks and children's books have not significantly changed the thinking of students about their future roles.

Sex Bias in Teacher Interaction: Elementary Through High School Years

From their classroom teachers, students also learn behaviors and expectations that expand beyond those learned at home or in the neighborhood. Teacher expectations for classroom performance and behavior of male and female students differ consistently at each level of schooling. Overall, teachers in the early years of schooling have higher performance expectations for females and assign them higher grades, across white, Hispanic, black, and Asian groups (Moore and Johnson, 1983). But before we assume that this means an "advantage" to female students (bestowed by a primarily female teaching staff), we should examine the "hidden curriculum" of covert, subtle behaviors in the schools.

Linda Grant (1986) found that elementary school teachers emphasize "motherwork" skills for their female students: nurturance, emotional support, care and loyalty, and deference to men. These expectations placed both black and white females at a disadvantage in having their abilities fairly assessed and enhanced within the classroom. In first-grade classrooms, teachers stated outright that they had higher expectations for girls than for boys, but added that these expectations were based on more than academic competence. For boys, teacher expectations were based on academic criteria such as knowledge, intellectual skills, and work habits. However, the criteria for assessing girls' skills were based equally on academic criteria and nonacademic criteria (e.g., grooming, dress, personal qualities, family connections). Other researchers have found that females are required by teachers to be calm, appreciative, considerate, dependable, and cooperative, while males are expected to be active, adventurous, aggressive, enterprising, and independent (Deem, 1978; Moore, 1983).

Teacher interaction with students in the elementary schools demonstrates patterns of reinforcement for gender hierarchies. Teachers are more likely to interrupt their female students, to call on males more often, and to give boys more time to answer a question. A review of other research indicates that teachers are more likely to encourage males to find an answer to their questions on their own, while they more often "give" the answer, or do the problem, for female students (Lips, 1989).

Educators reflect on the double jeopardy of their racial and ethnic minority female students, as well. Teachers' impressions of white girls are generally more favorable than those of black, Hispanic, or Native American males or females. White girls are encouraged to work independently, so long as they demonstrate loyalty to others (Grant, 1986). They learn to play domestic and occupational roles in a manner supportive of traditional gender-role relationships. For black females, Grant (1986) found that the emphasis by teachers is on service and deference, not on the acquisition of intellectual skills. Moore (1983) found that Hispanic females are held to high levels of conformity and passive norms as well and that teachers downgrade high-achieving Hispanic females who are perceived as independent or aggressive.

Grant (1986) also found that teachers were intolerant of nonconforming or defiant behaviors and dichotomized all female students into "good girl/bad girl" categories. "Bad girls" were described as "willful," "spiteful," or "time-wasters." Only one bad girl was also defined by the teachers as a low achiever, thus Grant concludes that it was the bad girls' failure to conform to feminine roles, rather than their academic performance, that drew teachers' negative assessments. Educational achievement requires increasing independence and activity at higher levels of schooling, as students prepare for adult vocations. This pattern of reinforced passivity by the schools and their representatives for female students is an important institutional barrier (Lips, 1989).

GENDERED TRANSITIONS: WOMEN'S CHOICES
IN SCHOOLING AND WORK

For those students who choose, or are encouraged, not to go on for formal college education, the vocational training patterns of schools are also important. These vocational programs are more likely to involve students from working-class backgrounds and set the educational and occupational patterns that will influence their adult activities. In high schools, the overwhelming patterns of vocational training suggest a continuation of the sex-segregated patterns of the labor market. Young women vocational students are more likely to be found in homemaking, secretarial, and business courses, whereas young men students are most likely to be found in automotive, agricultural, and other technical training classes (see Table 6-5). These patterns continue on into certification programs in community and junior colleges, as well.

TABLE 6-5 Percent of Vocational Education Units Earned, 1992

Field	Females (%)	Males (%)
Agricultural business and production	21	79
Business, general	65	35
Marketing and distribution	50	50
Health professions and related sciences	83	17
Home economics and vocational home economics	90	10
Mechanics and repairers	14	86
Transportation and material moving	42	58

Source: Adapted from U.S. Department of Education. National Center for Education Statistics. 1996. *Digest of Education Statistics 1996* (NCES 96–133). Washington, DC: U.S. Government Printing Office, Table 134.

In elementary and secondary education, powerful patterns of interaction, educational attainment, and expectations are set in motion. The coursework selected by students in their high school years may well affect their choices in the labor market or their transition into college. Significant deficiencies in mathematics and science prerequisites may delay entry into preprofessional programs in business, medicine, and law. Early socialization and coursework exposure will influence college entry, retention, and selection of programs.

As shown in Table 6-6, the areas in which women and men receive their degrees in college and university programs demonstrate significant segmentation, similar to the labor-force patterns discussed in Chapter Five. Anglo/white, Hispanic, and African American women are overrepresented in areas of psychology, home economics, education, and the health professions. They are underrepresented in engineering, computer/information technologies, and the physical sciences. Some interesting areas to watch for economic and social change over time are the greater participation of African American women in computer/information technologies and physical and social sciences, the greater participation of Hispanic females in language, and rising proportions of all women in law and business/management programs.

According to U.S. Census data from 1993, 15 percent of the highest earned degrees held by men were in engineering and only 2 percent of highest degrees held by women were in engineering. On the other hand, 19 percent of women reported their highest degree in education compared with only 6 percent of men receiving their highest degree in education. Nearly one out of five individuals received their postsecondary degrees in business/management (Bruno, 1996).

Sex Bias in Higher Education

At the college level, teacher interaction with students continues to be differentiated for male and female students. Hall and Sandler (1982) found in

TABLE 6-6 Bachelor Degrees by Major, Sex, and Race/Ethnicity, 1993–1994

Degree Area	White		Black		Hispanic		Asian/ Pacific Islander		Native American	
	M	F	M	F	M	F	M	F	M	F
Total percentage of B.A.s conferred	45.8	54.2	36.7	63.3	43.4	56.6	48.4	51.6	42.3	57.7
Business management and administrative services	54.2	45.8	39.1	60.9	48.7	51.3	45.0	55.0	45.8	54.2
Computer and information sciences	76.0	24.0	48.4	51.6	65.0	35.0	65.7	34.3	75.9	24.1
Education	22.6	77.4	23.4	76.6	22.6	77.4	24.1	75.9	26.9	73.1
Engineering	84.7	15.3	67.3	32.7	81.8	18.2	80.5	19.5	82.1	17.9
English language and literature/letters	35.0	65.0	25.5	74.5	32.3	67.7	31.5	68.5	35.5	64.5
Foreign languages and literatures	30.8	69.2	22.2	77.8	28.6	71.4	27.6	72.4	32.7	67.3
Health professions and related sciences	17.3	82.7	13.8	86.2	20.6	79.4	23.1	76.9	20.6	79.4
Home economics and vocational home economics	12.1	87.9	15.4	84.6	13.5	86.5	13.4	86.6	12.6	87.4
Law and legal studies	29.0	71.0	25.0	75.0	38.0	62.0	42.5	57.5	57.1	42.9
Mathematics	53.5	46.5	46.3	53.7	55.3	44.7	56.7	43.3	49.2	50.8
Physical sciences and science technologies	68.1	31.9	50.2	49.8	65.4	34.6	59.1	40.9	62.4	37.6
Protective services	64.7	35.3	46.9	53.1	56.5	43.5	69.5	30.5	60.0	40.0
Psychology	27.2	72.8	23.6	76.4	25.6	74.4	29.2	70.8	28.7	71.3
Social sciences and history	55.4	44.6	43.4	56.6	50.4	49.6	48.9	51.1	42.2	50.8

Source: U.S. Department of Education, National Center for Education Statistics. 1996. Digest of Education Statistics 1996 (NCES 96–133). Washington, DC: U.S. Government Printing Office, Table 260.

their study "The classroom climate: A chilly one for women?" that faculty are more likely to listen to male students, to credit men for ideas presented, and to further develop discussion around comments made by men. Among the subtle or covert behaviors by faculty were nonverbal cues: making eye contact more often with men, nodding and gesturing more often in response to men's questions, assuming an attentive posture (e.g., leaning forward), giving more detailed instructions to men, or allowing women to be "squeezed out" of lab demonstrations.

More overt behaviors by teachers documented in the study included excluding women from course-related activities such as field trips, because women were "too much trouble." Faculty also favored men in choosing teaching assistants and making recommendations for fellowships. Sexist comments used in the classroom that disparage women in general, belittle women's intellectual abilities, question women's scholarly commitments, and divert attention toward appearance rather than substance were catalogued. One common practice among teachers was to refer to males as "men" and to women as "girls" or "gals." Their study found that all of these practices lead to a negative learning environment for many women on college campuses.

The overlap of sexism with racism and classism on campuses is a significant factor in schooling. As Grant noted above, the treatment by teachers of racial or ethnic minority females is often a reflection of teachers' racist and gendered behavior. The emphasis on the Domestic Code is linked with overt and covert racist stereotypes and practices among teachers, administrators, and peers. Later in this chapter we identify the specific consequences of cultural capital, sexism, and classism for Chicana students.

Sexual Harassment: Educational Control

The whole gamut of verbal and psychological violence against women and minorities is also evident on campus, ranging from sexist or racist humor as a classroom teaching device, to verbal sexual harassment, racial slurs, racist violence, or sexual assault. *Sexual harassment* is, according to Russell, a form of social control that enables men to pursue their economic self-interests (Russell, 1984). The gender arrangement of power within schools provides men with a power base from which to harass women and protect their own resources. Sexual harassment in the educational system, then, is (1) a set of behaviors directed at individual women in the classroom, (2) a condition that contributes to a threatening educational environment, and (3) a dimension of power strongly related to women's minority status in schools.

Sexual harassment of students is recognized as a violation of Title IX of the Educational Amendments Act. These behaviors by faculty (and work or residence hall supervisors) include unsolicited verbal comments, gestures, or physical contact that is unwelcome by the recipient. The legal definition formulated by the Equal Employment Opportunity Commission has recently been extended by the U.S. Supreme Court to include behavior that creates a hostile or offensive work environment, even if it does not result in work-related losses. The availability of a supportive work environment overlaps with Title IX guarantees of equal educational opportunity for women employed and educated in the public schools.

Current estimates of sexual harassment of students on campus range from 10 to 30 percent. In one study, some 44 percent of harassed students reported that their feelings about work or class worsened; over 20 percent reported negative physical or emotional consequences; and 18 percent indicated that their classwork, attendance, or grades suffered as a result of the harassment (Moore and Hoover, 1987). Perpetrators of the harassment included faculty, campus job supervisors, and residence hall staff; and in 98 percent of the cases, the harassers were men. Dziech and Weiner (1984) note that the "professor-as-lecher" is so much a part of campus lore that the role appears often in popular literature. They also note that male faculty hold stereotypic attitudes toward women similar to those of the general male population.

Complicating the widespread problem of sexual harassment is the nature of student-faculty relationships that is fostered by the university environment. Professors are "gatekeepers" who can assist or impede academic progress and professional opportunities not only through grades but also by references for jobs, financial awards, and graduate school admissions. Thus, the potential for power abuse is significant (Dziech and Weiner, 1984).

Teacher-student interactions are affected not only by attitudes and behaviors but also by the content of the curriculum and the patterns of educational careers and teaching assignments that shape student expectations and role models. As we shall see in the next section, the structure of schools presents to students a pyramid of power and authority that is based on gender and race/ethnicity. The positions that women and women of color hold as teachers and administrators provide a daily map of the student and teacher relationships and reflect the larger social structures of racism and sexism.

SEX SEGREGATION IN THE SCHOOLS

The Feminization of Teaching

Teaching was a predominately male activity in the eighteenth century in the United States. Women worked primarily as volunteers in church charity schools for the poor. The entrance of women into teaching positions in the nineteenth century has been described as a social selection process into a "natural profession" for several reasons (Biklen and Brannigan, 1980). Women's educational work supposedly fit societal expectations for women and their "maternal destiny" of nurturance and social service, especially at the elementary school level. As women entered the teaching profession, the congruence of these roles led to acceptance of women as education workers. Lortie (1975) specifically described teaching as fitting contemporary feminine socialization patterns, meshing with family responsibilities, and appealing to the service aspirations of women. Today, the social role of teachers is imbued with certain "academic values," which vary with the educational level of work and the subject area and reflect gender biases.

The conflict theorists focus on the structure and demands of the educational market itself to describe the role of women in schooling. The entry of women into teaching in the late nineteenth century fit the financial constraints of expanding public education because women could be hired at lower salaries than men. These jobs offered some potential for autonomy and mobility above and beyond the factory setting. The graded or age-differentiated school brought a specific demand for women teachers, partly because they could be paid lower wages than men and partly because they had the required skills (nurturance and patience) to work solely with younger students in the elementary grades. Older students, requiring advanced training and intellectual stimulation, were perceived as more suitable for a male cohort of teachers (Danylewycz and Prentice, 1984).

The bureaucratization and expansion of public school teaching also precipitated occupational segregation of elementary and secondary schools (Strober and Langford, 1986). As teaching credentials were increasingly a requirement for employment and teaching loads were expanded to nine months of the year, most men dropped out, particularly from teaching the elementary grades. Men who once taught in the months they could not farm, now looked for more lucrative full-time occupations or moved to expanding numbers of administrative positions. The growing educational labor market absorbed women into a hierarchy of male dominance that fixed women at the bottom of a rapidly feminized occupation. This pattern is similar to that described in the last chapter for clerical workers.

According to Davies (1975), the concept of *feminization* describes increased proportions of women workers in a particular position with two concomitant labor-market effects:

1. A drop in the prestige of the occupation (and social esteem for the skills it involved)
2. A drop in the overall wages of workers in the field (including male workers who remain)

Lortie (1975) suggests that when teaching came to be seen as "women's work," the subordinate position of women in nineteenth-century society probably reduced the social rank of teachers in general.

Kelly and Nihlen conclude overall that the current authority and staffing patterns of schools "represent the type of inequality between the sexes that exists in the workforce in terms of status and income distribution" (1982:169).

Women's positions remain in general inferior to those of men in the educational hierarchy.

As noted by Banks and Banks (1989), the role of minorities in public school education is multidimensional and multicultural and brings a range of complex issues to the public schools. Included among these is the representation of minorities on the teaching and administrative staffs. Currently, the proportion of minority teachers is low (see Table 6-7) and dropping (Banks and Banks, 1989). Students have little access to minority teachers. White or Anglo students are even less likely to have contact with minority teachers than are minority students, because of the segregation of schools and teaching staffs. As demonstrated below, this racial/ethnic hierarchy and the sex stratification of the public schools results in lower wages of women and minorities in the education profession.

Sex Segregation

From 1950 to 1990, the highest concentration of women and minority teachers remained in elementary, prekindergarten, and kindergarten teaching. Women monopolized all of the special education positions in 1970 (see Table 6-8). In contrast, postsecondary teaching had the lowest percentage of females during the same time period. In sum, the largest increase in percentages of females occurred in the postsecondary category; the largest decreases were for elementary school and special education categories. Over time, male teachers have been avoiding secondary education and entering elementary and special education. Females are also decreasing their participation in secondary school teaching, but their increases in elementary education are not as large as for men. Females increased their postsecondary teaching from 1970 to 1990. With all of these shifts, it was still true that in 1994, 72.53 percent of all public and private school teachers were women (U.S. Department of Edu-

TABLE 6-7   Teaching Staff by Race/Ethnicity, 1993

Race/Ethnicity	Elementary/Secondary Teachers		College/University, All Ranks	
	N	%	N	%
Total	2,561,294		545,706	
Anglo/white	2,216,605	86.5	468,770	85.9
African American	188,371	7.4	25,658	4.7
Hispanic	108,744	4.2	12,076	2.2
Native American	20,064	0.8	1,997	0.4
Asian/Pacific Islander	27,510	1.2	25,269	4.6

Source: U.S. Department of Education, National Center for Education Statistics. 1996. *Digest of Education Statistics 1996* (NCES 96–133). Washington, DC: U.S. Government Printing Office, Table 66 and 221.

TABLE 6-8   Percent Distribution Across Teaching Categories by Sex, 1970–1990

Category	Males			Females		
	1970	*1980*	*1990*	*1970*	*1980*	*1990*
Postsecondary	29.35	27.11	28.76	6.64	8.12	8.57
Secondary	43.32	25.10	16.59	23.60	16.96	9.54
Elementary	19.72	38.22	40.12	56.74	60.99	63.76
Special education	—	0.68	0.68	0.07	0.79	1.37
Prekindergarten						
Kindergarten	0.23	0.44	0.36	5.92	6.16	7.08

Sources: U.S. Bureau of the Census. *Detailed Occupations of the Experienced Labor Force by Sex and Race.* Adapted from 1970, 1980 (PC-80-S1-15), and 1990 (Table 2) Census reports. Washington, DC: U.S. Government Printing Office.

cation, 1996) and 6 out of every 10 female teachers were in the elementary schools.

The concentration of female teaching staffs in the elementary schools and the lower representation in junior and senior high schools means that as the student becomes more adult, and is closer to entry into the labor market, women educators become less numerous (Kelly and Nihlen, 1982). In most parts of the world, there are more women than men in the teaching profession, but most women are primary school teachers. Until recent years, the predominately male secondary school teaching staff in the United States held a higher social status and earned a higher salary than the elementary school teacher (Havighurst and Levine, 1979).

Prekindergarten, primary, and secondary school teachers continue to be paid lower salaries than higher education teachers, and only recently have elementary and secondary school wages been set at the same scale. Strober and Best (1979) found that the male-female salary differentials in public school education in the late 1800s were lowest in those sectors with the greatest percentage of female teachers. So, too, were the median salaries lowest. Thus, men who continued to teach in feminized sectors of public education found their wages compressed when compared with men teaching in other sectors.

Today, feminization of salaries is most evident in two subcategories of public school education—prekindergarten and special education. Prekindergarten teachers continue to be disproportionately female (over 97 percent in 1988) and to be paid at or near the minimum-wage level (Trow, 1975; U.S. Department of Education, 1989). The average female prekindergarten teacher salary in 1980 was $8,390 (U.S. Bureau of the Census, 1984). In contrast, the small proportion of males in prekindergarten teaching made an average salary of $14,912. Thus, the lowest-paid sector of education continues as the most highly feminized.

In the special education field, growth since 1970 has been phenomenal—

from 453 teachers to 10,284 in 1980. The proportion of males moving into this field accelerated, and it rapidly became the most highly paid teaching specialty in the public schools. In 1970, the special education sector was 100 percent female; in 1980, this proportion dropped to 69 percent, and women earned an average of $11,322 in this field. Male representation quickly grew to one-third of employed teachers in this sector, and they earned $18,965 on the average in 1980 (U.S. Bureau of the Census, 1984).

At the top of the public school hierarchy are the administrators. Historically, women have been severely underrepresented in these decision-making positions. In 1988, women made up only 14 percent of elementary school principals, and 12 percent of secondary school principals (U.S. Department of Education, 1989). Among superintendents, there exists only a handful of women among the 17,000 positions throughout the United States. The educational pyramid is such that a small number of predominately male administrators makes decisions for a vast number of women educators.

Up the Education Ladder: Higher Education

In more recent times, higher education has cycled through periods of rapid expansion and then stagnation that affected staffing and economic patterns. The changes in job opportunities for academic workers have been tracked over the past three decades as the population of students has fluctuated. With the increased fertility rates of the post–World War II era, new schools had to be built at the elementary and secondary school levels. Added to that was an increased effort to provide educational opportunities as a solution to the 1960s War on Poverty, racial discrimination, and gender inequality. Schools at every level felt the pressure to increase staff numbers. In the early 1960s, higher education institutions were in a "seller's market," with many students and a demand for increased teaching staffs.

Then came the baby bust—a drop in the fertility rates during the late 1960s and early 1970s. Gradually, this influenced the closing of schools, restricted the number of new teaching slots open, and decreased the growth of the educational labor market. Now many of these institutions are in a "buyer's market," having fewer students and needing clients for their expanded academic labor force (Bernard, 1981). More than enough slots are available for those seeking admission as students, and women are now accepted into areas of professional and undergraduate training that had been closed by law or social custom in earlier U.S. history. Restrictions in teaching positions at public schools and in colleges came at a time when women were encouraged to pursue increasing educational achievements and to return to school to fill classes. In 1988, women made up 52.3 percent of all undergraduates, but 58 percent of all part-time students, suggesting an increase in the returning, nontraditional student among women.

Demographics in the 1990s suggest another trend. A mini baby boom has refilled the public school classrooms and has led to overcrowding and a concern about teacher shortages in the future. In addition, colleges and universities have successfully marketed the undergraduate degree to new, returning students at a time when retirement may remove a cohort of post–World War II faculty, with estimates as high as one-third of the professoriate retiring within the next decade. This trend may lead to increased job opportunities for M.A.- and Ph.D.-level students in the academic workforce.

Sex/race segregation in higher education.   The pyramid of gender segregation is evident in higher education teaching and administration. Trow (1975) found that 80 percent of all faculty in higher education are male. In 1989, women made up 33.6 percent of full-time faculty (Blackwell, 1989). When ranked by "quality" or prestige, highly ranked universities have greater proportions of male academics (90 percent male) than do community colleges (74 percent male), with associated decreases in median salary levels for male and female academic workers. More than two-thirds of all female academics teach at two- and four-year colleges, whereas men are equally divided between universities and other institutions (Trow, 1975), and those statistics hold true in 1989 (Blackwell, 1989:24). Women are concentrated in the lower ranks of instructional staffs and at lower-status institutions.

The patterns of minority participation as faculty in public schools are repeated in higher education (see Table 6-9). Minority participation in higher education teaching and administration is vastly underrepresented compared with their general population representation with the exception of Asian and Pacific Islanders in the faculty category. Blackwell (1989) highlighted the concern that few minority students are in the educational pipeline to fill faculty positions in the future. The number of African Americans in college dropped from 1,028,000 in 1980 to 995,000 in 1987. By 1993, only 8.3 percent of associate degrees, 6.7 percent of bachelor's degrees and 5.4 percent of master's degrees were awarded to African Americans.

Sex segregation by educational specialty.   As with most occupational segregation, it is not only interoccupational sex segregation but also intraoccupational segregation that influences women's labor-market experience. Fulton and Trow (1975) commented upon the "uneven distribution of the sexes within academia," identifying the semiprofessions as areas of high female concentration: social work, nursing, home economics, library science, and education. They also identified an intermediate group of subjects—fine arts and humanities—"in which women have traditionally had a legitimate interest, originating in their compatibility with Victorian notions of subjects fit for lady amateurs" (1975:208). These academic specialties have the highest proportion of women as well as the lowest status in the university community (ibid.). Thus, women are least likely (less than 10 percent) to be in the physical sciences, medicine, and law and participate in negligible proportions in engineering.

TABLE 6-9   Full-Time Faculty in Higher Education
by Race/Ethnicity, Fall 1993

Race/Ethnicity	% of Faculty
White, non-Hispanic	85.9
Black, non-Hispanic	4.7
Hispanic	2.2
Asian	4.6
American Indian	0.4

Source: U.S. Department of Education, National Center for Education Statistics. 1996. *Digest of Education Statistics 1996* (NCES 96-133). Washington, DC: U.S. Government Printing Office, Table 221.

The author concludes that due to gender segregation, women spend their intellectual lives physically and intellectually isolated from the core of the campus.

Riesman, Gusfield, and Gamson argue the centrality of some disciplines over others, noting that "A boyhood interest can lead a man to become a chemist or a zoologist, but rarely into French literature or anthropology" (1975:259). They identify the humanities and social sciences as places for those who want to become an "all purpose" intellectual or professor: "his [sic] students often speak for a society that regards what he does as unimportant, or at any rate not central" (ibid.). In the 1970s and 1980s, the restricted academic labor market strengthened the belief that certain educational work has little "exchange value" in the labor market outside of the ivory tower. These disciplines have only some restricted "use value" (they are subjects useful in a liberal arts, academic sense). The severe depression in academic hiring in humanities and social sciences during the 1970s and 1980s has countered any economic stability for these specialties.

In 1980, women made up about 36 percent of postsecondary educators, but they were disproportionately represented in health specialties, business, the fine arts, English, and foreign languages. Gains for women in postsecondary education have not been uniform across disciplines. Table 6-10 indicates that female participation is concentrated in the following categories: teacher education, nursing, English and literature, and foreign language.

In addition, women make up a large portion of the part-time faculty at universities and colleges throughout the United States. These are generally positions that do not offer the stability of tenure or any of the other benefits—i.e., health care benefits, retirement benefits, promotion and merit possibilities—that are afforded to full-time faculty. When institutions faced fiscal difficulties during the 1970s and 1980s, many began cutting back on hiring full-time faculty and supplemented their teaching staffs with part-time instructors. This has exacerbated the two-tiered system of employment in higher education and increasingly in some disciplines women are being relegated to the lower tier.

In the following specialties, over half of the part-time faculty are female: agriculture and home economics, communication, teacher education and other education, nursing and other health sciences, English and literature, foreign languages, and sociology. Evidence that this has created an environment in which women are a reserve pool of cheap labor for higher education is particularly telling in those specialties in which the majority of full-time faculty are male and the majority of part-time faculty are female. This occurs within the disciplines of agriculture and home economics, communication, education other than teacher education, health sciences other than nursing, and sociology.

In sum, postsecondary education has disproportionately large increases in female participation, relative to other teaching levels. This partially supports the notion that postsecondary education is becoming a feminized occupation.

TABLE 6-10 Percent Female Distribution of Full-Time and Part-Time Postsecondary Teaching Specialties, Fall 1992

Specialty	Full Time (%)	Part Time (%)
Agriculture and home economics	24.7	52.0
Business	31.1	30.0
Communications	34.6	51.8
Teacher education	57.1	76.7
Other education	48.0	60.9
Engineering	6.1	8.0
Fine arts	32.9	48.3
First-professional health sciences	23.0	30.9
Nursing	98.6	94.5
Other health sciences	47.7	59.9
English and literature	50.7	67.1
Foreign languages	51.7	63.9
History	23.3	31.6
Philosophy	13.2	26.1
Law	35.5	26.5
Biological sciences	23.8	42.6
Physical sciences	11.5	24.4
Mathematics	24.8	36.4
Computer sciences	20.0	21.3
Economics	15.4	17.3
Political science	17.4	19.5
Psychology	37.9	48.3
Sociology	25.2	57.7
Other social sciences	31.6	44.1

Source: U.S. Department of Education, National Center for Education Statistics. 1996. *Digest of Education Statistics 1996* (NCES 96-133). Washington, DC: U.S. Government Printing Office, Table 227.

However, the natural and medical sciences remain relatively impermeable to this shift at the college level.

Educational administration—the top of the pyramid.   Estler (1975) argues that male dominance patterns continue in educational administration as well. Though women are the majority of employees in education, they are the minority of administrators, and their numbers decrease with each step up the hierarchical ladder. This pattern of sex segmentation is deepening, as the proportional involvement of women as leaders in education at all levels has decreased over time (Estler, 1975:364).

Fewer than 3 percent of all top-level college and university administrators in 1972 were women. Those women who did administer were clustered at the four-year college and two-year college levels. The greater the proportion of women administrators, faculty, and full professors, the lower the prestige of the institutions—a pattern that partially affirms the notion of feminized educational markets (Simpson, 1976).

Sex Segregation and Salaries

From Davies's model of occupational feminization (see Chapter Five), we anticipate that patterns of gender dominance are linked with salary inequities. Table 6-11 presents median salaries for teachers in 1993–1994. Educators increase their salaries as they move up the educational hierarchy; female salaries have traditionally been below male salaries. In the elementary and prekindergarten categories, males increased their salaries (already above female salary

TABLE 6-11   Average Salaries for Full-Time
Teachers in Public Schools, 1993–1994

Selected Characteristics	Base Salary
Men	$36,182
Women	33,384
White	34,221
Black	33,889
Hispanic	32,996
Asian or Pacific Islander	36,134
American Indian or Alaskan Native	32,994
Elementary	33,517
Secondary	34,815

Source: U.S. Department of Education, National Center for Education Statistics. 1996. *Digest of Education Statistics 1996* (NCES 96-133). Washington, DC: U.S. Government Printing Office, Table 72.

levels in 1970) by 66 percent, females by 64 percent. Women who were making 81 cents to the male dollar in 1970 elementary school teaching slipped to 76 cents to the male dollar in 1980. In secondary schools, salary increases for male and female teachers were each about 64 percent, and women continued to make approximately 79 cents to the male dollar across the 1970–1980 time period. The gap narrowed between 1980 and 1994. Overall, in public schools women now make 92 cents to the male dollar. The larger increases for females were reflected in the elementary school systems.

In postsecondary education, the difference in male and female salaries was more pronounced. Between 1970 and 1980, female salaries increased by 66 percent, male salaries by 70 percent. Thus, in 1970, women were making 84 cents to the male dollar in postsecondary education. In 1980, this decreased to 70 cents to the dollar. However, across specialties and institutions women averaged 88 cents to 93 cents to the male dollar in institutions of higher education during 1993–1994.

Differences in salaries for males and females in postsecondary education may be tied to the interoccupational segregation of higher education. Table 6-12 presents salary levels by rank for postsecondary specialties along with the percent male and female within each of these specialties. Across all teaching specialties, women earn less than men. However, areas where more females are concentrated are often the lower paying of the academic specialties.

As illustrated in Table 6-12, the three highest-paying specialties in higher education included engineering (full professor average = $72,282), business (full professor average = $70,564), and computer science (full professor average = $68,346). Correspondingly, 93.9 percent of professors of engineering are male, 68.8 percent of business professors are male, and 79.9 percent of computer science professors are male. Looked at in another light, the lowest-paid full professors included fine arts (full professor average = $53,610), teacher education (full professor average = $54,743), and nursing (full professor average = $55,040). Among these lower-paid specialties, 32.9 percent of fine arts professors are women, 57.1 percent of teacher education professors are women, and 98.6 percent of nursing professors are women.

Through the 1980s and the beginning of the 1990s, salaries in postsecondary education increased, though this increase has been at a slower rate for females than for males. In addition, more than half of the professors in education, teacher education, health sciences, nursing, English and literature, and foreign languages are women. Today, women at all ranks in higher education still receive lower salaries than men. Table 6-13 illustrates that women are paid approximately 10 to 20 percent less than men at the same rank.

The scope and nature of sex segregation in education is changing. Sex segregation continues to show women concentrated in elementary and secondary education. These fields have been traditionally viewed as feminized occupations with a correspondingly lower reward structure than postsecondary education. We do find evidence that some interlevel segregation is taking

TABLE 6-12   Average Salary of Postsecondary Specialties 1995 and Gender Breakdown[a]

Specialty	Professor	Associate	Assistant	% Male	% Female
Agriculture and home	HE 58,605	HE 45,442	HE 37,166		
economics	AG 60,304	AG 45,895	AG 38,166	75.5	24.7
Business	70,564	57,428	51,322	68.8	31.1
Communications	56,932	44,908	36,687	65.4	34.6
Education	56,568	44,764	37,052	49.0	51.1
Teacher education	54,743	43,921	36,545	42.8	57.1
Other education	60,129	47,759	39,001	52.1	48.0
Engineering	72,282	55,954	48,101	93.9	6.1
Fine arts	53,610	42,096	34,912	67.0	32.9
Health sciences	62,192	47,988	39,795	49.9	50.2
Nursing	55,040	45,648	38,128	1.5	98.6
Other health science	56,160	46,088	40,533	52.4	47.7
Humanities	61,478	44,753	36,028	58.5	41.3
English and literature	56,242	43,576	34,973	49.3	50.7
Foreign languages	57,718	44,255	35,651	48.2	51.7
History	58,474	44,832	35,299	76.5	23.3
Philosophy	60,432	44,564	35,394	86.7	13.2
Biological science	59,572	46,150	38,231	76.2	23.8
Physical science	61,007	45,596	37,865	88.6	11.5
Mathematics	61,514	46,645	38,126	75.3	24.8
Computer science	68,346	55,382	47,222	79.9	20.0
Social science	57,044	44,914	35,363	72.5	27.5
Economics	66,919	52,131	45,308	84.5	15.4
Political science	60,397	45,640	37,057	82.5	17.4
Psychology	59,504	45,417	36,993	61.9	37.9
Sociology	56,860	45,034	36,302	74.6	25.2
Other social science	60,273	45,904	36,673	68.5	31.6

[a]Gender percent breakdown is based on 1992 data.

Sources: U.S. Department of Education, National Center for Education Statistics. 1996. *Digest of Education Statistics 1996* (NCES 96-133). Washington, DC: U.S. Government Printing Office, Table 227. Salary data by University Personnel Association. 1996. *National Faculty Salary Survey by Discipline and Rank in Public Four-Year Colleges and Universities, 1995–96.* Washington, DC: CUPA. For more information, call CUPA at 202-429-0311.

place, with men moving into special education in the public schools in astounding proportions. As more males enter this category of teaching, a rise in salaries follows.

At postsecondary levels, teaching was considered removed from the feminization process. Salary levels have remained higher than for other teaching categories, even during a time period of growth in the proportion of women. The disproportionate growth of females in the postsecondary category vis-à-vis other categories outstrips the general expansion of postsecondary education in the 1970s.

Women are still a minority in postsecondary teaching, but they are mov-

TABLE 6-13   Average Salary of Full-Time Faculty on Nine-Month Contracts in Higher Education by Academic Rank and Sex, 1994–1995

Academic Rank	Male	Female
Professor	$64,046	$56,555
Associate professor	47,705	44,626
Assistant professor	39,923	37,352
Instructor	30,528	29,072
Lecturer	35,082	31,677
No rank	43,103	38,967

Note: Preliminary data for 1994–1995.

Source: U.S. Department of Education, National Center for Education Statistics. 1996. *Digest of Education Statistics 1996* (NCES 96-133). Washington, DC: U.S. Government Printing Office, Table 229

ing disproportionately into areas such as health specialties, computer sciences, biology, business, fine arts, English, and foreign languages. In contrast, men have retained a disproportionate hold on the disciplines of natural and medical sciences.

In concluding this section on sex bias in the schools, it is evident that education is a patriarchal institution in its structure, process, and rewards. In the next section, we consider the notion that patriarchy affects the content of the school curriculum as well, by examining the effects of heterosexism in the schools.

HETEROSEXISM AND THE SCHOOLS

An important part of the information we receive from schooling is about who we are socially, politically, intellectually, and sexually. Feminist theorists argue that patriarchal societies are inherently homophobic and heterosexist and that these characteristics are in the hidden curriculum of the schools and become part of the cultural capital of our society. By *homophobia,* we mean the irrational fear of homosexuality (often based on ignorance and stereotypes of homosexual behavior), and by *heterosexism,* we mean a belief in the superiority of heterosexual behavior (Cruikshank, 1982). *Heterocentrism* is a parallel of the term *ethnocentrism,* the former indicating a cultural (as opposed to explicitly moral) domination by heterosexuals.

Coralyn Fontaine (1982) argues that heterosexism is the pivotal political and cultural mechanism employed by patriarchy to bind women (including their reproductive, spiritual, sexual, and cultural energies) to male-defined norms. Women often remain in abusive relationships because they are unaware of domestic violence shelters, laws against marital rape (in those states that have them), and the definition of date rape and abuse. Some feminists argue that all heterosexual relationships are by definition oppressive, because of the power held by men in patriarchal religious, legal, economic, and family structures (Dworkin, 1981). Schools do not acknowledge alternative lifestyles such as lesbian and gay relationships not solely out of moral repugnance, or even out of ignorance, but because they represent viable alternatives that threaten heterosexist dominance.

Two types of evidence can be used to establish heterosexist dominance in the cultural capital of the schools. On the one hand, evidence of homophobia in the classroom and in educational environments may reflect the prejudices against gays and lesbians (both as teachers and as students) that repress free exchange of information. Second, the deletion or distortion of information about lesbian and gay lifestyles or contributions by men and women in this and other cultures is also evidence that schools are heterosexist.

Lesbian and Gay Teachers and Students

Homophobia underlies the structure and process of teaching in the classroom. As a result, lesbian and gay students lack information about their history, culture, and contributions, as well as accurate portrayals of the health, economic, and social consequences of their lifestyles. Because lesbian or gay teachers may experience job, housing, and health insurance discrimination for being lesbian or gay, it is difficult for them to act as resources for gay and lesbian students.

Squirrell notes the difficulties of even contacting lesbian or gay faculty to assess the consequences of heterosexist schooling:

> The majority of us are professionally "in the closet" and fully intend to remain that way. The risk of doing otherwise is too great. . . . Here we cannot be sacked for being gay. Under section 99, we could only be sacked for conviction of a sexual nature. . . . Being open is impossible because any whiff of being gay would be the end of promotion prospects. There is no way that a known gay would be promoted. You could never prove, of course, that this was the reason for not being promoted. Yet it would be the case. If any rumor of being gay was spread among the parents, life would be unbearable. (1989:21)

The purpose of Squirrell's research was to examine the effects of lesbian or gay sexual orientation on teachers' daily lives in the staffroom and classroom. Many of the faculty were able to recount tales of dismissal or victimization as well as fears of being discredited. As one woman said, "Homosexuality puts into question all your other work. It makes it invalid and you don't get taken seriously." This creates a closeted or masked existence: "I always wear a skirt, it makes me feel safe." "But they say I couldn't be lesbian because I've got two grown children" (Squirrell, 1989:23).

This heterosexism is compounded by attitudes and stereotypes about feminism. A black lesbian teacher is quoted as saying that the staff believes all feminists are lesbians because "any woman who asserts herself is too aggressive and therefore must be a lesbian. The fact that a woman is a lesbian explains her views on any subject" (Squirrell, 1989:27). For both teachers and students, the fear of being labeled lesbian or gay in the adolescent subculture is so strong that same-sex friendships have artificial boundaries placed on their intensity. Janice J. Raymond (1986) notes that the power of the term *lesbian* is used to confront "any act of affection between women," not only because it excludes men and male privilege, but because it asserts women's authority and autonomy. This cultural restriction affects heterosexual women as well as lesbians, both of whom can claim the support of other women only with caution.

Toni A. H. McNaron (1989) mapped out the goals of lesbian students, particularly those in higher education. These goals were set in the larger context of visibility to guarantee attention to the educational lives and personal safety of lesbian and gay students. She exhorted student activism within school settings that recalled the early ethnic and women's studies battles for legitimation, not only of a curriculum, but of the rights of minority and women students to a place on campus.

Among discriminatory campus processes, she identified heterosexist language that renders lesbians invisible, including application and financial aid forms that omit information about committed partnerships. She cites the mistreatment of students in critical areas of physical health services and heterosexist counseling. In the first instance, lesbian students are pressured by heterosexual assumptions to reveal their sexual orientation or to put up with pressure to use birth control. One undergraduate reported a campus physician who noted her sexual orientation on her health card, and then indicated that "student *says* she is a lesbian, but appears to be well adjusted" (author's personal correspondence, emphasis added). In the second instance, the assumption that heterosexuality is the norm-active sexual orientation leads some counselors to treat the orientation of a lesbian client as "the root of the problem," rather than the problem presented by the student (stress, family issues, eating disorders, etc.).

In addition, the safety of lesbian and gay students on any campus was raised by McNaron in 1989. Data collected by the National Gay and Lesbian Task Force during the 1986–1987 academic year showed that the types of hate crimes against lesbians and gays on three campuses ranged from threats of physical violence to assault and sexual harassment. In 1995, there were 7,947 hate crimes reported to the police according to the Uniform Crime Report. More than one thousand of these were incidents based on sexual orientation bias. A more detailed description of bias-motivated crimes is included in Chapter Seven.

Finally, on many campuses, lesbians and gays are denied equal access to campus organizational opportunities and resources. Some campuses refuse to allocate space or legitimacy to lesbian and gay organizations. Others will deny funding to the organization from student fee resources. These campuses can be contrasted to those which have viable gay and lesbian student associations (including gay or lesbian Greek associations), culture clubs, and political advocacy groups. The formation of the Lambda sorority at the University of California, Los Angeles, and the creation of Project 10 at Fairfax High School in Los Angeles are examples of students and staff who work together to confront homophobia and provide support services.

Heterocentric Scholarship

The context of academic culture renders the history and social lives of lesbians invisible. Lesbian lives are rarely if ever mentioned in the public school curriculum (Squirrell, 1989). Where they are, the context is likely to be negative or the subject of legal and political challenges.

Lillian Federman (1982) asks: Who hid lesbian history? She reviews the biographies of women writers and identifies the homophobic deletions of letters and other materials by scholars who could not accept the woman-identified themes of their subjects. She writes a long complaint against the distortion of women's lives, including those of Emily Dickinson, Mary Wollstonecraft, and Edna St. Vincent Millay. Federman notes that the "loss of a much loved woman friend cannot be seen as 'drastic' by a heterocentric scholar" (1982:117). This is true not only of the scholar but of the homophobic teacher or counselor as well. She also issues a warning that "women's lives need to be reinterpreted and we need to do it ourselves."

Estelle Freedman (1982) provides resources for documenting lesbian history within the context of heterosexist institutions. Among her recommended resources for teachers and scholars are the following:

- Newspaper accounts of "passing women" (women passing as men)
- Obituaries that note "Boston marriages," "lifelong companions," and "friends"
- Records of "deviant" women in courts and prisons—women who are often immigrant, working class, and from the Third World
- Oral histories, literary histories, and diaries

Combatting Heterocentric Schooling

The invisibility of lesbian and gay students, staff, and teachers is reinforced and perpetuated by the lack of support for lesbian and feminist research. Students need opportunities to "map the connections" between lifestyles, cultural messages, and the teaching and scholarship processes. Teachers can devote class time to discussing the diversity of women's lives in ethnic studies courses, literature classes, and social science courses. McNaron (1989) also argues for more courses devoted expressly to lesbian culture and history. The syllabi for a number of groundbreaking lesbian studies courses are provided in Cruikshank (1982) and include such diverse course offerings as

Twentieth-Century Lesbian Novels, Lesbian Culture, Heterosexism and the Oppression of Women, and Relationships Between Women.

Finally, we must recognize the need for lesbian teachers and scholars who can provide role models for our heterosexual and lesbian students: "[S]tudents may find themselves more powerfully attracted to the lesbian teacher than to the usual male authority figure, since the lesbian teacher's energy and involvement in their mutually stimulating material is quite different" (Gurko, 1982:29). This teacher becomes not simply a model of alternative authority patterns but of "freedom, risk-taking (if she is open about her orientation) and some radically new ideas" (ibid.).

To move toward a schooling system that provides quality education for lesbian and gay students would require institutional statements that school administrators do not discriminate in hiring, promotion, or rewards on the basis of sexual preference. This would be a bare minimum in creating a safe environment. The active inclusion of curricular, social, and political resources for gay and lesbian students on campuses cannot be built without this guarantee. Such education programs would highlight the contradictions from homophobia in the larger society that deny lesbian and gay existence, or ignore all but their sexual behavior. Recently, the University of Wisconsin faculty recommended the exclusion of campus ROTC programs that exclude homosexuals as policy.

Gurko (1982) notes the parallels for racial/ethnic minority students and faculty who have struggled against racism. Although many minorities reject such parallels, progressive politicians such as Jesse Jackson and Angela Davis recognize the need for analysis of multiple dimensions of oppression (Davis, 1989). This is evident in the schools: "The dynamic created by any minority faculty person in an authority position in a major institution is explosive, because power in the classroom must be realigned and redefined quite drastically" (Gurko, 1982:30). While she discusses the majority/minority axis based on sexual preference, the presence of a racial/ethnic minority faculty member has its unique aspects of empowerment. The minority teacher gives minority students permission to have an accepted role, and majority students are forced to reexamine their assumptions about being right, having control and power within the realm of the school, and what kind of acceptance they can expect from this particular teacher.

CULTURAL COLONIZATION AND THE SCHOOLS

The intersection of gender, class, and ethnicity is readily apparent in the statistics and research cited earlier. Women of color are less likely to participate in formal education, experience a different process because of the devaluation of their gender and ethnic cultural capital, and receive fewer rewards even at equal participation levels when compared with minority males or white women. Yet by the year 2000, it is estimated that one of every three students in the United States will be from a minority culture. We next consider the cultural context of schooling for one Hispanic group: Chicanas.

The history of education for Chicanas overlaps and diverges in significant ways with the education of other women of color. Their educational attainment rates remain among the lowest, with only Native American women having lower participation rates across degree levels. Along with other Hispanic groups, their language has been treated by the dominant schooling system as a "barrier," rather than a resource. As among Southeast Asians, recent immigrants make up a substantial portion of the Chicano population, creating both cultural opportunities and economic pressures in the Chicano community.

For all racial and ethnic minority groups, certain issues are integral to ensure full participation for minority students and to educate Anglo students about their cultural environment. These issues include cultural pluralism in school curricula; desegregation and integration of minority and majority students; ability tracking that internally resegregates schools; involvement of minority parents in educational processes; and the presence of minority teachers, administrators, and counselors (Moore, 1989).

Earlier, we noted the underrepresentation of racial and ethnic minorities in the teaching and administrative staffs of schools. The educational achievements of Hispanics in general are reduced by these and other aspects of racism and colonization. In 1986, a California State University System study of educational equity indicated that Hispanics have the highest drop-out rates of all ethnic groups in California (Banks and Banks, 1989). Some school districts reported drop-out rates of 40 percent before the tenth grade. Nationwide, some 50 percent of Mexican American and Puerto Rican students drop out before completing high school; in large urban districts, that drop-out rate may exceed 70 percent (Banks and Banks, 1989).

Chicanos have a unique set of cultural, economic, and educational experiences among Hispanics. The term *Chicano* itself denotes those who claim a cultural tie to Mexico through their own recent migration into the United States, or colonization of their family three or four generations back through the annexation of Mexican lands (Colorado, Texas, California, New Mexico, and Arizona) by the United States. The term *Hispanic,* which refers to those with a Spanish/Latin linguistic and cultural background, masks the diversity among cultural groups.

Chicanas complete education at rates lower than Cuban women, have lower incomes, and are less likely to hold professional or managerial jobs (Mirande and Enriquez, 1979). Chicanas are also the most highly represented group among migrant and farmworker women, estimated at some 4 percent of all Chicanas. In 1970, migrant farmworkers in general had an average of fourth- or fifth-grade educational achievement, and 90 percent of migrant children never finished high school (Cotera, 1977). To understand the diversity of colonizing experiences and the overlap with patriarchal educational processes, we examine the formal and informal curriculum of the schools as they are experienced by Chicanos. We then assess a series of policy recommendations made for schools and communities by Chicana activists and Chicana feminists.

Formal Communication—Language

The United States is a language "laboratory" that includes over 206 surviving Native American languages; the major colonizing languages of the Western hemisphere, including English, French, and Spanish; and the languages of successive waves of immigrants, including Polish, Hmong, and Chinese. In addition to these autonomous languages are the indigenous language varieties that combine different language backgrounds, such as Louisiana French Creole and Gullah, an English and West African Creole. These have linguistic structures that set them apart from English, including functional patterns and styles. Though the schools seek to maintain English as the dominant language of instruction, these separate styles have at times been reinforced through de jure and de facto segregation of education in the United States (Ovando, 1989).

Ovando argues that a fair curricular process should build on the sociocultural and linguistic background the students bring with them. However, the use of Spanish or Gullah or other languages and dialects has had negative consequences for ethnic minority students. As we have seen above, many Chicanos have not prospered in the public school system, and educators have singled out their non-English communication patterns as an important part of their academic failure.

The English linguistic norm of the public schools enables communities and educators to blame the student, or the family, or the cultural community, for academic failure. Language capital (in Spanish) cannot be translated as readily as English into the mathematics, literary, and social skills used for student evaluation. This translation of skills is cut off by the monolinguistic nature of the teaching and administrative staffs. However, lack of English language skills on the students' part provides a function of "cooling out" ethnic minority parents and students who question the inequities in educational outcomes. It is the student who is deficient because she cannot speak English, not the school system or teacher that is deficient because they cannot take advantage of the students' cultural and linguistic skills.

One issue regarding the education of students who are linguistic minorities is whether their languages should be used formally in the classroom. Some educators interpret non-English skills as an educational impediment, arguing that students should discard their primary language and replace it with standard English, preferably by the time they leave kindergarten. As Ovando notes, this suppression of language is confusing to the student and detrimental to academic and social well-being. Repeated attempts to eradicate nonstandard English or non-English language use in the schools over the past fifty years has not been correlated positively with the achievement gains of language-minority students (Ovando, 1989:219).

In addition, Ramirez and Castaneda (1974) argue that bilingual children develop important bicognitive skills, including cooperation, a focus on the human dimension of information, and a personal attachment to the learning process. Ovando (1989:223) notes several principles that have produced excellent results in an integrated curriculum for language-minority students, including the following:

- Language development in the home language as well as English
- Language proficiency in academic tasks as well as in basic conversation
- Ability to learn an academic task in his or her home language prior to expectations to perform in English
- Acquisition of English language skills in a range of contexts
- Reciprocal social status, with English speakers learning the minority language and teachers and administrators using the minority language for noninstructional as well as instructional purposes

These linguistic and cognitive skills are a framework for cross-cultural communication that should enhance the educational experience of Chicanas and other ethnic minority students.

Informal Communication

Melendez and Petrovich (1989) note that Hispanic students in general, and females in particular, have culturally determined patterns of behavior that may be in conflict with the dominant culture. These include ways of dealing with authority figures, who are not expected to be friends nor to be called by their first names as a signal of respect. In addition, the expression of disagreement to an authority figure, or questioning the opinions of others, even in an intellectual discussion, may be perceived as a sign of disrespect. The professor or teacher, however, may interpret this silence as a lack of interest or independent thinking.

Even the nonverbal interaction patterns of Hispanics and females may contribute to communication barriers. In Anglo culture, direct eye contact is appropriate behavior when connoting assertiveness and honesty. For Hispanics, continuous eye contact "is a sign of challenge, or if between members of the opposite sex, seduction" (Melendez and Petrovich, 1989:63). Other factors that may complicate interpretations of behavior are differences in use of personal space, hand gestures, and touching. Research indicates that Mexican Americans use less personal space in their arm movements, in sitting, and in standing. They also use more touching, but the touching is not used as often as in Anglo culture to indicate dominance. Instead, the touching might be used to involve an individual more closely in a conversation.

Each of these factors may lead to errors of interpretation. Hispanics are less likely than Anglos to exhibit the styles of communication and behavior that are highly valued in academia in the United States: openly expressing disagreement, participating in classroom discussion, maintaining eye contact, thriving under conditions of individual competition. Chicanas in particular are likely to view Anglo teachers as alien. The elementary school teacher, likely to be female, "does not conform to her expectations of a feminine behavior. She finds it difficult to identify with the teacher as a woman because the latter does not act like other women she has known" (Mirande and Enriquez, 1979:132). She will find fewer female teachers and more Anglo male teachers as she progresses through school. The verbal and nonverbal cues expected of active, achieving students do not account for the cross-gender and cross-cultural biases brought about by school staffing patterns. The very qualities that schools model for Chicanas may be in conflict with their cultural expectations and behaviors.

Compounding this difficulty is the evidence that teachers do not respond positively to their Chicano students (Moore, 1983; Ortiz, 1988). Various studies indicate that Chicanos are often ignored in the classroom, given less time to respond, or have their names forgotten or mispronounced consistently. Ortiz (1988) also documents the differences in material resources (higher pupil-teacher ratios; fewer books; isolated classrooms; higher proportions of teacher aides, as opposed to teachers, assigned to work with language-minority students) allocated to programs that segregate students by culture (ESL programs) as well as within traditional classrooms. These patterns reflect the expectations of teachers and administrators that Hispanic students will perform less well and therefore deserve fewer resources.

Teachers and administrators must be reeducated about the differences in cultural codes between themselves as middle-class Anglos and ethnic minority students, how these codes operate in classrooms, and how schooling processes in and out of the classroom can be restructured to take into account bicognitive, bicultural considerations. This obviously can be accomplished best when minority teachers are well represented among staff and administrators. All teachers can be more effective when they understand the human value, not only of the individual Chicana, but of her cultural heritage.

Chicanas and the Public School Curriculum

What administrators, educators, and community representatives believe to be the essential knowledge and skills for all students to learn, how these are framed in terms of values, and how they are taught form the basic curriculum of the public schools. Revisionist historians argue that this educational "canon" is based on Anglocentric norms, history, and institutions that have essentially "colonized" minority group cultures and economies (McCarthy and Apple, 1988).

Chicano and Chicana activists argue that the history and current social conditions of their people have been particularly distorted: "Authentic studies about Hispanic America by North American scholars and journalists have not only been few, but even worse, much of what has been written has been distorted, incorrect and misinterpreted" (Jimenez-Vasquez, 1976:220).

Dual images and chicana culture.   Crucial to understanding Chicana contact with public schools in the United States is the historical role model for women in the larger Chicano culture. Three such role models stand out in the literature: Malintzin Tenepal, Sor Juana Ines de la Cruz (an intellectual and poet of seventeenth-century Mexico), and *la soldera* (the heroines of the 1910 Mexican Revolution). Consuela Nieto (1980) provides detailed descriptions of each. For our purposes, we highlight the dualistic image of Malintzin Tenepal in Mexican literature.

Malintzin was a woman sold into slavery by her family in the province of Coatzacoalcos. She was later given to Cortes, the Spanish conqueror of Mexico. She served as his translator and later as his mistress, eventually giving birth to the symbolic first *mestizo* of mixed Spanish and Indian heritage. Her union with Cortes is interpreted in Chicano culture as a traitorous act, and she is assigned the cultural title of *La Malinche* (the traitor).

Chicana feminists are revising this interpretation. They perceive her as first a victim of indigenous slavery among the Mayans, and then as a victim of Spanish colonization and patriarchy (Cotera, 1977; Nieto, 1980). Some point out that her work with Cortes was to build coalitions among Indian communities enslaved by the Mayans, which places her in the role of a patriot, a liberator of her own oppressed people. Only later was she betrayed by Cortes's colonial and patriarchal treachery.

A dual theme develops from these themes of betrayed alliances, enforced motherhood, and sexual union with a colonizer. This dualism parallels the virgin/whore dichotomy prevalent in the dominant Anglo-Saxon Protestant culture of the United States. On the one hand, women are stereotypically placed on higher moral ground because of the motherhood mystique and the nurturing, serving roles of women. On the other hand, women are viewed as potentially evil, particularly because of their sexuality. Malintzin is the "Eve" of the Chicano culture, La Malinche, but so too is she the mother of the mestizos, the Chicanos of North America. The combination of this indigenous dual role for Chicanos with the patriarchal and racist themes of the dominant schooling culture creates a "triple oppression" for Chicanas (Mirande and Enriquez, 1979).

To confront this triple oppression, Chicana feminists are attempting to revise dualistic stereotypes and to present new frameworks of information and interpretation. One result would be the valuing of women's roles as bearers of culture, and as contributors to the economic and social institutions of their communities—as mothers, wives, and daughters—without reference to distortions from patriarchy or cultural colonization.

Rarely are these visions of Chicanas part of the elementary and secondary school curriculum because of the double jeopardy of omission for being female and of a minority ethnic group. Some of this revisionist work has appeared in women's studies or ethnic studies programs in postsecondary education, but not without difficulty. Melendez and Petrovich (1989) note that Chicana interests in ethnic studies in higher education are often disparaged, considered "too narrow," not "objective," or "too personal" (which we read to mean too political). Women's studies classes, programs, and scholarships are criticized for omitting significant contributions by women of color (Zinn et al., 1986). But building on that which a student knows, her cultural capital, provides a far more exciting and challenging curriculum. The academic community needs an expanded literacy in other cultures, to retain and inspire Chicana students and faculty.

Heretical curricula: Teaching about women of color. Chicana advocates agree that an important implication for education is the inseparability of the many facets of Chicanas' lives, especially their self-fulfillment and their unique roles as women. "To say *Chicana* is to speak of a fusion, an inclusion of the energies of culture and womanliness, rather than a fragmenting of these" (Nieto, 1980:267). As Hull et al. (1982) trace the parallel development of black women's studies, they note the effects of three significant liberation movements: the black liberation movement, women's liberation, and the more recent black feminist movement. Each is unique, yet interconnected (Hull et al., 1982:22), as are the Chicano liberation and Chicana feminist actions for empowering "La Raza."[2]

Butler argues for the following heresies to challenge and ultimately displace the Anglocentric schooling process (Butler, 1989:154–55):

Heresy #1. The goal of interaction among human beings, action and ideas must be seen not only as synthesis, but also as the identification of opposites and differences. These may not be resolved.

Heresy #2. We *can* address a multiplicity of concerns, approaches and subjects without a neutral or dominant center. Reality reflects opposites as well as overlaps in what are perceived as opposites.

Heresy #3. It is not reductive to look at gender, race, class and culture as part of a complex whole. The more different voices we have, the closer we are to the whole.

Heresy #4. Transformation demands an understanding of ethnicity that takes into account the differing cultural continua and their similarities.

Heresy #5. Transformation demands we recognize that although not all -isms are the same, they are unified and operate as such; likewise their correctives.

[2]"La Raza," meaning "the race," is a self-identifying concept for Chicanos and Chicanas. It symbolizes the movement for political, economic, and social change. For more information see Ignacio Garcia's *United We Win: The Rise and Fall of La Raza Unida Party* published in 1989 by the University of Arizona Press in Tucson, and Elizabeth Sutherland Martínez and Enriqueta Longeaux y Vásquez's *Viva La Raza* published in 1974 by Doubleday in New York.

Heresy # 6. The Anglo-American norm must be seen as only one of many norms, and also as one that enjoys privilege and power that has colonized and may continue to colonize other norms.

Heresy # 7. Feelings are direct lines to better thinking. The intuitive as well as the rational is part of the process of moving from the familiar to the unfamiliar.

Heresy # 8. Knowledge is identity and identity is knowledge. All knowledge is explicitly and implicitly related to who we are.

For Chicanas, this means that their understanding of the schooling process includes their cultural and literary roles as women. The triple jeopardy of colonization, sexism, and racism affects staffing patterns, parental involvement in schools, and the formal and informal curricular norms. A heretical approach to schooling for Chicanas would include an assessment of their cultural norms of cooperation, emphasis on human interaction, and group identity as enhancements to the schooling of Anglo students.

PATRIARCHAL REPRODUCTION AND RESISTANCE

One of the challenges presented to feminist educators and activists is the ability to resist what appears to be oppression in the major institutions: schools, the law, the family, and the workplace. Kathleen Weiler (1988) critiques what she sees as "feminist reproduction theory," which suggests that these institutions are all-powerful. Many feminist theorists and educators share a common belief in the overriding power of material conditions, of the relationship of gender, race, and class, and of the economic and family oppression of women being uniformly reproduced without resistance by students in the schools. The statistical analyses presented earlier in this chapter can be tied too narrowly to sexist texts and discriminatory educational practices. Our focus is on the connection between sexist practices in the schools and women's oppression in the larger society, especially its economic outcomes (Weiler, 1988:31). This approach can fail to address the potential resources in women's individual consciousness, and can omit the possibilities of resistance.

McLaren describes in detail the process and problems of resistance in education. Working-class adult women students in Canada "presented themselves as individuals—and sometimes as rebels—of the real world" (McLaren, 1987:346). They did not passively accept the configurations of values and ideals presented by their parents and teachers. They actively struggled against the prospect of "dead end" jobs and "female ghettos." McLaren concludes that their inability to ultimately resist was because of a social structure that left too little room to maneuver, not because of socialization into feminine roles that dictated their later experiences.

Suzanna Rose (1989) makes more explicit the necessary role of resistance and protest in feminist theory, pedagogy, and praxis. This model borrows from the ethnic studies activism of the 1960s but identifies specific gains for women's studies students. In her own teaching, she includes an explicit assignment of community political participation. This helps students to translate vague dissatisfactions into specific targets for change. The planning of a protest, including letter-writing campaigns, teaches political strategy and practical information about representative democracy. These activities have significant effects on feelings of efficacy; they contribute to empowerment on individual and social levels.

Other hallmarks of feminist pedagogy potentially transform women's studies classrooms and may address the colonizing practices of schools as well. These include (1) cooperative, nonhierarchical teaching that reinforces a democratic exchange of ideas among students and between students and teachers and (2) the inclusion of personal experience as a starting point (Schniedewind, 1983). Both of these address the hierarchical structure set by competitive, patriarchal, colonized, or class-based schooling and the classroom processes that maintain that structure.

Finally, attention goes to those subject areas that are likely to be omitted or marginalized (Howe, 1987). Because they involve women's work (especially unpaid or marginalized work), the topics of housework, child care, and reproduction are rarely considered in traditional economic disciplines. Resistance to patriarchal education is accomplished by including the invisible or taken-for-granted ideas and actions of women. The colonized nature of minority cultures, languages, and norms can be explicitly cited as detailed challenges to Anglocentric history, social structures, and societal process. Finally, the class-based system of access to schooling demands a reassessment of sorting processes and the definition of "quality" education. These pedagogical themes support the critique by Weiler that our teaching about the structure of oppression need not cause our students to accept those structures.

USEFUL AND EXCHANGEABLE SCHOOLING

In the previous discussions, we have seen evidence of sexism, heterosexism, and racism in classrooms, curricula, and staffing. This points to a very real threat to women students, including lesbian and racial/ethnic minority members of society who seek information or try to provide information through the schools. It influences the quality of education, counseling, and social experiences of these students.

Research shows that sexism, heterosexism, and racism continue to affect the economic lives of adult women (Levine and Leonard, 1984; Blauner, 1972; Treiman and Hartmann, 1981). For lesbians, this becomes a double jeopardy, as their reproductive, social, and economic choices are restricted as women, and again as lesbians. For Chicana lesbians, and for lesbians of color, the triple oppression of racism, sexism, and colonization are compounded by the homophobia of both dominant and subordinate cultures.

The cultural capital of the schools is played out in a competitive, hierarchical process and structure that ensures that women, and especially women of subordinate ethnic and language groups, alternative sexual preference, or lower social class will be at the bottom of the educational ladder. The extent to which ethnic studies and women's studies programs can provide intellectual and practical tools for resistance will be the hallmark of our theory building and testing.

SEVEN

Women and the Law

In the previous two chapters, we have illustrated the influence of the institutions of education and economics on the lives of women. Now, we switch to an institution that permeates many aspects of women's lives—the law. The law, which some feminists embrace as a remedy for wrongs and the means of gaining legal rights in discrimination suits, is also an institution that reinforces the norm of patriarchal rule, protects capitalist enterprises, and reinforces racial and cultural biases. It has often reinforced a culture of violence against women that permeates many societies.

This chapter is divided into three parts. First, we will look at feminist issues as they relate to the sociology of law. Some of the issues we address include the historical development of law as it relates to women's lives, using protective legislation as a specific example; the history of women in law, policing, and correctional professions; and a contemporary analysis of women's place within these professions. Second, we will look at some feminist issues for criminology, including women's marginality as criminals, the use of official statistics, the incidence of female crime, women in correctional facilities, traditional theoretical explanations for female criminality, the role of status offenses in female delinquency, and the history of the sexualization of female crime. Finally, we will focus on women's survival in a culture of violence, especially violence perpetrated within families and across the life cycle.

FEMINIST ISSUES FOR A SOCIOLOGY OF LAW

Historically, women have been excluded from and trivialized in the analysis of law, the protection supplied by the forces of law, and in the enforcement of law.

This neglect was often attributed to the fact that few women were legal practitioners, legislators, and criminals. However, strong evidence indicates that women's lives, rights, and places in society have been affected by and have influenced the development of law.

History of Women and the Law

Woman as "nonperson." In 1779, Mary Wollstonecraft argued that women should hold equal rights with men because they possess the same capacities to reason (Wollstonecraft, 1779/1977). Rationality was the criterion used at that time to determine which men should gain privileges and rights in society. Mary Wollstonecraft's arguments were not well received by the philosophers and politicians of her day because the cultural beliefs, practices, and norms defined women as less intelligent, less rational, and even less human than males. Women were more likely to be viewed as the property of males (husbands or fathers) than as individuals in their own right.

In 1860, when seven women were refused admittance to the University of Edinburgh Medical School, they went to court. Their case became known as the "persons" case and the question simply became, Are women persons, as defined by British law? The seven women, led by Sophia Jex-Blake, met with strong opposition when they attempted to enroll in the medical school because it was believed to be an inappropriate place for a woman. At this time in England, there were two practicing women physicians: Elizabeth Blackwell, who had been trained in the United States and then came to England, and Elizabeth Garrett, who had slipped into medical school through a loophole. The presence of these women in the medical profession was causing discord among the male physicians, and this prompted strong opposition to allowing these seven women to attend medical school. When the case went before the courts, the women lost because it was argued that medical education is designed for men, and it would be too expensive to have separate classes for women.

> The "persons" cases, as they came to be called, were launched by feminists in the hope that their arguments needed merely to be stated to be upheld, namely, that an individual's gender was irrelevant to his or her factual or legal capacity, and that females were obviously to be included in the word "person." What was self-evident truth to feminists, however, was manifest absurdity to most of the judges. (Sachs and Wilson, 1978:6)

Even though we often attempt to use the courts as a mechanism to redress wrongs, traditional attitudes, beliefs, and values about women are reflected in the laws and the ways the laws are interpreted.

Class-privileged men have traditionally written the laws and interpreted them, often with the underlying concern of protecting family and community. Because of this, women have been defined in terms of their relationships to men—either in need of being protected by men or men needing to be protected from them. Clarice Feinman (1986) calls this the madonna/whore duality—women who are protected by men (husband, father, or even brothers) will be those the law is to protect, the "madonna." The "whore," on the other hand, is the open-territory woman, the one who has no legal male protector and is considered evil and seductive. The law is not designed to protect these women and is often used to punish them. The message of this dichotomy is that if women stay within their sphere of family and community, the patriarchal system will protect them (Feinman, 1986).

The other side of this argument is that women who stray from the traditional patriarchal family will suffer at the hands of the legal system. The witch-hunting crazes that occurred throughout Europe and in the United States are classic examples of this phenomenon. It is estimated that over nine million people were put to death for witchcraft between 1484 and 1784 (Gage, 1893/1972). The vast majority of these were women, and they were often unmarried women, divorced women, or others who lived outside the patriarchal norms of husband and family.

> For the targets of attack in the witchcraze were not women defined by assimilation into the patriarchal family. Rather, the witchcraze focused predominantly upon women who had rejected marriage (spinsters) and women who had survived it (widows). The witch-hunters sought to purify their society (The Mystical Body) of these "indigestible" elements—women whose physical, intellectual, economic, moral, and spiritual independence and activity profoundly threatened the male monopoly in every sphere. (Daly, 1978:184)

The consequence of this legal definition of women is that women are defined in the law similar to the way that property is defined—something to be protected, valued, appraised, insured, and if damaged, the perpetrator prosecuted and perhaps the property replaced. When women are seen as marital property, there are severe consequences for the way in which wife abuse and child abuse are seen by the courts. Local interventions to protect women from abuse have not been rapid. The disbelief on the part of judges concerning the level of abuse, women's inability to get and enforce restraining orders, the lack of arrest statistics for men who beat up their wives or partners, and the rising rate of women in prison who kill their husbands after long histories of abuse and of women who are arrested for abuse are all indicators that the premise behind the legal system is that women are the property of their husbands and the court should not interfere in the family sphere.

In addition to the notion of women as property, the madonna/whore duality also points out the explicitly sexual nature that is inherent in the descriptions of women as defined by law. Women are often defined in terms of their sexuality and are seen as sexual property belonging to a man. The history of the prosecution in rape cases reflects this belief. Women are often victimized not only by the sexual assault itself but by the hospitals and the courts.

It is much more difficult for open-territory women who have been victimized to gain a conviction against an offender than for women who are affiliated with a male—that is, as a wife, a daughter, or mother. The work in sexual harassment again reflects this same bias with women in both the workplace and in the schools finding it difficult to define themselves autonomously and force the institutional systems to provide safeguards and penalties against sexual harassers.

Although we cannot in the space of this chapter address the historical legal progress of each of the above concerns, we will examine one issue, protective legislation, that illustrates the interaction between the sexist bias in the justice system and how women are treated in the labor market.

Protective legislation.   In the 1820s, women, particularly those who suffered under the oppressive capitalistic factory system, began an unsuccessful attempt to organize themselves (Sachs and Wilson, 1978). The conditions of employment were notoriously bad, with long hours and extremely low pay. Women were used as a source of cheap labor, which maximized the profit of the capitalists.

Progressivism is a term that refers to a social reform movement that emerged in the late 1800s and early 1900s and sought to reform the capitalist system. Progressivists sought greater state involvement to curb long working hours, establish minimum wages, end child labor, and increase health benefits (Abramovitz, 1988). In the early 1900s, with a large increase in the number of white women in the labor force, progressivism centered some of its concerns on women's employment, focusing on the economic exploitation of women, the possible danger to women's reproductive capacity, and the potential for a loss in morality (Abramovitz, 1988). There was little concern about the working conditions for colonized women. Urban black women worked as cooks, seamstresses, domestics, and in other unskilled jobs under highly degrading circumstances, and rural black women often worked as sharecroppers. Protective labor laws were introduced to regulate white women's working conditions. Underlying the laws that regulated the hours of possible employment and the type of employment available to women was a concern that women in the labor force might disrupt the sex segregation of the labor market.

According to the Fourteenth Amendment of the U.S. Constitution, which was adopted on July 28, 1868:

> No State shall make or enforce any law which shall abridge the privileges or immunities of citizens of the United States; nor shall any State deprive any person of life, liberty or property, without due process of law; nor deny to any person within its jurisdiction the equal protection of the laws.

The Fourteenth Amendment struck down many existing labor laws (Baker, 1925). However, because of the vagueness of the amendment, it has been interpreted with some elasticity. For example, laws that abridge the privileges or immunities of citizens can be upheld if they are viewed as necessary for public welfare. The greater liberty of all the people is weighted against the right of the individual.

Therefore, it was ruled in some cases that certain arenas of women's lives could be regulated and controlled. Employment for women was deemed one of those areas where women's reproductive function needed to be protected by the state from the capitalists. In *State* v. *Muller,* 48 Oregon 252 (1906), Oregon passed a law stating that women could not work longer than ten-hour shifts. Muller violated the law and had women working longer shifts. The ruling of the Oregon court in 1906, upheld by the U.S. Supreme Court in 1908, supported the limitation of hours for women as a class. Some of the Court's findings are worth repeating here since they clearly illustrate the assumptions of women's worth as defined only in terms of mother and wife.

> That woman's physical structure and the performance of maternal functions place her at a disadvantage in the struggle for subsistence is obvious. This is especially true when the burdens of motherhood are upon her. Even when they are not, by abundant testimony of the medical fraternity continuance for a long time on her feet at work, repeating this from day to day, tends to injurious effects upon the body, and as healthy mothers are essential to vigorous offspring, the physical well-being of women becomes an object of public interest and care in order to preserve the strength and vigor of the race.
>
> Still again, history discloses the fact that woman has always been dependent upon man. He established his control at the outset by superior physical strength, and this control in various forms, with diminishing intensity, has continued to the present. . . . Differentiated by these matters from the other sex, she is properly placed in a class by herself, and legislation designed for her protection may be sustained, even when like legislation is not necessary for men and could not be sustained. (Sachs and Wilson, 1978:114)

Even though the judges were attempting to protect women from capitalists whose only motive for long days and cheap labor was to maximize profit, the outcome of protective labor legislation was to restrict women's ability to compete in the labor market equally with men and to earn a living on an equal basis with men, thereby effectively decreasing women's exchange value. It is interesting to note that while the *Muller* argument worked to decrease the number of hours women could work and later similar arguments managed to keep women out of certain occupations entirely, the Court would not accept arguments that women would then require higher pay than men because of their mothering and reproductive roles.

Policing and Correctional Professions

The field of criminal justice, including law, corrections, and policing, has traditionally been dominated by men. This is not surprising given that most professions that hold political or economic power have been traditionally male domains (Morris, 1987). The history of women entering the legal professions mirrors that of the medical and scientific professions, in which various mechanisms, both legal and social, were introduced to prevent women from entering these fields (Sachs and Wilson, 1978).

Under the guise of protective legislation, women were defined as inappropriate workers for the tasks of policing, law, and corrections, unless their tasks were specifically tied to the mothering role. In 1873, Myra Bradwell wanted to practice law in the United States and was barred from doing so because she was female. She took her case to the U.S. Supreme Court and lost.

Bradwell *v*. Illinois, *16 Wall 130, 141 (1872)*.[1]   Myra Bradwell had petitioned the Illinois Supreme Court to admit her to the bar, the prerequisite to being a lawyer. Although Myra met all the usual criteria (education, testing on the law, of good moral character), the Illinois Supreme Court predicated its decision on laws that precluded women from entering contracts independent of their husbands. If Myra were to make a "lawyerly" act that might prompt a lawsuit, her husband would be sued. This was a prospect the court held to be radical and ludicrous. On appeal to the U.S. Supreme Court, Justice Bradley's concurring opinion illustrates the unbridled sexism of the time.

> The natural and proper timidity and delicacy which belongs to the female sex evidently unfits it for many of the occupations of civil life. The constitution of the family . . . founded in divine ordinance, as well as in the nature of things, indicates the domestic sphere as . . . the domain and functions of womanhood.
>
> *Bradwell* v. *Illinois,* 16 Wall 130, 141 (1872)

In 1872, the Supreme Court upheld the Illinois decision to prevent Myra Bradwell from practicing law. The social ideas of the time were the foundation for Justice Bradley's opinion, ideas that remained relatively immutable until the ratification of the Nineteenth Amendment in 1920, which gave women the right to vote. There were three social ideologies that helped shape the Supreme Court's refutation of Myra Bradwell's "right" to practice law:

1. Women were not "designed by God" for any significant function beyond that of wife and mother
2. Defining interaction between races was a volatile concern at the time and was to be explored only with great caution
3. Postwar tensions transcended race issues, encompassing a very entrenched states'

[1]The case citation method is distinct from that used in the social sciences. The names indicate the parties to the case (Bradwell, the **appellant** has stated a cause of action against the State of Illinois, who is the **respondent** or **appellee**). The first number (16 in this case) refers to the volume number of the "reporter" in which the case is published (Wall stands for Wallace, a now-extinct reporter). The number immediately following the name of the reporter indicates the page in this volume where the case begins. If a second number appears (141 in this example), it specifies the pagination for quoted or paraphrased material. The number in parentheses is the year the court made its decision. Subsequent references to the same case directing you to the specific page include: ***Id.***, at _____ [*Id.* is the abbreviation for ***idem***—the same reference previously made (words of Latin origin are italicized)]; ***supra,*** at _____ (above) refers to a previous part of the book and is synonymous with ***ante,*** at _____ (before); ***infra,*** at _____ (below or within) is the opposite of ***supra*** and refers to a subsequent part of the book. With the exception of ***Id.***, at _____, an alternative style omitting "at" is permissible, i.e., ***supra,*** 141.

rights agenda that sought to nullify the intrusive federal question inherent in the Fourteenth Amendment

In addition to the gender issues raised by the *Bradwell* case, it would take an additional twenty-five years to fully resolve the matter of admitting African Americans to the bar.

This attitude reflects the arguments put forward to support protective legislation for women and children. In 1850, more than half of the workforce were women and children, and most jobs were performed by both men and women (Morris, 1987). However, in the early 1900s, jobs were scarce following the depression of the 1890s, and protective legislation served to close certain occupations to women. Protective legislation ruled that women were not suited to certain types of work and should be protected from harsh labor, as should children. Yet, a double standard existed, as women were considered suited to factory work but were considered unsuitable to the professions of law and medicine.

During the middle to late nineteenth century, women began their work in criminal justice as volunteers, as part of the philanthropic movement for moral reformation where women visited workhouses, prisons, schools, and refuges. This voluntarism was viewed as a natural extension of women's mothering and family duties. The first women admitted into the professions of policing and corrections were hired to fulfill feminine roles, which were essentially custodial in nature. Women were employed primarily as caretakers of juveniles and female offenders.

Alice Stebbins Wells, a social worker and theology student, was the first regularly appointed American policewoman. She was appointed in 1910 in Los Angeles. She received her appointment after circulating a petition to the city council and police commissioner urging the appointment of a woman police officer to work with women and children (Price and Gavin, 1982). By 1915, twenty-five cities in the United States employed women in policing, primarily to deal with juveniles, female offenders, and female victims. Today, it is now required that women and men be recruited and employed on an equal basis. This has met with rigorous opposition by both the males and females on the police forces. The women police officers argued they wanted the specialization, particularly because it often prevented them from having to take night-shift work, so that they could balance working on the police force with raising their families. Male officers, on the other hand, argued that women were a liability whenever there was trouble because they felt their female colleagues needed "protection" in a traditional chivalrous sense. Male officers also argued that partners developed close working relationships that they felt would be impossible given the sexual tension that would likely arise if they were required to work closely with a female partner. Male officers also expressed a fear that women police officers would take over policing, especially since female applicants were generally better qualified and performed better on the standardized exams. The research that has followed the progress of women in policing shows these fears to be unfounded. Even though policewomen often face problems of overprotectiveness, verbal and physical harassment, or abuse from their male colleagues, overall studies indicate that women are fully effective and competent as police officers (Bloch and Anderson, 1974; Sichel et al., 1978).

A Contemporary Look

Certain occupations can still be denied to women on the basis of sex, although this has become exceedingly more difficult since Title VII of the Civil Rights Act of 1964, which disallows discrimination on the basis of race or sex, as well as the Equal Employment Opportunity Act of 1972. However, sex must be a bona fide occupational qualification in order for women to be excluded simply on the basis of sex. This means that it must be proven that persons of one sex cannot perform the duties of the job because of their sex. The military uses sex as a bona fide qualification to prevent women from some active military combat positions. Overall, it has proven extremely difficult for employers to define a job as male or female only. In *Frontiero v. Richardson* (1973), the court ruled that sex should be treated as an inherently suspect category. The impact of this case was to call into question any job description that excludes females or males. However, even with legislative and court rulings, the fields of law, corrections, and policing remain primarily white male labor markets.

Table 7-1 illustrates the percentage of women and minorities in adult and juvenile correction occupations as of June 30, 1994. Thirty percent of employees in adult correctional systems were women, and 35 percent of employees in juvenile correctional systems were women. Women and minorities were more

TABLE 7-1   Employees in Adult and Juvenile Correctional Systems by Race, Ethnicity, and Sex as of June 30, 1994

	Total	White	Black	Hispanic	All Others
Adult Correctional Systems					
	352,847	252,086 (71.4%)	69,420 (19.7%)	20,370 (5.8%)	8,631 (2.4%)
Percent male	69.7	72.1	62.3	73.1	70.5
Percent female	29.6	27.9	37.7	26.9	29.5
Juvenile Correctional Systems					
	39,376	25,351 (64.4%)	10,598 (26.9%)	2,651 (6.7%)	776 (2.0%)
Percent male	64.7	66.4	60.8	64.5	65.3
Percent female	35.3	33.6	39.2	35.5	34.7

Source: American Correctional Association. 1996. *Directory of Juvenile and Adult Correctional Departments, Institutions, Agencies, and Paroling Authorities* (Lanham, MD: American Correctional Association), Pp. x1ii, x1iii. As cited in U.S. Department of Justice, Bureau of Justice Statistics. 1996. *Sourcebook of Criminal Justice Statistics 1995.* Washington, DC: U.S. Government Printing Office, Tables 1.87 and 1.88.

likely to be employed in juvenile correctional systems than adult systems. Twenty-eight percent of employees were minorities in the adult systems and 36 percent of employees were minorities in the juvenile systems.

In policing, women made up only 5.8 percent of all public service police officers and detectives in 1983. By 1994, 24.4 percent of all police employees were women. However, only 9.5 percent of sworn officers were women. The largest percentage of women in law enforcement were working as civilian employees. Table 7-2 indicates that a higher percentage of sworn women police officers were employed in larger cities and urban areas. The percentage of female officers in these areas ranged from 12.6 percent to 15.4 percent of all sworn officers. Fewer women were employed in smaller cities with populations ranging from under 10,000 people to 50,000 people.

However, women made up 27 percent of bachelor's degree candidates in law enforcement and 40.5 percent of criminal justice studies graduates in 1994 (see Table 7-3). Taking all the protective service degrees into consideration, women were awarded 38 percent of all bachelor's degrees in 1994 and minorities were awarded 24.4 percent of all protective service degrees (see Table 7-4). More black females than black males are receiving bachelor's degrees in both law (see Table 7-5) and the protective services.

Overall, even though women and minorities are increasingly being trained into criminal justice and legal professions, they are not as readily being absorbed into the labor market. Many women training in law enforcement find themselves unable to get positions with police departments and end up working traffic, security, or dispatch jobs. Many factors can explain these discrepancies, including the culture of the occupation and individual and structural discrimination.

Occupational culture. One of the first obstacles that women face as they enter the profession of criminal justice is its masculine character. Crime control, as crime itself, has been primarily a masculine endeavor. The characteristics describing individuals who have succeeded in these professions include being a "tough cop," or a "forceful judge"—roles that emphasize aggression, activity, self-reliance, and so on (Morris, 1987). Women, as they enter these professions, are often faced with stereotypical assumptions concerning their lack of these "required masculine characteristics." Because of this, they often experience exclusion and testing by their colleagues. As in any profession where one is a distinct minority, they suffer the classic problem of tokenism.

The occupational work culture in policing and corrections has had a history of nonacceptance of female workers. This pattern has been shown to exist from the training, education period (Austin and Hummer, 1994) and continues on the street (Martin, 1980) and in the correctional facilities (Martin, 1996).

In 1994, Austin and Hummer conducted a study of the attitudes of male criminal justice majors toward female police officers. They found that almost

TABLE 7-2 Full-Time Law Enforcement Employees by Sex and Population Group, October 31, 1994 (1994 estimated population)

Population Group	Total Police Employees			Police Officers (Sworn)			Civilian Employees		
	Total	Male (%)	Female (%)	Total	Male (%)	Female (%)	Total	Male (%)	Female (%)
Total agencies: 13,124 agencies; population 244,517,000	782,110	75.6	24.4	561,543	90.5	9.5	220,567	37.7	62.3
Total cities: 10,010 cities; population 164,313,000	474,663	77.1	22.9	368,441	90.7	9.3	106,222	30.3	69.7
Group I									
65 cities, 250,000 and over; population 46,841,000	171,751	73.6	26.4	133,714	85.8	14.2	38,037	30.8	69.2
9 cities, 1,000,000 and over; population 21,338,000	93,193	72.6	27.4	72,703	84.6	15.4	20,490	30.1	69.9
19 cities, 500,000 to 999,999; population 12,329,000	40,492	76.0	24.0	32,029	87.2	12.8	8,463	33.6	66.4
37 cities, 250,000 to 499,999; population 13,174,000	38,066	73.6	26.4	28,982	87.4	12.6	9,084	29.8	70.2
Group II									
133 cities, 100,000 to 249,999; population 19,542,000	47,779	75.3	24.7	36,206	90.8	9.2	11,573	26.6	73.4
Group III									
352 cities, 50,000 to 99,999; population 24,110,000	54,285	77.8	22.2	41,868	93.1	6.9	12,417	26.2	73.8

Group IV 680 cities, 25,000 to 49,999; population 23,463,000	52,351	79.3	20.7	41,073	94.0	6.0	11,278	25.7	74.3
Group V 1,680 cities, 10,000 to 24,999; population 26,444,000	60,650	81.3	18.7	48,555	94.8	5.2	12,095	26.9	73.1
Group VI 7,100 cities, under 10,000; population 23,913,000	87,847	80.5	19.5	67,025	93.6	6.4	20,822	38.4	61.6
Suburban counties 852 agencies; population 51,457,000	190,760	72.3	27.7	117,669	88.6	11.4	73,091	46.0	54.0
Rural counties 2,262 agencies; population	116,687	74.9	25.1	75,433	93.0	7.0	41,254	41.9	58.1
Suburban areas[a] 6,204 agencies; population 99,617,000	322,513	75.6	24.4	219,778	91.1	8.9	102,735	42.5	57.5

[a]Includes suburban city and county law enforcement agencies within metropolitan areas. Excludes central cities. Suburban cities and counties also are included in other groups.

Source: U.S. Department of Justice, Bureau of Justice Statistics. 1996. *Sourcebook of Criminal Justice Statistics 1995.* Washington, DC: U.S. Government Printing Office, Table 1.56.

TABLE 7-3 Bachelor's Degrees Awarded in Protective Services by Field of Study and Sex, 1993–1994

	Males	Females
Corrections/correctional administration	388	317
Criminal justice/law enforcement administration	4,490	2,777
Criminal justice studies	6,959	4,743
Forensic studies	96	62
Law enforcement/police science	1,317	482
Criminal justice, other	670	444
Criminal justice and corrections, total	13,920	8,825
Fire control and safety	221	8
Protective services, other	28	7
Protective Services Total	14,169	8,840

Source: U.S. Department of Education, National Center for Education Statistics. 1996. *Digest of Education Statistics 1996* (NCES 96-133). Washington, DC: U.S. Government Printing Office, Table 244.

TABLE 7-4 Bachelor's Degrees Awarded in Protective Services by Race and Sex, 1993–1994

	Males	%	Females	%	Total	%
White non-Hispanic	11,254	79.4	6,139	69.4	17,393	75.6
Black non-Hispanic	1,634	11.5	1,848	20.9	3,482	15.1
Hispanic	798	5.6	614	6.9	1,412	6.1
Asian or Pacific Islander	280	2.0	123	1.4	403	1.8
American Indian/Alaska native	96	0.7	64	0.7	160	0.7
Nonresident alien	107	0.8	52	0.6	159	0.7
Protective services Total	14,169		8,840		23,000	

Source: U.S. Department of Education, National Center for Education Statistics. 1996. *Digest of Education Statistics 1996* (NCES 96-133). Washington, DC: U.S. Government Printing Office, Table 260.

TABLE 7-5 Law Degrees Awarded by Sex, 1993–1994

	Bachelor's Degree		Master's Degree		Doctor's Degree	
Degree	Male	Female	Male	Female	Male	Female
Pre-law studies	120	119	0	0	0	0
Paralegal/legal assistant	154	874	70	27	31	5
Law and legal studies, other	374	530	1,538	797	32	11
Law and legal studies, total	648	1,523	1,608	824	63	16

Source: U.S. Department of Education, National Center for Education Statistics. 1996. *Digest of Education Statistics 1996* (NCES 96-133). Washington, DC: U.S. Government Printing Office, Table 244.

half of the students surveyed harbored unfavorable attitudes toward women as police officers.

These patterns continue even though women have been patrol officers in the United States for over twenty-five years and yet they make up less than 10 percent of police officers nationwide (Martin, 1991). Affirmative action, both court ordered and voluntary, have had significant influence on hiring but not on the promotion of female officers (Martin, 1991).

Structural discrimination. In addition to the individual distrust of women entering into this male enterprise, organizational barriers exist that exclude or create hostile environments for women. Females entering the legal professions may have to be better qualified than male entrants. The American Bar Association in 1983 reported that female lawyers were better qualified and worked harder than male lawyers, yet they earned less (Morris, 1987). For many years, height and weight requirements for police and corrections officers automatically excluded women; however, these requirements have been eliminated as not job related. But strength and agility are still required of candidates and are defined in masculine terms.

The Veterans Preference System used in hiring police officers and corrections officers serves to discriminate against women, because fewer women have direct military experience. In England, police officers cannot work part-time, and women find it impossible to combine police work with family commitments (Morris, 1987). In the United States, the full-time requirement, along with shift work, often creates a situation that makes it impossible for women to combine a police career with family responsibilities. In defining the work pattern for legal professionals, the male career pattern is considered the norm, and it takes no account of women's career patterns (Morris, 1987). The "mommy track" is a typical example of this pattern. Women are being tracked differently from men in order to accommodate both home and professional responsibilities. The positive outcomes of this tracking include shorter working hours and more flexible work schedules. However, the negative consequences include less seniority, lower salaries, and fewer opportunities for promotion.

FEMINIST ISSUES FOR CRIMINOLOGY

Some will argue that regardless of whether one is female or male, a criminal act is a crime and should be prosecuted. However, a more cautious look at the issues relevant to female criminality gives a more complex portrayal than that oversimplified approach to criminality. Existing theories of delinquency and criminality have proven inadequate in explaining female delinquency and criminality. They do little to clarify official police, court, and correctional reactions to females who enter penal institutions as delinquents or prisoners.

Many issues are gender specific, including the invisibility of the female criminal or delinquent, the roles of the status offense (defined as an act that is against the law for juveniles but not for adults, such as running away or incorrigibility) in female delinquency, and the sexualization of female delinquency and criminality.

Invisibility of the Female Actor—Women's Marginality as Criminals

As we have stated earlier, girls and women are less likely to commit crimes than are men, according to official crime statistics. Because of this, females have been omitted from policy and research and their problems trivialized because their crimes are not considered serious ones.

Although there has been an overall increase in the female crime rate in the United States, the exact nature of this increase in terms of its size, its relations to increases in the male crime rate, its cause, and its specifics in terms of types of crime are not quite as clear. First, we will look at the crime rate itself and what the statistics suggest about increases and decreases, and then we will assess traditional explanations of overall female criminality as well as theories explaining contemporary crime patterns.

Use of Official Statistics

The vast majority of data that have been used to depict women's increasing crime rate have come from the Uniform Crime Reports (UCR) (Nettler, 1974; Simon, 1975b; Adler, 1975; Datesman and Scarpitti, 1980; Steffensmeier, 1981a), although some information has been gathered through victimization survey data (Hindelang, 1979) and self-report delinquency studies (Gold and Reimer, 1975).

A comment should be made at this point concerning the advantages and disadvantages of using these measures of criminality. The Uniform Crime Reports are one of the most frequently used tools describing and categorizing criminal activity in the United States. However, the UCR's primary focus is on crimes that are known to the police and are founded (or accepted) by the police. They do not account for unreported crimes (e.g., many rapes). The discrepancy between actual or "real" crime rates and arrest rates is still unknown (Savitz, 1982). Also, many factors outside the realm of criminal activity can affect the crime statistics, such as changes in the techniques of reporting (Seidman and Couzens, 1974); the interaction between the police and the complainant (Black, 1970); technological advances (Savitz, 1982); increases in efficiency and training (Maltz, 1975); and changes in the legal code, administration, and so on.

Crime statistics are susceptible to misuse, particularly in the areas that are suspected of being highly underreported. There are suspicions that women are grossly underestimated in arrest statistics (Pollak, 1950; Datesman and Scarpitti, 1980). Pollak (1950) contends that women commit many more crimes than are reflected in crime statistics, because women's crimes are often not reported to the police, and when they are reported, police are likely to dismiss them.

Therefore, it is also important, especially in the area of women and crime, to look at victimization survey data and, if possible, self-report delinquency data to get a clearer portrayal of women's participation in criminal activity.

Women's Crime Rate

The majority of published reports concerning the issue of women's criminal participation have used the UCR as the basis for their claims concerning an increase in the women's crime rate. It would appear appropriate, then, to take a close look at these figures.

It is generally accepted, with one notable exception (Pollak, 1950), that women commit crimes less frequently than men. In a cross-cultural analysis, Nettler (1974) concluded that in all known cultures, young men make higher contributions to the crime rate than do older persons and women. However, the "disparity between the sexes fluctuates with class of crime, with time, and with social setting" (Nettler, 1974:101). Industrial societies are beginning to see a noteworthy increase in the number of women being arrested for different types of criminal offenses. According to Simon (1981), in 1932 the ratio between males arrested and females arrested for property crimes in the United States was 1 to 19, whereas, in 1972 this ratio was 1 to 4.7, with the largest increases beginning in 1967.

The increase in the women's crime rate has been due primarily to increases in property crimes. In fact, the percentage of females arrested for violent index crimes, which include the crimes of murder, forcible rape, robbery, and aggravated assault, has remained virtually constant over the last two decades (Adler, 1975; Datesman and Scarpitti, 1980).

Arrest rates comparing males and females for 1986 and 1995 appear in Table 7-6. The largest percentage increases for women's crimes among the index offenses occurred for aggravated assault, up 104.2 percent, and motor vehicle theft, up 64.0 percent. The largest percentage increases for males were also in aggravated assault, up 45.5 percent, and motor vehicle theft, up 13.6 percent. However, these percentages are not directly comparable. Since the base figures (1986 arrest rates) for females are significantly lower than for males, this will artificially inflate the percentages for women. If we look at the actual increase in number of crimes, a different picture emerges. The most frequently committed crime for women is larceny-theft, with 351,580 arrests in 1995. While the increase in aggravated assault increased for women by 36,207 arrests, this figure increased by 102,756 arrests for men. In terms of violent crimes, women were arrested for 84,760 crimes in 1995, 39,236 more arrests

TABLE 7-6 Arrests for Index Crimes by Sex, 1986–1995

	Females				Males			
	1986	1995	% Change	Increase (n)	1986	1995	% Change	Increase (n)
Murder	1,725	1,457	−15.5	(268)	12,572	13,927	10.8	1,355
Forcible rape	268	297	10.8	29	26,016	23,809	−8.5	(2,207)
Robbery	8,800	12,068	37.1	3,268	104,871	116,741	11.3	11,870
Aggravated assault	34,731	70,938	104.2	36,207	225,720	328,476	45.5	102,756
Burglary	26,403	29,868	13.1	3,465	297,599	236,495	−20.5	(61,104)
Larceny-theft	301,636	351,580	16.6	49,944	687,289	704,565	2.5	17,276
Motor vehicle theft	11,012	18,058	64.0	7,046	104,886	119,175	13.6	14,289
Arson	1,780	2,156	21.1	376	10,918	11,413	4.5	495
Violent Crime[a]	45,524	84,760	86.2	39,236	369,179	482,953	30.8	113,774
Property Crime[b]	340,831	401,662	17.8	60,831	1,100,692	1,071,648	−2.6	(29,044)
Crime Index Total[c]	386,355	486,422	25.9	100,067	1,469,871	1,554,601	5.8	84,730

[a]Violent crimes are offenses of murder, forcible rape, robbery, and aggravated assault.
[b]Property crimes are offenses of burglary, larceny-theft, motor vehicle theft, and arson.
[c]Includes arson.

Source: U.S. Department of Justice, Federal Bureau of Investigation. 1996. *Crime in the United States: Uniform Crime Reports for the United States 1995.* Washington, DC: U.S. Government Printing Office, Table 33.

than in 1986; men were arrested for 482,953 violent crimes in 1995, 113,774 more arrests than in 1986.

Invisibility of Women in Correctional Facilities

We know that fewer women than men and fewer girls than boys are arrested, and an even smaller number are incarcerated. Therefore, little attention has been paid to the programs and facilities that house women and girls. Moreover, Chesney-Lind (1988) questions whether these numbers have been traditionally so small or if, in fact, women and girls have simply been ignored by traditional criminologists. Also, it is assumed that the justice system serves to screen out hard- and soft-core criminals so that only the hard-core women offenders end up in prisons. The likely explanation, however, since the majority of women who go to prison are poor and black, is that court chivalry may work to the benefit of white middle-class women and girls but works to the disadvantage of minorities and poor women.

Explanations of Female Crime

Women's emancipation.   One of the arguments that attempts to explain the increases in women's arrest rates has been the notion that as women become emancipated, they develop an equality with men and thereby gain access to criminal outlets that have traditionally been unavailable to them (Pollak, 1950; Simon, 1975b; Adler, 1975, 1980). The claim that the emancipation of women would have dire consequences for law and order in society is not a recent one. In 1899, Lombroso spoke about the dangers involved in educating women, thereby releasing them from the constraints of maternity and domesticity. This, he claimed, would allow for the "innocuous semi-criminal" present in all women to emerge and wreak havoc on law and order (Smart, 1976). W. I. Thomas, in *The Unadjusted Girl* (1923), stressed the immorality of the time and placed the cause of immoral behavior at the doorstep of the women's emancipation movement.

Otto Pollak (1950), in his theory concerning the masked character of female crime, was the first major theorist to claim that women were grossly underestimated in crime rates. He believed that women's low official rates were due to the underreporting of offenses committed by women, lower detection rates as compared with male offenders, and greater leniency shown to women by the justice system. Pollak contended that women were capable of maintaining their hidden criminality due to the deceitful, cunning, and manipulative capabilities that he considered inherent in all women. The woman's emancipation movement was seen by Pollak as a mechanism whereby women could expand their opportunities for crime:

> Thus, with her burden of social functions increased, it seems probable that her opportunities for crime have not just changed but increased correspondingly.

> Only against the background of this sociological consideration is it possible to accept the suggestion of the material so far available that the total volume of female crime has increased as a result of the progressing emancipation of women in our society. (Pollak, 1950:75)

Although Pollak's theory has come under much criticism, more recent writers, including Simon (1975a) and Adler (1975, 1980), put forth explanations citing women's emancipation movements as a main influence on the increase in women's criminality.

Before going into further detail on the emancipation argument, it is necessary to outline the underlying assumptions concerning women's criminality that are incorporated in these writings. Two important assumptions need to be addressed. First, it is apparent in the work of Simon (1981) and Adler (1975) that they assume that UCR figures represent real increases in female criminality. This assumption is empirically untested. Second, there is an implicit assumption that the women's movement represents an attempt to emulate masculine behavior (Smart, 1976). This is reflected in attempts to portray women as becoming more involved in "masculine" crimes. This latter argument also has little empirical support. Based for the most part on what could be termed "role theory," the main assumption accounting for women's criminality is that as women's roles change and become more highly associated with the tensions and opportunities of the male role, women will engage in more crime (Smart, 1976).

Deming claimed that "the greatest single causative factor in the increase of female criminality has been the women's liberation movement" (1977:74). He also claimed that the increasing freedoms women are winning will increase female criminality until eventually the rates of women's criminality will approximate men's. Adler (1975, 1980) is perhaps the best-known proponent of the emancipation argument. In her book *Sisters in Crime,* she uses UCR arrest statistics to portray dramatic increases in women's criminality. This is combined with personal accounts from a variety of law enforcement officers, probation officers, and other justice officials claiming an alarming new trend among woman offenders. This trend takes the form of females attempting to emulate masculine behavior. The fear, as in Lombroso's writings, is that once a woman has had an opportunity to commit the ultimate "masculine" crimes, she will never wish to return to the mundane "feminine" ones:

> Like her legitimate-based sister, the female criminal knows too much to pretend, or return to her former role as second-rate criminal confined to "feminine" crimes such as shoplifting and prostitution. She has had a taste of financial victory. In some cases, she has had a taste of blood. Her appetite, however, appears to be only whetted. (Adler, 1975:15)

Adler uses UCR data to fit the emancipation theory she advances. When confronted with the actual rates for murder and aggravated assault, which remained virtually the same for men and women, Adler's only comment was "murder and aggravated assault, *curiously*, remain the exception" (Adler, 1975: 16; emphasis our own).

Simon's (1975a, 1975b, 1981) main emphasis links women's criminality and women's increased participation in the labor force, a topic that will be dealt with in greater detail in the next section. However, it is important to mention it at this point because women's increased labor-force participation is often viewed as a result of the efforts of the women's liberation movement. There are two important claims made by Simon concerning women's criminality and women's emancipation. First, Simon (1981) claims that the women's movement has created increased opportunities for crime because more women are working outside the home. Greater opportunities to embezzle, to commit fraud, and to steal are now available. Second, she claims the women's movement has in some respects brought about its own troubles.

> Women themselves have been largely responsible for their increased notoriety. Having organized into a visible and vocal social movement, whose objectives are the attainment of greater freedom and more responsibility, they have also succeeded in drawing attention to themselves. (Simon, 1981:19)

The strengths of the emancipation argument lie perhaps more in the eloquence of its writings than on the basis of empirical findings; however, its value lies more in its direction for future work than in its quantifiability. Through the work and insight of individuals such as Adler and Simon, there has been an increased awareness of female criminality. Also, with the large volume of articles and books that have appeared, some of which were written as a direct challenge to this argument, a new set of appraisals of women's criminality has been created. The women's emancipation movement is an important issue in the discussion of female criminality; however, instead of viewing it as a phenomenon that simply causes dissatisfactions, it could be seen as an expression of existing and experienced injustices and inequalities (Smart, 1976).

Another important contribution made by the emancipation argument is that it raises the question of differentiating between male and female criminals. Earlier theorists tended to ignore female criminals entirely or simply assumed they fit the same models proposed for male criminals.

> Certainly the tendency of sociological theorists of the 1950s and 1960s to restrict their theories to males *by design* (e.g., Cohen, 1955; Cloward and Ohlin, 1960; Matza, 1964) represented a decision to focus on residual variance (after sex had been controlled—i.e., ignored) and thereby represented a missed opportunity to include in theoretical explanations a powerful predictor of involvement in illegal activity. (Hindelang, 1979:154)

Although emancipation theories differentiate male and female criminals, they are still bound up in defining female deviance in relation to patterns observed in the male normative role and its place in the social structure. "Thus a much more meaningful approach would take female deviance as an aspect of the female sex role and its relationship with social structure" (Heidensohn, 1968:170).

The main weakness of the emancipation argument is the lack of empirical evidence to support the claims that there is a dramatic increase in women's criminal activity, particularly in "masculine" crimes. Datesman and Scarpitti (1980), using both UCR and self-report data, found that women's arrest rates are increasing but not dramatically. Female percentage rates of arrests increased most for larceny and fraud and to a lesser extent for forgery, counterfeiting, and embezzlement, with counterfeiting and embezzlement representing only a small percentage of total female arrests. They found that the largest increases in female percentages of arrests were for more traditional "female" crimes such as welfare fraud as opposed to traditional male crimes. They conclude by stating that although women may be playing more active roles, "one possibility is that changes in female sex roles have not been extensive enough or in a direction that would lead to changes in female criminality" (Datesman and Scarpitti, 1980:359). Steffensmeier (1981b) comes to a similar conclusion, noting that the relative increases in arrests for larceny, fraud, and embezzlement merely represent an extension of traditional female role expectations.

> In sum, our analysis of UCR arrest statistics suggests that the new female criminal is more a social invention than an empirical reality and that the proposed relationship between the women's movement and crime is, indeed, tenuous and even vacuous. (Steffensmeier, 1981b:54)

In summary, the arguments claiming the women's emancipation movement led to increased female crime rates do not appear to be supported by the evidence. However, defining sex differentiation in the study of crime is an important component in understanding criminality in general.

Increased opportunity. Another explanation for women's increasing criminality that has arisen from the cited literature on the women's movement is that since women's labor-force participation has increased, their opportunities to engage in criminal activities have also increased. Simon is the major proponent of this argument, stating that "women's participation in selective crimes will increase as their employment opportunities expand and as their interests, desires, and definitions of self shift from a more traditional to a more liberated view" (1981:24). From this premise, Simon hypothesizes that the increases should be in certain types of property offenses, financial offenses, and white-collar offenses.

The assumptions that underlie this argument are similar to those stated in the emancipation argument. First, there is the assumption that UCR data represent real increases in female criminality. Second, again there is the assumption that "liberation" is to be assessed by participation in "masculine" crimes, although these "masculine" crimes are now those connected with increased opportunity in the labor force, such as embezzlement. The third, and perhaps most puzzling, assumption is that somehow the women's movement has succeeded in making great gains in terms of women's labor-force participation. Adler (1980) and Simon (1981) both utilize women's increased participation in the labor force as indicative of accomplished goals in the emancipation movement; however, increased female labor-force participation is not necessarily a reflection of the increasing influence of feminist movements. Since women have traditionally been defined as a "cheap" source of labor, this increase is more likely to be a consequence of economic factors. In fact, in industrial societies, increases in female labor-force participation can result in even greater relative inequality due to exploitation of women in low-wage jobs.

In her analysis of UCR data between 1932 and 1972, Simon (1981) found that the proportion of women arrested in 1972 was greater than that for each of the three preceding decades. She found that the increase was greatest for serious offenses such as property crimes, particularly larceny, embezzlement, fraud, and forgery. Simon concluded that these data supported her hypothesis that expected increases in economic and financial types of offenses reflected women's increased participation in the labor force.

The strength of Simon's argument lies in the necessary connection between women's criminality and the economic institution. Although this is a valuable insight, it should not be viewed as a singular influence. It is important in that it raises the right questions concerning women's economic position in society and the influence this could possibly have on female criminality.

The weaknesses, other than those already identified in the assumptions, again focus on the empirical manipulations of the UCR data. The category of fraud/embezzlement is a particularly interesting one in relation to this discussion. Steffensmeier et al. (1980) claim that increased employment of women in the labor force after World War II helped to alter the traditional sex-related divisions of labor, thereby giving women more responsibility in managing family finances as well as increasing the number of female heads of households. Contrary to Simon's (1981) argument depicting more women gaining access to white-collar crime opportunities, Steffensmeier claims that welfare fraud and other forms of traditional female crimes are driving the dramatic increases in the fraud/embezzlement category. Until 1964, fraud and embezzlement were categorized under one heading; however, if one looks at the male-female ratios from 1964 to 1979 for each category, Steffensmeier's claim is supported with a more dramatic female increase in fraud participation than in embezzlement.

Steffensmeier (1981a) listed five reasons he did not believe one could link labor-market opportunities with increases in women's arrest rates. First, even if there was a marked increase in the number of women working, crimes such as employee theft or occupational fraud are unlikely to be found in the UCR. Second, new occupational roles have not freed women from their traditional domestic roles. Although their paid-work opportunities may increase, the time and energy needed to work the double day leave little if any time for criminal scheming. Third, work and the additional income and benefits may actually lessen females' inclinations toward crime. Fourth, occupations vary greatly in terms of their access to criminal outlets, and women are not making large gains in the traditional male occupations. Finally, even with the few openings available to women, they are unlikely to gain access to the "old boy" network, especially those connected with organized white-collar crime and corporation crime (Steffensmeier, 1981a).

In summary, although Simon's argument is important in terms of drawing the economic institution into the analysis of women and crime, it cannot be viewed as a singular explanation for increases in women's arrest rates.

Multidimensional explanations.   Steffensmeier and Cobb (1981) conclude that there are two factors that explain the increases in female petty property crime: first, changes in the opportunities for petty thefts and fraud; and second, changes in the social control agencies and law enforcement agencies.

There are some important differences in terms of assumptions underlying their analyses. They do not assume that the UCR data necessarily reflect actual increases in female crime. They claim that the data could more likely be a result of increases in arrest probabilities of women, which indicate the increased likelihood that women will be caught and arrested, than increases in "real" female crime (Steffensmeier and Cobb, 1981). They do, however, assume the traditional emphasis placed on "masculine" crimes but extend it one step further than most by defining "masculine" crimes rather than assuming that there exists a common definition of them.

Steffensmeier's (1981b) basic premise rests on the notion that the dramatic increase in female crime is more apparent than real. It appears to be a phenomenon created rather than discovered. Although there are certainly increases in the female arrest rates, these are examined by types of offenses and explanations given for specific categories, as opposed to the umbrella explanation given by Adler. As stated earlier, Steffensmeier claimed changes in opportunities and changes in social control agencies as the two primary explanations for increases in petty property crimes. The opportunities are reflected in the greater reliance on such things as self-service marketing and increased use of credit, which open up more opportunities for crimes such as shoplifting and credit card fraud. The social control agencies include those elements in the business sector who are more willing to prosecute, are utilizing computerized records, and are investing in improved detection devices, thereby increasing the number of individuals arrested for shoplifting, credit card fraud, bad checks, and so on.

> In sum, the most crucial point, perhaps, is that trends in female criminality, as is true of male crime, appear *linked to broader economic, legal, technological* and *law enforcement changes than to specific changes in sex roles.* (Steffensmeier, 1981b:63)

The strength in Steffensmeier's argument lies in his attempt at a multidimensional approach to the study of women's arrest rates. As he states in his article with Cobb (1981), it is now necessary to go beyond the summary statistics of the UCR and to incorporate other forms of studies, such as victim surveys and self-report studies. However, more emphasis should also be placed on the interaction between the agencies of control and the female offender. Issues such as discretion and the decision to prosecute both by law enforcement agencies and the business sector should be analyzed in terms of sex differences.

There are two important weaknesses that can be seen not only in Steffensmeier's argument but in the others as well. First, these explanations of women and crime ignore the historical context of female criminality, especially in terms of understanding how the issue of women's oppression influences or is affected by changes in the image of the female offender as well as changes in the legal structure.

Second, the majority of criminologists have ignored women's own voices. Any explanation of women's participation in criminal activities should begin with listening to the accounts of women who have come into conflict with the law. If the emancipation theory is correct, one would expect the number of emancipated women in prisons to be increasing. However, many of the women in prison feel estranged from the popular women's movement and believe strongly in traditional women's roles. There has been a recent move toward recording women's accounts of their own lives. Campbell (1981, 1984) has documented the lives of young women in gangs. *Criminal Women,* by Carlin et al. (1985), is a collection of essays written by ex-offenders.

Since women have traditionally committed fewer crimes and are more likely to behave in socially conforming ways, Heidensohn argues that there are good reasons to focus on women rather than excluding, ignoring, or trivializing their lives.

> Sex is therefore a crucial variable, indeed the crucial variable in predicting criminality. You might expect, then, that students of crime, its causes, consequences, and remedies, would have used this observation frequently in their work of explaining criminality; that it provides an obvious touchstone for all theories of criminal behavior, a vital litmus test for the validity and reliability of all types of studies; that the remarkable conformity of females, as well as the sex differences, would stimulate considerable research. (1989:88)

Role of Victimization in Understanding Female Crime

The culture of violence that permeates women's everyday existence in society contributes to the patterns of behavior that can lead to female criminality. For women, previous violent experiences can both contribute to as well as result from crime (Lake, 1993, 1995). Women who enter into criminal behavior often exhibit a pattern from victim to survivor to offender (Gilfus, 1992).

The Role of Status Offenses in Female Delinquency

Males commit as many status offenses as females, yet status offenses accounted for 25.2 percent of all girls arrested in 1986 and only 8.3 percent of boys arrested (Chesney-Lind, 1989). According to Chesney-Lind, girls are more likely to be charged with running away from home, incorrigibility, or as being a person in need of supervision (PINS). When they are arrested for a status offense, girls are given harsher sentences than boys or girls who are charged with criminal activity (Conway and Bogdan, 1977; Chesney-Lind, 1986).

In her article on female delinquency, Chesney-Lind discusses this growing discrepancy between male and female status offenders and the subsequent large number of females who had been institutionalized in reformatories for status offenses. This led to the Juvenile Justice and Delinquency Prevention Act of 1974, which mandated specific actions to deinstitutionalize status offenders. As a result, the number of females in detention was dramatically reduced for a time. The total number of girls institutionalized in juvenile detention centers fell 39.4 percent between 1974 and 1979 (Chesney-Lind, 1986). However, this was not to last, and the numbers leveled off between 1979 and 1982. According to Chesney-Lind (1986), the National Council of Juvenile and Family Court Judges effectively lobbied in 1980 to reclassify a youth who violated a court order as a delinquent. The consequence of this was that running away from home once again became a delinquent act. In addition, acts that would earlier have been defined as a status offense were redefined in criminal terms. For example, taking food from one's parent's house in order to run away was now burglary (Chesney-Lind, 1986). See Table 7-7 for illustrations of differences in arrest patterns for male and female juveniles. In 1991, the top five offenses for juvenile males included larceny/theft, burglary, vandalism, non-aggravated assault, and disorderly conduct. By 1995, drug abuse offenses became the second most frequent offense for juvenile males. For females, the top five offenses in 1991 included larceny/theft, runaway, non-aggravated assault, liquor law violations, and disorderly conduct. The only change between 1991 and 1995 was the inclusion of curfew and loitering violations in female juveniles' top five offenses. Patterns of arrest for juveniles have remained fairly stable since 1977 with a couple of notable exceptions including a higher frequency of vandalism among juvenile males between 1986 and 1991 and the increase in the number of arrests for drug offense violations.

When comparing male and female arrest patterns over time, some notable patterns develop. The two status offenses of running away and curfew and loitering violations rank in the top five for juvenile females in 1995 but not for juvenile males. Females are not only more likely to be arrested for status offenses, they are also more likely to be institutionalized for nondelinquent reasons, including status offenses.

In 1991, there were 51,282 males and 6,379 females held in juvenile correctional facilities (U.S. Department of Justice, 1993). Ninety-seven percent of juvenile males were incarcerated for committing a delinquent act and 81 percent of juvenile females were incarcerated for delinquent acts. Thirteen percent of the juvenile females in the facilities were there because of a status offense, neglect or abuse, emotional disturbances, or voluntary admissions, compared with 2 percent of the males.

Supporters of this system claim a chivalrous need to protect status offenders from themselves or the "world out there." They also claim that status offenses are the stepping stones to further criminality. However, little evidence supports this claim (Datesman and Aicken, 1984). Clearly, chivalry and paternalism both play a role in defining delinquency for young females. The perceived need to protect them from the evils of the world and, as the history of juvenile justice illustrates, from their own sexuality was a basis for the juvenile institution.

History of the Sexualization of Female Crime

The Progressive movement, organized primarily by upper-class women, sought to establish the need for separate institutions for young offenders based on the concerns they had with such social evils as prostitution and white slavery (Chesney-Lind, 1989). As with their beginning work in policing, women were seen to be the legitimate champions of the moral sphere, which became the territory of the family courts. These "childsavers," as they were called, saw it as their duty to protect young girls, particularly immigrant girls, and to prevent them from straying from a proper moral path (Chesney-Lind, 1986). In the early family courts, nearly all of the girls were charged with immorality or waywardness (Chesney-Lind, 1989; Schlossman and Wallach, 1978). Females were more likely than their male counterparts to be institutionalized in the reformatories and training schools, where gynecological exams were made routinely to verify their virginity (Chesney-Lind, 1989). In the early 1900s, there was a large increase in the number of girls' reformatories to meet the needs established by the courts. These institutions focused on the perceived precocious nature of the young females' sexuality and isolated the females from all contacts with boys. The institutions were in the countryside, away from the evil influence of the cities, where the girls performed domestic chores until they were of a marriageable age (Chesney-Lind, 1989). In contemporary correctional institutions for juvenile females, treatment often focuses on adjustments to one's female role in society, and training is often geared toward traditional female occupations.

The sexualization of female delinquency has a number of consequences for the status of female delinquents. First, criminal activities are overlooked if the girl appears to be under parental control (Smith, 1979). Second, status offenses become the official charge for females who are outside the control of their sexual guardians. Third, the theories of female delinquency focus on sexuality, and criminal acts are redefined in sexual terms. Finally, the sexualiza-

TABLE 7-7 Juveniles Arrest by Sex and Offense Type, 1991–1995

Offense Charged	1991 M	1991 F	1995 M	1995 F	% Change M	% Change F
Total	1,110,455	324,934	1,292,152	431,159	16.4	32.7
Murder and nonnegligent manslaughter	2,291	110	2,063	130	−10.0	18.2
Forcible rape	3,782	67	3,334	69	−11.8	3.0
Robbery	29,889	2,900	35,025	3,598	17.2	24.1
Aggravated assault	38,513	6,888	40,771	9,588	5.9	39.2
Burglary	84,250	8,113	73,552	8,321	−12.7	2.6
Larceny-theft	212,741	85,780	214,157	102,397	0.7	19.4
Motor vehicle theft	55,792	7,110	44,771	7,691	−19.8	8.2
Arson	5,102	496	5,887	845	15.4	70.4
Violent crime[a]	74,475	9,965	81,193	13,385	9.0	34.3
Property crime[b]	357,885	101,499	338,367	119,254	−5.5	17.5
Crime index total[c]	432,360	111,464	419,560	132,639	−3.0	19.0
Other assaults	75,499	23,594	97,875	36,851	29.6	56.2
Forgery and counterfeiting	3,428	1,694	3,631	1,988	5.9	17.4
Fraud	7,325	2,704	12,607	4,316	72.1	59.6
Embezzlement	471	256	461	329	−2.1	28.5
Stolen property: buying, receiving, possessing	27,114	3,099	24,971	3,440	−7.9	11.0
Vandalism	78,757	7,141	80,556	9,505	2.3	33.1
Weapons; carrying, possessing, etc.	30,930	2,053	34,353	2,907	11.1	41.6

Offense						
Prostitution and commercialized vice	449	471	433	434	−3.6	−7.9
Sex offenses (except forcible rape and prostitution)	11,291	862	9,858	769	−12.7	−10.8
Drug abuse violation	46,663	5,743	108,620	15,847	132.8	175.9
Gambling	681	15	996	48	46.3	220.0
Offenses against family and children	1,653	867	2,543	1,534	53.8	76.9
Driving under the influence	9,028	1,432	7,306	1,359	−19.1	−5.1
Liquor laws	54,401	20,995	53,141	21,707	−2.3	3.4
Drunkenness	11,880	2,171	11,710	2,152	−1.4	−.9
Disorderly conduct	61,271	15,975	84,151	27,660	37.3	73.1
Vagrancy	1,765	253	2,311	287	30.9	13.4
All other offenses (except traffic)	163,814	43,792	205,994	59,707	25.7	36.3
Suspicion (not included in totals)	2,040	560	894	227	−56.2	−59.5
Curfew and loitering law violations	41,777	15,040	73,540	30,992	76.0	106.1
Runaways	49,898	65,313	57,535	76,688	15.3	17.4

aViolent crimes are offenses of murder, forcible rape, robbery, and aggravated assault.
bProperty crimes are offenses of burglary, larceny-theft, motor vehicle theft, and arson.
cIncludes arson.

Source: U. S. Department of Justice, Federal Bureau of Investigation. 1996. *Crime in the United States: Uniform Crime Reports for the United States 1995*. Washington, DC: U.S. Government Printing Office, Table 35.

tion of female criminality maintained the myth that delinquency was a natural act for boys who were just having a bit of fun or that it was committed by a "romantic rogue."

> For their part, academic students of delinquency were so entranced with the notion of the delinquent as a romantic rogue male challenging a rigid and unequal class structure, that they spent little time on middle-class delinquency, trivial offenders, or status offenders. Yet, it is clear that the vast bulk of delinquent behavior is of this type. (Chesney-Lind, 1989:17)

From this we see that girls are treated differently from boys in the juvenile justice system. They also contact the system in a different manner than do boys. In the past, parents were often the ones who insisted upon a girl's arrest. Even today, girls are more likely to be brought before the courts by someone other than the police. Parents are often committed to two standards of behavior, one for girls and one for boys. Gender-specific socialization has not changed dramatically over the years, particularly for girls.

Therefore, girls are treated differently, often more severely, from boys by individuals who bring them before the courts and by the courts themselves. The question remains: Are the causes of delinquency in girls the same as the causes for boys?

WOMEN'S SURVIVAL IN A CULTURE OF VIOLENCE

Although women's participation rates for criminal activities are minor compared with men's, and women are more accepted in the fields of law, policing, and corrections today, the frequency with which they are the victims of crime, especially such violent crimes as rape, marital abuse, and incest, is alarming. In this section we will outline how the forces of law reinforce and protect a misogynist cultural system.

Misogyny

We define *misogyny* simply as the hatred of women. Although this appears an extreme and bold concept to use in this circumstance, it helps to illustrate the state of siege that all women feel at one time or another. The consequence of a misogynist society is to keep women, particularly protected women, off the streets and in the homes of their protectors, behind locked doors. Even in today's enlightened world, we hear of cases in court where rapists are given light sentences or let off because the victim wore provocative clothing or went someplace inappropriate "for a lady." The outcome of this culture of violence, which is perpetuated by the legal structure and the criminal justice system, is that women live with a constant level of fear. Sometimes with newspaper accounts and information passed by word of mouth about attacks, fear can rise to debilitating levels.

Men have little comprehension of what it is like to live with this fear and often greet it with a trivializing comment such as "you worry too much" or "aren't you exaggerating a little" or a chivalrous "don't worry, I'll escort you, protect you." Trivializing the situation denotes the fear as typically irrational and unworthy of attention. Offering to protect the woman places her in a vulnerable and childlike position.

Joan Smith, in her book *Misogynies,* analyzes cases in England, including the case of the Yorkshire ripper and various rape and assault cases. She shows how even the most extreme cases, along with reactions of the police and the courts, reflect an overall cultural misogynist belief.

> The discrimination and denigration and violence that women suffer are no historical accident but linked manifestations of this hatred; I inhabit a culture which is not simply sexist but *occasionally lethal* for women. Misogyny wears many guises, reveals itself in different forms which are dictated by class, wealth, education, race, religion, and other factors, but its chief characteristic is its pervasiveness. (1989:xix)

She claims that although many cases of excessive violence were extreme behavior for individual males, their very existence and the reactions of authorities to them were influenced by the fear and loathing the male culture has toward women. In addition, the literature on characteristics of rapists shows us that many cases of rape are not carried out by men who are psychologically ill, but rather, by ordinary men carrying out what they perceive to be a normal function of their manliness (Brownmiller, 1975).

Victims of Bias-Motivated Crimes

Since the late 1980s, the issue of hate crimes has gained national attention. Referred to as bias-motivated crimes, the FBI in their Uniform Crime Reports began keeping separate statistics on these crimes. Table 7-8 identifies the incidence of bias-motivated incidents reported in 1995 by the number of incidents, number of offenses, number of victims, and whether the victim knew the offender. There were 7,947 hate crimes reported to the FBI during 1995. The 7,947 incidents involved 9,895 separate offenses, 10,469 victims, and 8,433 known offenders. The largest number of reported incidents were from California with 1,751 total reported incidents. The second highest was from New York with 845 reports. Sixty-one percent of the incidents were motivated by racial bias; 16 percent by religious bias; 13 percent by sexual-orientation bias, and 10 percent by ethnicity/national-origin bias.

Lesbians were the target of 146 reported incidents, and 131 of the victims knew the offender. An additional 18 incidents were motivated by antibisexual bias. Seventy-two percent of the reported incidents motivated by sexual-orientation bias were targeted at male homosexuals.

As illustrated in Table 7-9, crimes against persons accounted for 72 percent of hate crime offenses with intimidation being the most frequently re-

TABLE 7-8   Number of Incidents, Offenses, Victims, and Offenders by Bias Motivation, 1995

Bias Motivation	Incidents	Offenses	Victims	Known Offenders
Race	4,831	6,170	6,438	4,751
Religion	1,277	1,414	1,617	437
Sexual orientation	1,019	1,266	1,347	1,273
Ethnicity/National origin	814	1,022	1,044	958
Multiple bias	6	23	23	14
Total	7,947	9,895	10,469	8,433

Source: Adapted from U.S. Department of Justice, Federal Bureau of Investigation. 1996. Criminal Justice Information Services (CJIS) Division, Uniform Crime Reports. *Hate Crime—1995,* Table 2. http://www.fbi.gov/ucr/hatecm.htm

ported hate crime offense, accounting for 41 percent of the total. In 1995, twenty people were murdered in hate-motivated incidents.

Hate crimes are most often targeted against individuals. In 1995, 83 percent of all reported bias crime victims were individuals and 17 percent were businesses or organizations.

TABLE 7-9   Types of Hate Crimes by Number of Offenses, Victims, and Offenders in 1995

Type of Offense	Offenses	Victims	Known Offenders[a]
Crimes against persons	7,144	7,144	7,708
Murder	20	20	26
Forcible rape	12	12	12
Aggravated assault	1,268	1,268	2,045
Simple assault	1,796	1,796	2,537
Intimidation	4,048	4,048	3,088
Crimes against property	2,725	3,299	1,524
Burglary	96	131	57
Robbery	194	225	447
Larceny/theft	53	53	39
Motor vehicle theft	5	5	3
Arson	62	81	40
Destruction/damage Vandalism	2,315	2,804	938
Other[b]	26	26	39

[a]Will not add to total number of offenders in Table 7-8 because some are connected to more than one offense.
[b]Includes offenses other than those listed that are collected in the National Incident-Based Reporting System.

Source: U.S. Department of Justice, Federal Bureau of Investigation. 1996. Criminal Justice Information Services (CJIS) Division, Uniform Crime Reports. *Hate Crime—1995,* Table 3. http://www.fbi.gov/ucr/hatecm.htm

Victimization and Fear of Crime

Although criminal victimization can occur to women of any age, younger women are particularly vulnerable, especially to violent sexual crimes. In a study of forcible rape victims, 57 percent of the victims were under eighteen and 16 percent were under age twelve (Langan and Harlow, 1994). According to Langan and Harlow (1994), there were 17,000 girls under the age of twelve who were forcibly raped in 1992. In 46 percent of these cases, a family relationship was involved (Langan and Harlow, 1994). Domestic violence is also a significant factor in many women's lives.

Victimization by crimes of violence serves to instill fear in women. Estimated victimization rates from 1994 indicate that 43.1 out of every 1,000 white women were victims of a violent crime and 60.1 out of every 1,000 black women were victims of a violent crime (see Table 7-10). The victimization data on the

TABLE 7-10   Personal Victimization Rates by Type of Crime and Sex and Race of Victim, United States, 1994[a] (per thousand persons age 12 and older)

Type of Crime	Male		Female	
	White	Black	White	Black
All personal crimes	60.4	71.7	43.1	60.1
Crimes of violence	58.6	68.5	40.7	56.2
Completed violence	14.2	29.3	13.0	20.7
Attempted/threatened violence	44.4	39.2	27.6	35.4
Rape/sexual assault[b]	0.2[c]	0.5[c]	3.5	4.5
Robbery	6.5	18.4	3.2	10.3
Completed/property taken	3.3	14.8	2.0	7.7
With injury	1.2	5.6	0.9	1.7
Without injury	2.1	9.3	1.1	6.0
Attempted to take property	3.3	3.6	1.2	2.6
With injury	0.8	0.6[c]	0.4	0.8[c]
Without injury	2.5	3.0	0.8	1.9
Assault	51.8	49.5	34.0	41.3
Aggravated	14.6	20.5	7.4	13.3
With injury	3.3	7.9	2.3	3.8
Threatened with weapon	11.2	12.6	5.1	9.6
Simple	37.2	29.0	26.6	27.9
With minor injury	7.5	6.2	6.5	6.5
Without injury	29.7	22.8	20.1	21.4
Purse snatching/pocket picking	1.8	3.2	2.4	3.9
Population age 12 and over	NA	NA	NA	NA
(N)	88,009,110	11,695,970	92,535,360	13,934,130

[a]Detail may not add to total shown because of rounding.
[b]Includes verbal threats of rape and threats of sexual assault.
[c]Estimate is based on about 10 or fewer sample cases.

Source: U.S. Department of Justice, Bureau of Justice Statistics. 1996. *Sourcebook of Criminal Justice Statistics 1995.* Washington, DC: U.S. Government Printing Office, Table 3.8.

crime of rape indicates that approximately 4 women out of every 1,000 were raped. Overall, men—particularly black men—are more likely to be victims of violent crime, with the exception of rape.

The fear of crime and violence serves to control women. It defines where they can go and when. It limits their abilities to work and travel freely. It makes it difficult for them to travel alone. If tomorrow it were announced that all men would have to travel in twos or threes everywhere they go as soon as it is dark, there would be an outcry. Yet, effectively this is the culture imposed on women. In fact, men often make fun of women traveling in groups, calling out and ridiculing them for not being able to go out on their own.

The court system has served to perpetuate and at times exacerbate this process. In fact, Carol Smart (1989) argues that in processing rape cases, the courts go beyond simply reinforcing cultural values and norms surrounding women's sexuality and disqualify women and their sexuality. Through disqualification of women's sexual nature, the courts effectively disempower them.

Survival in a World of Physical and Sexual Abuse

One of the factors that clearly stands out in the research on female delinquents and women who are arrested for crimes is a likelihood of physical and sexual abuse in their backgrounds.

Of the victims of child sexual abuse, 70 percent are female. Female child abuse starts earlier and lasts longer than abuse against males, and girls are more likely to be assaulted by a family member, particularly a stepfather (Chesney-Lind, 1989). The effects of this abuse are varied but include depression, fear, anxiety, increased sexual behavior, and, not surprisingly, running away from home (Chesney-Lind, 1989).

In a study of girls in juvenile institutions in Wisconsin in 1982, 79 percent of the girls had suffered physical abuse resulting in injury; 32 percent had been sexually abused by their parents or some other individual connected with the family; and 50 percent had been sexually assaulted (Phelps et al., 1982, as reported in Chesney-Lind, 1989). McCormack, Janus, and Burgess (1986) found even higher rates of sexual abuse in a study of individuals in a runaway shelter where 73 percent of the females and 38 percent of the males had been sexually abused.

Men often define daughters and stepdaughters as their property, and societal norms require females to stay close to home where their victimizers have the greatest access to them. Even the social control agencies often work together to keep families "intact"—keeping girls at home and vulnerable (Chesney-Lind, 1989). If girls do run away from sexual or physical abuse at home, they often wind up in the streets, where survival can depend on prostitution, drugs, and other forms of abuse. They are then likely to come into contact with the law.

We see a similar pattern developing among adult women. Abused or neglected women are twice as likely as women with no such background to have an adult criminal record (Chesney-Lind, 1989). Men with abuse backgrounds are also likely to have criminal records, but often as the perpetrators of abuse. The women are more likely to be involved in property crimes or order offenses such as disorderly conduct or loitering.

DOMESTIC VIOLENCE

The largest cause of injury to women in the United States is domestic violence (National Coalition for the Homeless, 1996). More than 6 million women a year are affected by this form of violence. In 1992, 20 out of every 1,000 white females over the age of twelve were the victims of assault and 28.5 out of every 1,000 African American females over the age of twelve were victims of assault. According to the American Medical Association, in 1992, 1 in 3 women would be assaulted by a domestic partner, accounting for 4 million assaults in any given year (Smolowe, 1994).

Women commit murder at much lower rates than do men. In 1993, men accounted for 90.7 percent of all arrests for murder and women accounted for only 9.3 percent (see Table 7-6). Since 1984, the number of women arrested for homicide has decreased by 10.8 percent and, correspondingly, the number of males arrested for homicide has increased by 30 percent. Clearly, women are motivated to kill far less frequently than men, and when women do kill, they often kill a family member, generally their legal spouse, common-law spouse, or ex-spouse.

In a study on motivations for murder, Christine Rasche found that males primarily listed possessiveness, abuse, and arguments; whereas females primarily listed self-defense (Rasche, 1993). When women kill, they often kill family members, and often the victim is a man who has battered. According to a report in the *Boston Globe,* as many as 90 percent of women in jail for killing men had been battered by those men (Bass, 1992:27).

Estimates from research on women incarcerated for murder indicate that 40 to 50 percent of these women killed because of battering. According to the National Coalition Against Domestic Violence, the average sentence for men charged with murdering their women partners is two to six years; yet, the average sentence for women who kill their male partners is fifteen years.

Although killing an abusive spouse is a dramatic and final solution, alternatives for women in abusive situations can be very limited.

Domestic Violence and Homelessness[2]

The effect of domestic violence is widespread, interacting with all aspects of victims' lives including their economic livelihood, their housing, their mental and physical health, and their ability to care for their families. Many social problems that affect women are related to the problem of domestic violence.

---

[2]Information for this section was used with permission from the National Coalition for the Homeless World Wide Web Site. WWW address is http://nch.ari.net/domestic.html

As we discussed earlier, women who have been incarcerated for criminal activity have often had histories of abuse and violence. In addition, one of the leading causes of homelessness among women and children is domestic violence.

About 40 percent of the sheltered homeless population is made up of family members and the vast majority of these are headed by women (National Coalition for the Homeless, 1996). A recent Ford Foundation study found that 50 percent of the homeless women and children in the United States are fleeing abuse. Because of the vast extent of the problem and the dwindling of resources to provide safe shelters, many women who are fleeing abusive situations have nowhere to go. Many of the battered women's shelters are filled to capacity. For example, New York's domestic violence program turns away 59 percent of the women and children seeking shelter (National Coalition for the Homeless, 1996). Also, the shelters are, for the most part, set up to shelter women and children only for a few days to a few weeks on an emergency basis. Long-term housing is much harder to locate, with waiting lists for low-income and subsidized housing as long as seven months to a number of years. Studies in three urban areas have found that 33 percent of women return to their batterers, and a study in Michigan found that 60 percent of those that returned did so because of a lack of affordable housing. Therefore, we are often forcing women to choose between battering and the street. The following set of statistics gathered by the National Clearing House on Domestic Violence illustrates the widespread nature of this concern across the United States.

- 26 percent of homeless families in Seattle are homeless because of domestic violence
- 27 percent of homeless women in Minnesota left their last home in Minnesota because of abuse
- 35 percent of homeless women in New York State are survivors of domestic violence
- 25 percent of heads of homeless families in New York City are battered; 20 percent left because of battering or abuse
- 53 percent of homeless families in Denver list abuse as a primary or secondary problem; 30 percent left their last housing because of it
- 44.6 percent of the children in emergency centers in Rhode Island were with mothers who had been battered in the last six months; 25 percent of homeless women were fleeing abuse
- 31 percent of women in Chicago shelters were there because of partner abuse; 46 percent had to leave their homes at some time because of abuse
- 24 percent of the homeless population in Wyoming are homeless because of abuse (National Coalition for the Homeless, 1996:1–2)

CONCLUSION

The institution of the law reinforces the norms of patriarchal rule as it protects capitalism and reinforces class, race, and cultural biases. The history of the law as it relates to women portrays a clear pattern of protecting class interests. Women's criminality was perceived to be of little importance and was often ignored. Current criminological research includes women as subjects, but this research must take into account women's positions and oppressions. An understanding of women's lives in a culture of violence is imperative.

The intersection of the capitalist and legal systems has been comprehensively documented. The extent to which the law responds to new demands for equality, justice, and compensation and provides material resources for workers within the criminal justice system is critical. Poor and minority women have been disproportionately sanctioned for their economic oppression. Given few resources, they are poorly represented in an adversarial legal system. The definition of women as sexual property in a system of capital has complicated issues of sexual assault, parental surrogacy, and legal reproductive rights.

Under patriarchy, women lack authority in the political and the legal systems, which set the parameters of sanctions for defendants and victims alike. To recoup mental and physical health, women are dependent upon a system of men to sanction other men.

Patriarchal authority lines influence the appointment of judges, the hiring of law enforcement personnel, and the policies that set criminal investigation in sexual assault and other violence against women, including partner abuse and sexual harassment on the streets and in the workplace.

Colonized women have less access to the courts. Their status as victims is questioned by a system that has questioned their status as human beings, and yet they are governed by the same laws as privileged, property-holding whites. Exclusion from the voting process, from legal training programs, and from economically accessible representation in the courts exacerbates the economic factors that drive survival activities such as prostitution, shoplifting, and welfare fraud.

Finally, the destruction of indigenous political and normative systems has saddled colonized women and men with the dominant definitions of deviance and justice. The variations across societies in what is "fair" and reasonable compensation, who is responsible for the economic or physical degradation of others in the social group, are derived today in the United States from English common law. These laws frame the economic and sexual relations of individuals on the basis of marital status, sexual preference, and economic resources.

EIGHT

Women and Aging

Our final topic for this book focuses on the aging process and its consequences for women. We shift our concentration from the structural oppressions of the educational, economic, and legal systems to the process of aging and the discrimination experienced by elderly women. We demonstrate in this chapter that as women age, the oppressions of a lifetime become exacerbated. We demonstrate in this chapter that the oppressions felt by elderly women are not simply a product of aging but rather a result of the culmination of discrimination in the workplace, devalued education, and structural limitations. For example, the poor health and shortened life expectancy for minority women are a result not only of improper medical facilities and care throughout their lifetimes but also of hard, underpaid labor in the workforce, lack of proper insurance and retirement schemes, and the lasting effects of childbirth. Although recent reports indicate an overall rise in the standard of living for the elderly, this rise is not reflected in the lives of all elderly women.

Aging is studied within the discipline of gerontology. We will first discuss the discipline itself, outlining some of the well-known theoretical models that have been developed. We will then address five issues specific to the life quality of elderly women, including the influence of culture on body image; the impact of marriage, widowhood, and divorce; the problem of housing; the issue of sexuality; and the problems of elderly women's physical and mental health. As stated earlier, the problems experienced by elderly women are exacerbated by a lifetime of oppression in various spheres. However, it is not a simple additive model. The intersection of colonization, patriarchal oppression, and capitalism with age creates a complex network of multiple jeopardy.

There will be more than 418 million elderly, defined as individuals age 65 or older, in the world by the year 2000. In 1994, there were 357 million elderly in the world. Persons aged 65 and over represent 6 percent of the world's population, and the annual growth rate for the elderly between 1993 and 1994 was 2.8 percent compared with an annual average increase of 1.6 percent for the total world population. Every major region in the world expects increases in the proportion of the population that will be 65 or older by 2020. This is primarily due to declines in fertility rates, infant and maternal mortality, as well as declines in mortality from infectious and parasitic diseases. In 1994, thirty nations had elderly populations of at least 2 million. Mainland China had the most with 71.1 million, India was second with 36.3 million, and the United States ranked third with 33.2 million (Hobbs and Damon, 1996).

As illustrated in Table 8-1, there are significantly more older women than there are older men. For all ages, the ratio of males to females worldwide in 1994 was 105.1 to 100; and for those 65 years of age and older, this ratio drops to 75.2 males per 100 females (Hobbs and Damon, 1996). This is primarily due to the difference in life expectancies between women and men. Overall, women live longer than men. In the United States, women live on the average 6.9 years longer than men.

In 1994, there were 33.2 million elderly individuals in the United States (defined as 65 or older). This represented one-eighth of the country's total population. Of those 65 and older, 18.7 million were aged 65 to 74, 11 million were 75 to 84, and 3.5 million were 85 or older.

The fastest-growing group of the older population is the "old-old" segment. This includes individuals who are 85 years of age or older. Currently they make up 14 percent of the world's elderly, and women constitute the majority

TABLE 8-1 World Population by Age and Sex, 1994 and 2000 (population in millions)

Year and Age	Both Sexes N	%	Male N	%	Female N	%	Males per 100 Females
1994							
Under 15	1,790	3.17	917	32.3	873	31.2	105.1
15–64	3,492	61.9	1,771	62.3	1.722	61.5	102.9
65 and older	357	6.3	153	5.4	204	7.3	75.2
Total	5,640	100.0	2,841	100.0	2.798	100.0	101.5
2000							
Under 15	1,877	30.5	962	31.0	915	29.9	105.2
15–64	3,866	62.7	1,959	63.1	1,907	62.4	102.8
65 and older	418	6.8	182	5.9	236	7.7	77.1
Total	6,161	100.0	3,103	100.0	3,057	100.0	101.5

Source: U.S. Bureau of the Census. 1996. Current Population Reports, Special Studies P23-190. *65+ in the United States.* Washington, DC: U.S. Government Printing Office, Table 2-6.

TABLE 8-2   Percent Elderly by Race and Hispanic Origin,
1990 and 2050

	1990	2050
All Races	12.5	20.4
White	13.4	22.8
Black	8.2	13.6
American Indian, Eskimo, and Aleut	5.6	12.6
Asian and Pacific Islander	6.0	15.3
Hispanic origin	5.1	14.1

Source: U.S. Bureau of the Census. 1996. Current Population Reports, Special Studies, P23-190. *65+ in the United States.* Washington, DC: U.S. Government Printing Office, Figure 2-17.

of persons in this category. From 1960 to 1994, the "oldest old" in the United States increased by 274 percent, compared with a 200 percent increase of those 65 and older, and a 45 percent growth for the total population. The "old-old" population in the United States is expected to reach 7 million by the year 2020. In the United States, there were 3.5 million old-old individuals in 1994. When women reach the age of 85 or older, there are 259 women for every 100 men (Hobbs and Damon, 1996).

White elderly outnumber minority elderly; however, there is a faster growth rate among elderly minorities. As illustrated in Table 8-2, about 8.2 percent of the black population, or about 2.5 million people, are 65 years of age or older; about 5.1 percent of the Hispanic population are 65 years or older; 6 percent of Asians and Pacific Islanders are age 65 or older; and 5.6 percent of American Indians, Eskimos, and Aleuts are 65 and older.

THE DISCIPLINE OF GERONTOLOGY

Gerontology is a multidisciplinary field of study that brings together individuals from sociology, social work, medicine, psychology, psychiatry, and other related disciplines who wish to focus their work on the problems, conflicts, and interactions involved in the aging process.

Within sociology, there are a number of theories that attempt to explain the aging phenomenon.[1] The theories fall into three basic types: functionalist theories, which focus on the discontinuities in the aging process and the loss of status; theories that focus on aging individuals and their interactions with society and their environments; and critical theories, which address the structural factors that influence the elderly. Functional theories include role theory (Cottrell, 1942), activity theory (Havighurst, 1968), and disengagement theory

[1]For a more comprehensive review of gerontology theories, see Kart, C. S. 1990. *The Realities of Aging,* 3rd ed. Boston: Allyn & Bacon.

(Cumming and Henry, 1961). Theories that focus on the individual and society include socioenvironmental theory (Gubrium, 1973, 1975) and exchange theory (Dowd, 1984). Critical theories include age stratification (Riley, 1971, 1977; Riley, Johnson, and Foner, 1972; Foner, 1975) and the political economy of aging (Estes, Swan, and Gerard, 1984; Phillipson, 1982).

Functionalist Theories

Role theory. The key components of role theory as applied to the field of gerontology are role loss and the adjustment or maladjustment to new old-age roles. Roles change as individuals proceed through the life cycle; and role theory identifies the consequences of these changes for older people (Cottrell, 1942). These changes can often be quite dramatic. Extensive research has been conducted on the role changes that occur following retirement when independent work roles are replaced with dependent forms of social relationships (Cavan et al., 1949).

One premise of role theory is that women adjust more easily to old-age roles because they have a smoother transition into dependent roles in general. Research on sex roles finds that feminine traits are often very similar to old-age traits—dependency, childlike behavior, domesticity, and nurturing. It is not surprising that researchers find that traditional females and males who are able to adapt to feminine traits adjust better to old age (Reichard, Livson, and Peterson, 1962). In fact, Monge (1975) concludes that as women and men grow older, they become more androgynous.

There are many criticisms of role theory. In brief, role theory tends to perpetuate dominant cultural values and portrays an oversocialized picture of women in society (Beeson, 1975). Retirement is the most widely researched topic within this theoretical framework simply because retirement is seen to cause the most conflict for men (Russell, 1987).

Activity theory. Activity theory is also referred to as the *implicit theory of aging* (Kart, 1990; Kart et al., 1988). This theory posits that there is a positive relationship between social and physical activity and life satisfaction. According to Havighurst (1968), even though the social world may attempt to withdraw from the aging person, the elder who is most able to stay active, thereby resisting the pressure to withdraw, is the one who will have the highest life satisfaction.

Interestingly, Longino and Kart (1982) found that informal activity did have a tendency to increase life satisfaction; however, formal activity such as planned recreational activities had a tendency to decrease life satisfaction. Not only is the type of activity important but also the extent to which the individual chooses or controls the activity. A formal dance or card game that all residents of a home or project are expected to attend is less likely to increase the quality of life for an elderly individual than is a quality conversation around the kitchen table with an old friend.

The primary criticism of activity theory is that it assumes that individuals have some element of control over their social world. It ignores issues of gender, poverty, or racial discrimination. Some individuals or groups have more power than others to control their own activities. In addition, activity alone will not replace certain losses. There is also a discernable difference between quality and quantity of activity. Repetitive domestic tasks may have a different influence on life satisfaction than paid labor in the workforce, which can noticeably increase life satisfaction.

Disengagement theory. Disengagement theory is one of the most prominent in the gerontological literature. Introduced by Cumming and Henry (1961), it purports that decreasing social interaction is expected of aging individuals and that there is a mutual withdrawal between elderly and nonelderly persons within the social system. Aging persons supposedly accept this disengagement from society. This is a traditional functionalist approach to the issues of aging. Disengagement is seen as both inevitable and universal, and it functions to maintain social stability by avoiding the disruption of sudden withdrawal of members from the social system (Cumming, 1963). It also provides for the recycling of work and social resources to the young.

There has been much criticism of disengagement theory and researchers have found little or no support for its propositions (Youmans, 1967; Palmore, 1968). Hochschild (1975) outlines three problems with the theory: First, it allows for no possibility of dispute because Cumming and Henry (1961) posit ad hoc explanations for all individuals who do not quite fit the theoretical propositions; second, the major variables of age and disengagement are too broad, making operationalization of the theory extremely difficult; and third, the theory denies an individual's own view of the aging process and his or her own perception of social disengagement.

Socioenvironmental Theory

Jaber Gubrium (1973, 1975) focused on the influence of the older person's social and physical environment on their social activities, interaction patterns, and life satisfaction. Specifically, he developed a model addressing age-homogeneous and age-heterogeneous environments and their connections with social interaction. This theory focused on individuals and their interactions with neighbors and family. The perceptions and meanings that the elderly person places on her or his daily life is an important component in this theoretical model.

It was hypothesized that an age-homogeneous social environment will generate the highest amount of quality interaction. This theory recognizes the importance of the social context in defining and generating normative behavior patterns. However, it does not address the fact that different individuals with varying resources have different amounts of control over their environment. In addition, what part does the relationship between age and sex play in defining quality interaction? Since the majority of individuals in age-homogeneous communities are also women, how does this influence the interaction? Perhaps gender-homogeneity itself influences the patterns of interaction.

Exchange theory. Exchange theory is a popular sociological theory explaining the interaction between individuals within a social group or between individuals and a social group. The focus is on individuals as they interact and attempt to maintain a balance as they exchange rewards, punishments, and friendship. The *norm of reciprocity* refers to how people will help those who have helped them (Gouldner, 1960). Older people receive support from friends, family, and neighbors (Sussman, 1976; Shanas, 1979), and they also provide support to others (Riley and Foner, 1968; Sussman, 1976).

However, the exchange between various age groups is not always considered a balanced exchange. Dowd (1984) claims that while the norm of reciprocity holds for the young-old, with the old-old, this norm is replaced by *beneficence,* a state where every person will receive as much as is needed, regardless of that person's ability to reciprocate.

Homans (1958, 1974) argues that social exchange activities are governed by *distributive justice.* This means that if the exchange becomes unbalanced and someone is giving more than she or he gets or is getting more than she or he gives, that person will become offended or dissatisfied and may withdraw from the exchange.

For elderly women, exchange is often negotiated in terms of volunteerism or other forms of unpaid labor. A large number of elderly women provide unpaid child care and domestic labor for their children and grandchildren. In fact, a woman's fulfillment in old age is often depicted as involving perpetual domestic chores, baby-sitting, housework, and other mundane tasks (Delamont, 1980). These are often in exchange for maintaining ties with a loving family.

Dowd (1975, 1978, 1980) addresses the more general question of the social exchange between the aged and society. For elderly persons in industrial nations, their social power decreases. They are expected to become economically and socially dependent and to comply with the social-structural constraints that have been placed upon them. Retirement exemplifies this process in that a worker who at one point was exchanging skills and labor hours for wages must now comply with retirement in order to receive health care benefits, pensions, and Social Security.

Critical Theories

Age stratification. Social stratification analyzes the strata, typically based on class, that divide individuals and groups within some social order. These strata have differential access to rewards, resources, and power. In the discipline of gerontology, age stratification depicts strata in society that are created on the basis of one's age. Different resources, rights, and privileges are accorded to members of the society based on age. Matilda White Riley (1971, 1977) argues that the concepts of age strata and aging are analogous to the social stratification concepts of social class and social mobility.

Political economy of aging.   Within this conflict perspective, the aging phenomenon is viewed in terms of social-structural aspects rather than as an individual concern. Estes, Swan, and Gerard (1984) argue that differential treatment and discrimination against elderly people reflects the distribution of power, income, and property in the overall social structure. Capitalism plays a key role in defining a social structure in which elderly individuals are dehumanized and become consumers of products such as health and nursing care for which they have few lifelong resources. The needs of elderly people by definition become a low priority in a system based on capitalism and the search for profit (Phillipson, 1982). Analyzing the health care system in America, Navarro (1984) concludes that the poverty of today's elderly people is a function of the capitalist system's ability to control the political, economic, and social institutions.

There is a significant relationship among class, gender, and age. As Parker concluded, "those who are privileged socioeconomically are also privileged physically and psychologically when they retire" (1982:114). Individuals who have economic resources are better able to mitigate the problems of aging, both individual problems such as health and social problems such as loss of status, than are aging individuals with limited resources. Generally, elderly women and minorities lack these scarce resources. Markson's (1983) survey identified three groups among elderly people: the "enjoyers," the "survivors," and the "casualties." The enjoyers were healthy and financially secure and lived with a spouse; the survivors were coping with the lack of one or two of the above factors; and the casualties lacked good health, financial security, and a spouse to care for them. The significance of this research was that the enjoyers were mostly men and the casualties were mostly women.

ISSUES SPECIFIC TO ELDERLY WOMEN

We next address five issues that clearly influence the quality of life of elderly women. These issues include the culture of youth and its influence on elderly women and body image; marriage, widowhood, and divorce and their influence on the lifestyles of elderly women; the problems of housing in contemporary society; sexuality; and physical and mental health care.

Culture and Body Image

The image of older women has often been negative and at times personified as evil as in the case of witches. Historically, witches were primarily women and most were old widows. There was a belief that women following menopause were likely to become witches. Therefore, old women, particularly the poor and ugly, were suspect. In contemporary terms, the image of the witch at Halloween still embodies an image of an ugly old woman (Grambs, 1989). The concept of *hag* exemplifies a contemporary view of old women. Although the concept hag derives from Greek, meaning "holy one," in today's Webster's dictionary it is defined as "an old, ugly woman; a witch."

In American culture, a double standard of aging exists (Sontag, 1972): Aging often improves men's resources and life chances and decreases women's. Also, our social impressions of old age are different for men and for women. Women are perceived as "old" fifteen to twenty years earlier than men (Bell, 1976). Women are defined as sexually and socially desirable in terms of their physical attractiveness. Men's desirability is defined in terms of intelligence, charm, success, and financial resources (Russell, 1987).

Age therefore increases men's power and appeal because they are being valued on criteria that are independent of biology. Women, with such a strong societal emphasis on physical appearances, find they have few resources with which to fight the aging battle other than plastic surgery or expensive and unproven creams and lotions. Overall, individuals in society value youth and define physical attractiveness in terms of youth, and this becomes a powerful oppressor for women at all ages (Russell, 1987).

Marriage, Widowhood, and Divorce

Women do, on the average, outlive men. Women not only have longer life expectancies at birth, they also have lower death rates throughout the life cycle. As a result, as the population ages, the percentage of women within each age category increases (Garner and Mercer, 1989). The average life expectancy for a white female in 1991 was 79.6 years compared with 72.9 years for a white male. The average life expectancy for a black female was 73.8 years and for a black male, 64.6 years (Hobbs and Damon, 1996). Overall, by the year 2050, women can expect to live about 81 years and men can expect to live 71.8 years (Garner and Mercer, 1989).

These differences in mortality rates and life expectancies help to explain why aging is primarily a social issue affecting elderly women. The majority of elderly, widowed, old-old, institutionalized, or older homeless people are women. Helena Lopata's research on widowhood (1987a, 1987b, 1979) addresses the difficulties and adjustments made by widows throughout the world. She focuses on resources and support systems available to women after their husbands have died. Her work focuses on three factors that affect all women's support networks: (1) the society in which she lived; (2) the community in which she lived, and (3) her personal resources (Lopata, 1987a). She defines a support as "any object or action that the giver and/or receiver define as necessary or helpful in maintaining a style of life" (Lopata, 1987a:4). In maintaining the support networks of widows in the Middle East, Asia, and the Pacific, she found that

> A main difference in what happens to a woman when her husband dies appears to be whether she herself must reorganize her support systems and lifestyles, as is typical for modern women in urban, more developed centers, or whether her social integration is provided by others. In many societies undergoing major transitions, a gap develops between how a woman was socialized and how she now must live. (Lopata, 1987:22)

Widowhood particularly affects women because (1) women live longer than men, (2) women generally marry men who are older than themselves, (3) older men are more likely than older women to remarry, and (4) strong social norms exist against older women marrying younger men as well as norms against older women remarrying (Garner and Mercer, 1989). In a survey of marital status in countries that maintain data, the median rate of widowhood for women 80 years or older was 75 percent. This compares with 39 percent for men 80 years or older (Torrey et al., 1987). Given these figures it is not surprising to find that elderly women often end up as caretakers for elderly men.

In addition to the difficulties of widowhood, there are more separated and divorced older women than older men. Divorced persons represented only about 4 percent of older people in 1986; however, 4 percent of elderly people constitutes 1.1 million people, and this number is increasing rapidly (Garner and Mercer, 1989).

Housing

In 1995, 32 percent of persons 65 and over lived alone. In 1993, in the United States, 41 percent of women over the age of 65 lived alone. For men in this same age category, only 15.5 percent lived alone. The same figures hold true in Great Britain where 80 percent of the elderly who live alone are women. This is clearly related to cultural and social factors since in Japan, 75 percent of the elderly live with relatives. Research that compared the health status of women who live alone with the health status of those living with someone (such as husbands, other relatives, or friends) demonstrated that elderly women living with persons other than their husbands are most likely to be in poor health. However, poor health was not a consequence of living arrangements; rather, those who were in need of extra assistance due to health difficulties were more likely to live with others (Magaziner et al., 1988).

As illustrated in Table 8-3, it is clear that elderly women are more likely to live alone than elderly men. This trend has been increasing over the past decade especially for women 75 years of age and older. In 1993, 51 percent of women (compared with 18.3 percent of men) 75 to 84 years of age were living alone. Among those 85 years of age and older, 57 percent of women and 29 percent of men were living alone. The Census Bureau projects that women will maintain 77 percent of the households run by persons 75 years and over in the year 2000 (Day, 1996).

Today's women, aged 65 to 74, who are living alone are in relatively good health and better able to afford living alone than has been true in the past (Hobbs and Damon, 1996). However, other factors beyond economics and health influence an older person's choice to live alone. Some of these factors include a desire for independence, intergenerational family ties, interaction with friends, and kinship networks. In an analysis of racial differences and living arrangements, family-related factors were "the most important factors in the living arrangement decision of widowed elderly women of color" (Choi, 1991:496).

Living alone is a common experience for elderly women. So too are the problems that individuals face when they live alone. Fear of crime, difficulty getting repairs done, and the danger of home accidents are everyday experiences for many elderly women. Elderly women have a higher fear of crime than women and men of all other age categories even given their relatively lower victimization rates (Ollenburger, 1981).

One of every three nursing home residents is a woman 85 years of age or older. As would be expected, the likelihood of living in a nursing home increases with age. The size of the elderly nursing home population increased by 29 percent between 1980 and 1990. In 1990, 1.6 million people aged 65 or older were housed in nursing homes. These institutionalized elderly are primarily old-old, female, and widowed or never married. However, only 5.2 percent of the elderly in the United States are residents in a nursing home (Hobbs and Damon, 1996). Throughout the world, the elderly who require additional care are more likely to be cared for by family members—usually adult daughters or daughters-in-law.

Sexuality

One of the popular misconceptions about elderly women is that they are not sexually active. This is related to the emphasis on youth and youth culture, where beauty is defined by youth and physical attractiveness. Elderly women by definition are seen as unattractive and not sexually desirable. Goodwin and Scott (1987) listed the following five myths about women, sex, and aging:

1. Older people are no longer interested in sex and sexuality and no longer engage in sexual activity. Sex is for the young.
2. Changes in hormone levels which occur during and after menopause create a "deficiency disease" that causes women to find sex uncomfortable and unpleasant.
3. Women who are beyond childbearing years lose their desire and their desirability.
4. In order to have a full and complete sex life, a woman must have a male partner.
5. The only truly satisfying and acceptable sex is through intercourse, culminating in mutual orgasm. All other sexual activity is "foreplay" and doesn't count. (1987:80–81)

TABLE 8-3 Living Arrangements of the Elderly, 1980 and 1993

	1980 Percent Distribution			1993 Percent Distribution		
	Total	Men	Women	Total	Men	Women
65 Years and Older						
Living alone	29.3	14.6	39.4	30.3	15.5	40.8
w/Spouse	52.9	75.2	37.4	54.7	74.6	40.6
w/Other relatives	16.1	8.4	21.4	12.8	7.1	16.8
w/Nonrelatives	1.7	1.7	1.7	2.2	2.8	1.8
Total	100.0	100.0	100.0	100.0	100.0	100.0
	n = 24,157[a]	n = 9,889	n = 14,268	n = 30,870	n = 12,832	n = 18,038
65 to 74 Years						
Living alone	24.5	12.0	34.0	23.6	12.9	32.0
w/Spouse	61.7	79.8	47.8	63.6	77.8	52.3
w/Other relatives	12.4	6.6	16.7	10.8	6.5	14.2
w/Nonrelatives	1.5	1.6	1.4	2.1	2.8	1.5
Total	100.0	100.0	100.0	100.0	100.0	100.0
	n = 15,302	n = 6,621	n = 8,681	n = 18,362	n = 8,114	n = 10,249

75 to 84 Years

Living alone	37.1	18.6	48.4	38.1	18.3	51.0
w/Spouse	41.5	69.5	24.5	46.4	72.0	29.7
w/Other relatives	19.4	10.0	25.2	13.3	6.8	17.6
w/Nonrelatives	1.9	1.8	1.9	2.2	2.9	1.8
Total	100.0	100.0	100.0	100.0	100.0	100.0
	$n = 7,172$	$n = 2,708$	$n = 4,464$	$n = 9,918$	$n = 3,925$	$n = 5,992$

85 Years and Older

Living alone	38.8	25.9	45.2	48.3	28.8	57.0
w/Spouse	21.9	48.9	8.4	23.5	53.8	10.1
w/Other relatives	36.1	22.3	43.0	24.9	14.8	29.4
w/Nonrelatives	3.2	2.9	3.4	3.3	2.7	3.6
Total	100.0	100.0	100.0	100.0	100.0	100.0
	$n = 1,683$	$n = 560$	$n = 1,123$	$n = 2,590$	$n = 792$	$n = 1,798$

Note: Numbers in thousands. Civilian noninstitutional population.

Source: U.S. Bureau of the Census. 1996. Current Population Reports, P23-190. 65+ in the United States. Washington, DC: U.S. Government Printing office, Table 6-3.

Research conducted independently by the Kinsey Institute and the well-known team of Masters and Johnson found that individuals engage in sexual relationships at all stages of their life cycle, and these sexual patterns change very little in old age (D'Emilio and Freedman, 1988). Menopause does not create a "deficiency disease"; in fact, menopause is a normal part of growing older for women and has virtually no influence on a woman's sexuality. Although menopause will end the fertility years for a woman, fertility and sexuality are not linked biologically. Many women may feel more sexual following menopause given that the fear of pregnancy will no longer be an issue (Doress and Siegal, 1987). It is a heterosexist assumption that elderly women will become asexual due to the lack of available men.

Physical and Mental Health

According to Fowles (1987), in 1986 older people made up 31 percent of all hospital stays and they average more visits to a physician compared with younger groups.

Elderly women, compared with elderly men, have higher rates of morbidity (Russell, 1987), even though they have lower mortality rates. Women of all ages are more likely than men to be hospitalized, undergo surgery, consume more drugs, and become institutionalized (Marieskind, 1980).

Older men tend to stay longer in the hospital once they are hospitalized; older women are more likely to require nursing home care or home-care services (Lewis, 1985)—often because elderly women do not have spouses to provide those home-care services. When elderly men become ill, they often have a spouse in the home who can care for them. In fact, Oliver (1983) found that the presence of a wife in the home meant that men were likely to be discharged earlier from the hospital and were less likely to receive home visits by aides or nurses because it was assumed that the wife would become the home-care provider. Eighty-two percent of disabled elderly people live at home and are taken care of by the unpaid labor of female relatives (Russell, 1987). This is one explanation for the high cost of medical care for elderly women. When elderly women become ill or in need of care (either hospital or home-health services), there is often no one to provide these services although this same woman may have provided the same services for her partner or her parents and received no compensation for her labor.

Elderly women spend one-third of their median income on medical expenses (Garner and Mercer, 1989). The cost of medical care is one of the most common reasons that older persons do not seek health care when they need it (Harris and Associates, 1981). Pat Keith (1987) found in her study of unmarried older women that the primary reason that women postponed seeking health care services was because of distress over finances. Health care expenses for elderly people are extremely high and are rising at surprising rates.

On a per capita basis, [yearly medical expenses] amounted to $4,200 per elderly person in 1984. Medicare paid just under half of this amount ($2,050); Medicaid contributed 13 percent ($540); the elderly paid one-fourth of the total through out-of-pocket expenditures ($1,060); and the remaining $550 was absorbed by other public and private programs. Obviously, these sums represent large portions both of the incomes of many elderly persons and the budgets of federal and state governments. On average, elderly persons devoted 15 percent of their incomes to health care expenses in 1984, up from 12 percent in 1977. (Rix, 1984:191–92)

Poverty is a serious problem for elderly women and the rising costs of health care contribute to this significantly. Women are often required to "spend-down" their life savings in order to qualify for Medicaid to help meet the costs of their or a spouse's illness. This can force elderly middle-class families into poverty (Sidel, 1986). Recent changes in the Medicaid system allow non-ill spouses to keep a larger percentage of their assets after their spouse is placed in a nursing home; however, elderly persons who live alone and become ill must still liquidate virtually all their assets to qualify for Medicaid. Since the majority of the elderly who live alone are women, this adversely affects the economic status of many elderly women.

Black elderly people have higher levels of chronic diseases, functional impairment, and hypertension and, overall, are more likely to be sick, disabled, or simply in poor health (Garner and Mercer, 1989). Blacks over the age of 75 have significantly higher rates of poverty and poor health as compared with whites (Agree, 1987). Black women have higher rates of hypertension, obesity, heart disease, diabetes, nutritional deficiencies, ulcers, gastritis, and cirrhosis of the liver as compared with white women (Garner and Mercer, 1989). Blacks have less access to quality health care, especially rural blacks whose conditions are exacerbated by extreme poverty, bad water, and poor sanitation (Marieskind, 1980).

Among the Hispanic, elderly people do not use formal long-term health-care services, although Agree (1987) found that 85 percent of the 65-or-older age group reported at least one chronic condition. Hispanic elderly suffer from high incidence of arthritis, hypertension, cardiovascular conditions, obesity, and anemia (Garner and Mercer, 1989). The interrelationship between poverty and health is particularly acute for the large group of Hispanic women who work as migrant workers. This often puts them in contact with potentially harmful pesticides, further damaging their health (Marieskind, 1980).

Loneliness and depression are also more common among elderly people, particularly among widows (Evers, 1983). Szinovacz (1983) claims that widows particularly become lonely and depressed because they have been socialized into a dependence upon their husbands, coupled with the normative cultural values that discourage women, particularly elderly women, from going out in public places unaccompanied. Once the husband has died, the widow may lead a very restricted social life. Lopata (1973) argues that this dependence on the husband can also result in ignorance about financial matters and a deficiency in basic decision-making capabilities.

It was believed that aging and mental health were clearly related, with elderly individuals suffering greater mental health difficulties than other age groups. However, contemporary research indicates that age is not the key variable in assessing the likelihood of suffering from a mental illness (Beck and Pearson, 1989). The variables most likely to be related to mental illness among older persons include low income, widowhood, and social isolation (Beck and Pearson, 1989). Because of the influence of these variables, it is not surprising to find that elderly women suffer higher rates of mental illness than elderly men given that they are more likely to be living in or near poverty, are more likely to be a widow, and are more likely than men to experience a state of social isolation. However, elderly persons are not likely to use mental health services and, in fact, are likely to underutilize the mental health services available to them. Only a small proportion of all mental health services are provided to elderly women as they have few economic resources to purchase these services.

THE INTERSECTION OF RACE, CLASS, AGE, AND SEX

Although some issues may affect all elderly people, clearly they do not affect them all to the same degree. One's race, class, or sex may temper the impact of a severe illness or may be the determining factor in whether or not home care is to be provided after hospitalization. In this section, we raise three issues that point out this intersection of race, class, age, and sex. First, we will look at the multiple jeopardy that minority elderly women face in their day-to-day activities. Second, we will address the specific economic circumstances of growing older in the United States, including the issues of poverty among elderly people, employment, and retirement, as well as pensions and Social Security. Third, we will look closely at the issue of caregiving and the mother-daughter conundrum of caretaking.

Minority Elderly People

Multiple jeopardy. As we mentioned in the theory section, we can use a multiple-hierarchy stratification model to characterize the quality of life and the differences in life chances between ethnic minority elderly persons and nonminority elderly persons. The double jeopardy hypothesis claims that the discrimination, prejudices, stereotypes, and disadvantages that minorities share become greater in old age as compared with middle age or youth (Dowd and Bengtson, 1978). A multiple jeopardy will occur when the elderly person is female, lesbian, or living in poverty in combination with her minority status.

> Since ethnic minority status, female gender, old age, and low social class are at the lower end of the system, the bottom of the hierarchy is occupied by poor, el-

derly women of ethnic minority backgrounds, while the top is occupied by middle- or upper-class, middle-aged (or younger) White Anglo-Saxon males. Other combinations fall somewhere in the middle. (Markides and Mindel, 1987:31)

The demographics for elderly minorities demonstrate that the elderly minorities are growing at a rate in the United States faster than elderly whites. It is projected that by the year 2050, 19.7 percent of the older population will be minorities (Gould, 1989). Because of the multiple jeopardies experienced by these individuals, their quality of life in old age will reflect and intensify in the types of inequality and discrimination that they faced throughout their lives (Gould, 1989).

Older minority women are some of the poorest individuals in American society (Gould, 1989). In 1985, 80 percent lived with incomes below $2,000 per year (Lowry, 1985). Black women make up a large proportion of individuals who are living in poverty or near-poverty (Minkler and Stone, 1985). Their primary source of income is Social Security, with very few (in 1984 less than 5 percent) receiving income from private pensions (Gould, 1989). This is in spite of the fact that many elderly black women are employed; however, the type of employment available to elderly black women is often low-paying, domestic employment primarily as private household workers and service workers (Gould, 1989).

Aging Lesbians

Those women over 65 who compose the elderly lesbian population may number over 834,000 (Adelman, 1980), but the older members of the lesbian community are for the most part hidden from us. Lesbians in their forties and fifties have few role models. Younger lesbians

> do not know if lesbians over sixty-five have found creative and unusual living arrangements; what they do for recreation; whether lesbians of color over sixty-five have needs and concerns not shared by white lesbians their age; whether older lesbians would like more interaction with younger lesbians or what kind of support from a younger community of women would be helpful to them. (Poor, 1982:166).

Poor (1982) reviews some of the literature by and about older lesbians but notes that much of it is fragmented or unknown to the larger lesbian community.

An older lesbian woman experiences a triple jeopardy—as a woman, as an older person, and as a lesbian. However, this triple jeopardy may be interpreted differently depending upon generational experiences. Marcy Adelman's (1980) interviews with older lesbians indicated that many were integrated into mainstream culture and would not want to use services that were designed for lesbians. This may have been due to the lack of women-identified social services during most of the years of these women's lives so that they believe their only choice is to hide their identity and integrate into the dominant culture. This makes things particularly difficult for those who are coming out in their later years and need the same support systems claimed by younger lesbians: social, medical, and legal programs that meet their special needs.

Doress, Siegal, and the Midlife and Older Women Book Project (1987) report that they were unsuccessful in contacting many of the oldest lesbians in writing their landmark resource book, *Ourselves, Growing Older.* The authors attribute this to isolation and to fear from repressive circumstances. Poor (1982) describes the efforts of a number of groups aged forty-five and over that have organized support groups for older lesbians.

Economics and Elderly People

Poverty.   Elderly women, particularly minority elderly women, single elderly women, and widowed elderly women are more likely than other age categories or elderly men to live in poverty or in near-poverty (Russell, 1987; Gould, 1989). Some recent research has illustrated that poverty today is not as severe for elderly persons as it was in the 1950s due to growth in Social Security benefits and pensions (Ross, Danziger, and Smolensky, 1987). In general, elderly people today have more assets than nonelderly people. Although 35 percent of adults 65 and older were poor in 1959, by 1992 the proportion dropped to 18 percent (Hobbs and Damon, 1996). However, these increases have primarily benefitted elderly men and nonminority elderly people. The poverty rates fell at a much slower rate for women than for men, and they are still substantially high for women in the old-old age category (Holden, 1988). In addition, the largest number of elderly women who are living in poverty are living alone (Holden, 1988). Clearly, lack of adequate income is the number one concern amongst today's elderly people (Estes, Gerard, and Clarke, 1976).

As indicated in Table 8-4, poverty rates in 1992 were 33 percent for elderly African Americans and 22 percent for elderly Hispanics. Older black women and older Hispanic women have the highest rates of poverty, with 42.8 percent of black women 75 and older living in poverty and 32 percent of Hispanic women 75 and older living in poverty. Of all women 65 years of age or older, 15.7 percent are living below the poverty line. Although women make up 58.4 percent of the entire elderly population, they account for 71.3 percent of the poor elderly population (Hobbs and Damon, 1996).

Widows are particularly vulnerable to poverty, especially those who are recently widowed. Many factors contribute to this condition, including a lack of adequate survivor pension benefits, reductions in Social Security benefits, and the loss of a spouse's earnings (Shaw, 1983). In addition, there has been an assumption in research and by social policy workers that older, widowed women have more economic problems because they are poor money managers (Hyman, 1983). However, other research has shown that, first, widowed women

TABLE 8-4   Incidence of Poverty Among Persons Aged 65 and Older by Sex and Race, 1992

	Persons with Income Below the Poverty Line (%)
All groups (total)	12.9
Male	8.9
Female	15.7
Whites (total)	10.9
Males 65–74	6.5
Males 75+	8.1
Females 65–74	10.3
Females 75+	17.8
Blacks (total)	33.3
Males 65–74	23.3
Males 75+	34.8
Females 65–74	34.5
Females 75+	42.8
Hispanics (total)	22.0
Males 65–74	16.7
Males 75+	18.8
Females 65–74	21.6
Females 75+	32.0

Source: U.S. Bureau of the Census. 1996. Current Population Reports, Special Studies, P23-190. *65+ in the United States.* Washington, DC: U.S. Government Printing Office, Table 4-5 and Figure 4-9.

are not as inexperienced with money as had been suggested and, second, the likelihood of being poor had little to do with money management skills (Morgan, 1986).

Employment and retirement.   It has long been assumed that men retire and women simply continue being housewives. The premise of disengagement theory is that women have a smoother transition into old age because they do not have to experience the dramatic shift from the workplace into an environment lacking in social responsibility and linked with social isolation. "Retirement is not an important problem for women because . . . working seems to make little difference to them. It is as though they add work to their lives the way they would add a club membership" (Cumming and Henry, 1961:144). These assumptions ignore the obvious intersections among race, class, and sex. The opportunity to maintain women as unpaid labor in the household has always been a privilege for the white middle and upper classes. Therefore, the assumptions being made about the lack of adjustment problems for women in old age are assumptions about one group of women. Even amongst this group, the assumption that they are willing to carry on the domestic unpaid labor into old age has not been validated.

Minority women, on the other hand, often work throughout their lives and into old age, not because they necessarily choose this life course, but because they must survive economically. They are often employed in service and domestic labor positions that offer little in terms of retirement benefits, and therefore they must literally work until they no longer can or they die. Of all black women who are employed as private household workers, 41 percent are 65 years of age or older (Gould, 1989).

While retirement is seen as the major life transition for men, widowhood is seen as the major life transition for women (Russell, 1987), and research in the fields of retirement and elderly labor-force participation reflect this bias. However, employed women actually do have difficulty with retirement—they have more retirement problems than men and often take longer to adjust than men (Szinovacz, 1982). Research has found that most men find retirement to be a satisfactory experience (Sheppard, 1976). Of course, class plays an important role in whether or not any individual will find retirement difficult. Those who have economic resources are more likely to find retirement less difficult and are also likely to experience fewer physical and psychological problems in old age (Parker, 1982). This is due to class privilege, which allows individuals with economic resources to have lifelong access to health care services as well as to live overall healthier lives with proper nutrition, less economic stress, and access to preventative and early treatment services. In addition, because of the high number of women who work part-time and their accumulated lower wages, they are less likely than men to have adequate retirement benefits and pensions.

Caregiving and Elderly Women

As mentioned earlier, disabled and frail elderly men are more likely than elderly females to have a spouse to care for them. Since most males are older than their spouses, they are more likely to receive care from these spouses. The wife is often left either to live alone when she is elderly or to be institutionalized when living alone is no longer a possibility. The other alternative often available to her is to live with or be taken care of by her children. The caregiver is most often a daughter or a daughter-in-law. It is an expectation in this society that adult female children will take care of aging widows (Russell, 1987).

In the United States, daughters and daughters-in-law will spend more of their adult lives caring for elderly parents than caring for dependent children. The average woman caregiver will spend eighteen years caring for an aging parent and seventeen years caring for a dependent child (U.S. House Select Committee on Aging, 1987). Women provide 72 percent of the caregiving for elderly parents and they are on the average 57 years old, live in the same household with the aging parent, are in poor or frail health, and live in poverty or near poverty (Grambs, 1989).

There exists a "grandmother" stereotype that depicts an elderly woman surrounded by her loving family. However, if we look closely at this picture, we see that this grandmother is often pictured doing things for other people, such as washing dishes, cooking meals, baby-sitting, reading stories to children, or sweeping. Elderly women are often expected to provide unpaid labor to their children's families on a regular basis (Delamont, 1980). This grandmothering role is, in fact, simply an extension of the mothering role, where unpaid labor is assumed and is expected to be carried out with a minimum of complaints. After all, the reward is love and compassion rather than economic resources. Approximately 4 million grandchildren lived in the home of their grandparents in 1995 (U.S. Census Bureau, 1995).

Working-class women are more likely to spend their elderly years in caregiving because of the likelihood of illness and poor health amongst working-class men who also have fewer insurance and retirement resources. Poor health is the primary reason for early retirement for men (Parker, 1982). Often this care is long-term and can last five to ten years or more (Abel, 1986). One consequence of social policies that have sought to deinstitutionalize elderly people has been to increase the burden to the family of caring for frail elderly individuals (Abel, 1986). "Relatives already provide 80 percent of long-term care of dependent elderly . . . two-fifths of the people who care for an elderly person in their own homes do the equivalent of full-time jobs" (Abel, 1986).

CONCLUSION

Research and theory focusing on the aging process for women need to take into account not only the oppressions felt by elderly women but also the culmination of discriminations faced throughout their lifetime. Oppressions of race, class, and sex do not form a simple additive model as one ages. We must address the intersection of colonization, capitalism, and patriarchal oppression as a complex network of multiple jeopardy.

Economic factors for women intertwine the lifelong process of wage-earning and nonwage caretaking. Low incomes, high proportions of part-time jobs with no pension benefits (what proportion of women do earn these?), and dependence upon male-generated resources (welfare, housing, property accumulation) exacerbate women's vulnerability to poverty. For women who live their lives in poverty, the increased resource demands of the aging process associated with health care and wage losses are without a cushion or "safety net."

Because of the demands of capital and patriarchal family structure, women's care-giving activities do not decrease and may in fact increase. Women do not retire from housework, and expectations that women provide care for their elderly spouses, elderly parents, and dependent children and grandchildren layer the economic and labor drains on their resources.

Coupled with this is the automatic patriarchal devaluation of women who have passed their core reproductive and sexual roles assigned in a sexist system. The objectification of women as older, desexed, wombless, and roleless varies across cultures, but retains its power to label. Contrasting the condition of women in non-Western and developing nations to the condition of women in the United States reminds us that contradictory expectations abound for women in a variety of cultural contexts.

For women of color within and outside the United States, we are reminded that colonization has distorted the values of indigenous cultures and reduced the structure of resources to support older societal members. Where women may once have held honored roles for their expertise in medical, spiritual, and domestic activities, the Western industrial expropriation process has reduced those role resources. Forced internal migration within countries breaks the caretaking resources within families across all age groups. The lack of housing and health care has exacerbated the reproductive and productive demands on women, so that in many countries, the mortality advantage of being female has been severely reduced.

NINE

The Intersection of Gender, Class, and Race

We began this inquiry into the sociology of women from a feminist sociological base. This feminist sociology stands in antithesis to the tradition of androcentrism in sociology. By recognizing the power of the researcher and the theorist, we highlight the potentially biased frameworks that have been placed over women's own interpretations. These biased frameworks arise from the prior questions asked in sociology and the dominance of some methods used to gather information from respondents.

We note the predominately male profession of sociology in its history, authoritative voices, and contemporary structure. We also identify key problems in the functionalist model that hold women in the status quo of helpmate and family functionary. By expanding the substantive areas in which women are considered beyond the family, we have access to a range of conflict models that reveal the "line of fault," a disruption in our understanding of everyday life, that Dorothy Smith (1987) takes as a starting point for feminist understanding of oppression and action.

We draw on the particular experiences of women and embed those in the social organization of work, schooling, law, and aging. The stories of women's lives are drawn from a variety of qualitative and quantitative sources. Our intent is to triangulate this information, to compare qualitative to quantitative to theoretical accounts, to identify key structures and experiences that resonate with the diversity of women's experience.

Our framework emphasizes the subjective meaning of social action (use value) and the empirical relations of exchange in the market (exchange value). These concepts enable us to assess the nexus of capitalism, colonization, and patriarchy, without prejudging the priority of one over the other in particular contexts. However, we state as a proposition that a sociology of women is work undertaken by, for, and about women in their diversity.

We also examine the individual or group response to the subjective meaning of women's work and quality of life, again noting their variations. So too, the irrational relation of exchange value to women's status and activity is evaluated. Our guiding proposition is that a synthesis of the structural and interpretive approaches reveals theoretical relationships of the value concept that are hidden in androcentric theory and methods.

WOMEN AND WORK

Women and Exchangeable Work

In our chapter on women and work, we consider the evidence for a challenge to the current economic definition of value. As homeworkers, volunteers, and paid workers, women's productive contributions are marginalized through the historical processes of feminization and the split of the public and private spheres of production. The exchange value of women's labor has yet to be calculated effectively, nor have women been compensated in terms of lost wages and benefits, opportunities for career development, and access to leisure time. The usefulness of this labor has been degraded by a patriarchal and colonizing culture that labels such work as "women's work." Yet, that degraded work has produced useful services for people—education, health care, spiritual or emotional support, and dependent care of the elderly or children—hallmarks of our self-definition as a "civilization."

In analyzing the history of women's work, we show the devaluation of women's exchange value through inequitable returns to education and training, employer and co-worker stereotypes, and the exclusion of women through protective labor legislation and the construction of feminized labor markets. When the proportions of women change in a specific occupation, we find concomitant feminizing effects on exchange value—wages and prestige also change. In the examples of clerical work and special education workers, we find contrasting illustrations. Over the last century, women moved into the clerical force and men moved up into new management positions. The bureaucracy of capitalism changed the nature of the work and wages were depressed. In the more recent past, as men moved within public school education, they flooded into special education. The wage increases in this area reflect the economic power of men within the public school sector.

Quantitative empirical methods are used to reveal the striking monolithic hierarchies of public and private enterprises. The disproportionate representations of women and men, the inequities in salaries associated with distorted personnel categories, and the international dimensions of women's productive labor point to a patriarchal frame of work. The overlap of colonizing efforts to exploit the labor of indigenous or enslaved people creates a documented intersection with capitalism and colonization both within and exported outside of the United States. Women of color labor in the secondary, marginalized markets of the world, as well as in the homes and fields of their families, without adequate compensation for survival or opportunities for self-determined labor.

Some feminist researchers continue the important documentation of this marginalization and devaluation across economic and cultural contexts of class, political structure, and economic organization. Questions that remain include the following: What are the effects of paying women their worth? Are these effects only "costs" to national or corporate budgets? What are the potential benefits to a social system? What are the effects of pay equity on capitalist, socialist, or centralized economies? What are the advantages to worker conditions and humane survival in providing a living, equitable wage to workers who are today underpaid or excluded from the exchange process by their homework?

Women and Useful Work

The qualitative analysis of the caretaking world of women addresses both use value and exchange value themes. Some caretaking takes place within the framework of exchange. If the occupation has not been fully professionalized, the consequence of providing service to others is to suffer minimal wages and benefits in high turnover, unstable markets. These latter service jobs are marked by the higher proportions of women of color, as in the nursing home caretakers observed by Diamond, or in the private child-care sector.

Other caretaking occurs in the private sphere, as mothers care for their children and children care for their parents at the extreme ends of the life cycle. Throughout, this caretaking is accompanied by the day-to-day homeworking routines of women who live alone, or with a partner. Whether she is poor, a woman of color, a lesbian, or white and middle class, she will take care of the home. Only the privileged elites afford themselves the services of another woman to provide for their domestic needs. The usefulness of the double day is evident in capitalistic and patriarchal contexts, and the colonization of others to do the domestic service of the dominant group is also in evidence throughout the world.

Women live their days in a context of double burden. The burden of providing unpaid caretaking and homeworking services and the burden of providing economic survival through wage work is the norm for women. There is no rational separation of the two: They are seamless activities for women, except under capitalism, colonization, and patriarchy. This intersection of exchange and use value has been highlighted by women, yet a number of questions remain: What are the actual costs to women of providing care and service in the home? How much has this contributed to the structure of the exchange market and women's subordinate position within it? What are the benefits of compensating women's nonwage labor, in creating healthy environments for the care of dependents and guaranteeing individual survival and security? What are the social and economic obligations of men to the care and service of a society?

WOMEN AND SCHOOLING

Schooling in the United States is tied to the economic and cultural contexts of capitalism, patriarchy, and colonization. An open, competitive system is the official description of our prekindergarten through college formal education structure, which is then tied to the exchange market. However, we see evidence of a hierarchical teaching and administrative staff that is divided on the basis of gender and race. The curriculum of the schools is biased toward an Anglo-Saxon Protestant heritage that is true to the history and culture of a dwindling ethnic majority and omits the contributions of the women.

The outcome of unequal educational completion rates for minority students and the segregated patterns of educational concentration for women reinforce the larger economic inequalities discussed in Chapter Five. As women and minorities continue to major in occupations that are "semiprofessional" or that lead to service-related jobs, the social justification for unequal salaries and diminished careers is produced by these early educational distortions.

The context of education for women of color is framed by the colonizing practices of the dominant racial/ethnic group. At the onset, the creation of public charity schools to correct the "negative effects of the home environment" were prompted by a mixture of ethnocentric morals and economic concerns for a disciplined workforce. Yet many local schools in rural areas developed non-English cultural and language curricula. As the diversity of the workforce became more of a concern to industrialists, the national push for compulsory, monocultural, Anglocentric education intensified. Today, the small local schools conducted in German or Czech or Spanish have disappeared from the landscape, and our schoolchildren become monolingual to a fault and are encouraged to assimilate the dominant norms and beliefs.

For Chicanas in the public schools, the triple jeopardy of patriarchy and capitalism, the racism of the dominant group, and the images of women in indigenous Chicana culture intersect. The result is often negative evaluations from teachers for Chicanas (and for African Americans as well) whose autonomous behavior challenges the dominant sex roles, or whose academic achievements challenge racist norms of genetic inferiority. Those same teachers may disdain the circumspect interaction of Chicanas that is valued in the home. As troublesome is the loss of language and cultural integrity that becomes the obligatory ticket to mainstream "success." The lowered rates of college and high school completion for Chicanas testify to the burden of these complex expectations.

Finally, the dualistic cultural images for Chicanas, the mother/whore dichotomy, present unique challenges to Chicana students and scholars who explore outside of their traditional roles. To fulfill one's intellectual and emotional interests may lead to a status as a traitor. The forced juxtaposition and lack of integration among these roles generates a cultural and economic dilemma that is successfully challenged by only small numbers.

Heterocentric Schools

The educational lives of lesbian students and teachers are shrouded by the homophobia of the dominant society. In contrast to heterosexual students, lesbian students are presented with heterosexist social activities, have little or no political representation in the student organizations, have inadequate, heterocentric counseling and health programs, and are less safe on campus. In scholarly work, an accurate, objective, or subjective evaluation of lesbian and gay contributions to the arts, history, politics, and other social movements is omitted.

For lesbian teachers and staff, the legal discrimination against homosexuals puts their job, housing, and child custody at risk. In most instances, this results in a range of education workers who are unwilling to advocate for the needs of their lesbian students. As lesbian students advocate for their own interests in the traditional disciplines and in women's studies and ethnic studies, the challenges to the schooling system are myriad.

Schooling Questions

From these heterocentric and colonized experiences, we can address a number of research questions: What are the effects of creating a bilingual, bicultural schooling system? Are the positive effects of bicognitive ability sketched by Ramirez and Castaneda (1974) generalizable to other subordinate ethnic and racial minority groups in the United States? What are the consequences of exporting our educational hierarchical structure to Third World nations? How are we to encourage gay and lesbian scholarship in a society that is legally homophobic? What are the positive effects for both heterosexual and homosexual students when they take into account the formerly hidden lives and contributions of sexual minorities, or make an informed choice among lifestyles?

WOMEN AND THE LAW

In our chapter on women and the law, we raise a number of research questions concerning the role law plays in defining women's experiences, structuring inequality, and reinforcing the discriminatory patterns of a patriarchal judiciary system.

Women Policing the Crisis

In analyzing the history of women in policing, we show the historical focus on women's use value as volunteers to perform tasks related to mothering, familial duties, and acting as moral guardians. When the numbers of women in policing were extremely low, they had little influence on the market value; however, as the numbers increase we predict a feminization process as women police officers begin to influence the market value of the policing occupation. As women took on exchange value, there was rising opposition against their participating in policing that took the forms of employment discrimination, tokenism, and general hostility from male officers. This hostility reflects the treatment of policing as a scarce resource that is maintained by the patriarchal structure.

Contemporary research questions would include the following: How do women's and men's exchange value in policing differ? Do use value qualities such as empathy in sexual assault investigations play an important part in policing? Can they be regarded? Methodology considerations would include better data collection on the number and diversity of women in policing. An in-depth look at women in policing would question how they see themselves, how they value themselves, and the place self-esteem plays in the roles involved in policing.

Cultural and ethnic diversity issues must become a part of the feminist research agenda on women and the law. For example, what is the consequence of lie detector tests on lesbians applying for policing positions? How are women of color in law enforcement perceived by their own communities? How is the issue of co-optation by a dominant cultural, patriarchal legal structure addressed?

Exchange Value and Women's Criminology

The criminality of women and sanctioning of "deviants" concern both feminist sociologists and criminologists. We would suggest a reanalysis of the theories of criminality in terms of use value and exchange value. For example, in Simon's (1975b) and Adler's (1975) emancipation arguments, increases in women's criminality could be a reflection of their increased exchange value. Exchange value increased as women's criminality became more visible and more important in terms of the value placed on it by the patriarchal judicial system.

Juvenile status offenses are use value crimes that are tied to expectations of juvenile females. This is reflected in the *parens patriae* status of the state, which functions to protect the "value" of virginal children for an eventual marriage market in the interests of the patriarchal family structure.

Many of the crimes by women and girls such as prostitution, welfare fraud, and shoplifting can be analyzed in terms of their interaction with the exchange value of the market. The emancipation model can be viewed in terms of the fear of the effect that women's crime will have on the exchange system, particularly for crimes such as embezzlement or computer fraud.

A feminist methodology in the area of women and crime would by necessity take a different focus from the traditional male-centered definition of criminality that attempts to fit women into that definition. Such a male-centered definition is reflected in criminology data collection, as well as theory. A feminist criminology would challenge the androcentric assumptions of traditional criminological research. Different questions can be posed and new definitions formulated: How do women in prison see themselves? Why are they unwilling to see themselves as emancipated even though some theorists have claimed this to be the case? What are the differing perceptions of status offenses by juveniles and adults? What is the purpose of status offenses in terms of protection and use value of the family or individual "girls"? Why do corrections facilities focus on training women for use value activities when increasing their exchange value in the labor market would certainly be more useful outside the prison walls?

Cultural and ethnic diversity issues for women's criminality must go beyond the numerical accounting of minority women in prison. We must address the intersection of class and race and its influence on all aspects of women's criminality, including the ability to change laws and sanctions. These issues, added to those others raised in Chapter Seven, will arise as part of the feminist interactive research agenda for a sociology of law.

WOMEN AND AGING

In our chapter on women and aging, we tie together the biological, social, legal, and economic questions concerning the structural forces that influence women's experiences in aging.

Use Value and Mothering

In analyzing the place for women in the labor market and the impact of aging on women's work, we found that women are valued in old age according to their use value. Cross-culturally, the grandmother role is an unpaid labor role. Women are expected to perform domestic duties for their immediate family and relatives, particularly their children and spouses. In the United States, the elderly woman also constitutes a threat to the exchange value of the family because when her dependency needs become too great, she loses all her use value and becomes an economic liability with few resources to address them herself.

Contemporary research questions would ask this: How do we measure the value of a lifetime of labor (nonwage labor and wage labor) at a societal level (gross national product), and at an institutional level (state and local legislation), and at an individual level (just compensation and the value of grandmothering).

What are the colonization effects on economic stratification among elderly people? How have diverse ethnic groups and cultural and ethnic diversity issues become a part of the feminist research agenda on women and aging?

Culture, Body Image, and Sexuality Questions

The societal values of youth and beauty influence the lives of aging women. Sexuality is tied with use value—the "value" of youth, virginity, and beauty. As men age, they increase their exchange value through their employment, increased financial success, political strength, and social power. Women's exchange value decreases as they age due to the accumulation of low wages and few benefits, as well as other factors associated with their sexuality.

A feminist research agenda might address the question of why men are marrying younger women. Is it for their sexual use value, for their caretaking use value, or is it a response to the threat of middle-aged women's exchange value? How do age differences compound the gender dominance patterns in families?

A feminist methodology in the area of women and aging would take on a different focus than traditional gerontological work. It would address who is asking the questions and raise the issue of distortions as cultural beliefs and ageist stereotypes are incorporated into the research enterprise.

BUT WHAT ABOUT THE (WHITE/ANGLO) MEN?

Women's studies, feminist scholarship, and a sociology of women exist because we recognize that the sociological enterprise is not a neutral, objective enterprise. Nor are the teaching, policy making, writing, and consulting activities of sociologists that flow from our original research and theory activities. The sociological enterprise mirrors society as it omits, distorts, and devalues women. We see a sociology of women as an academic base for contesting the pervasive ideology that men are the "norm" that defines women as "other."

In a sociology of women, men are considered within the dialectical process as a social group with disproportionate formal and informal power in all major institutions. It is true that at times we oversimplify "men" by not taking into account the diversity of race, ethnicity, sexual preference, age, and social class that affects their lives as well. Socialist feminists note that we must carefully consider the effects of class relations on male access to power, particularly when looking at working-class women's lives. To the extent that working-class men do not have access to research, policy making, and political power, their lives, too, have been distorted and their value in the economic and social system reduced. Under the colonization process, the work and culture of indigenous men have also been subordinated and distorted by the combined effects of capitalism and racism.

However, radical-feminist theorists note that all men gain from patriarchal privileges, whether they accept those privileges or not. Their position as male is more apparent in some dimensions (pay inequity, sexual assault, domestic violence, street harassment) than is their class or race/ethnicity.

A sociology of women is likely to be challenged as "reverse discrimination" against an understanding of men and their diverse experiences or intentions. Such a charge ignores the relevance of power and privilege in the definition of academic, political, or social enterprise. For women to exclude men who do not share their sex oppression may be "a necessary stage in building a power base, whereas those in power exclude the oppressed in order to retain resources and privileges" (Bright, 1982:98).

Kanter (1977) notes the structured inequalities of the workplace that contribute to gender differences. These include positions held by women that have accountability, but lack power; the exclusion of women from sponsorship networks that give access to formal and informal power; access to organizational visibility, but mostly as tokens; and the emphasis on individual competition for scarce resources and opportunities. The exclusion of men may well involve building intellectual, political, and economically segregated activities that enhance communication among women and allow for the abandonment of androcentric, racist, bureaucratic, and distorted structures and practices.

An example might be the concern over all-male clubs. These clubs are often "social" or "recreational" clubs that have the latent effect of providing communication networks outside of economic and political organizations. Domhoff (1971) documents these clubs at national and regional levels as providing insider information and access to positions that women are excluded from by membership restrictions (the use of racial/ethnic, economic, and religious exclusions are also obvious). What appears to be an organization that focuses on the use value of summer camping, golf, or epicurean dinners for its members is in fact a significant arena for exchange value.

Some have argued that "parallel" exclusion of men from women's organizations is equally discriminatory, in reverse. However, a careful rethinking of the use and exchange value concepts demonstrates that this is not parallel. For example, participation in an all-female altar society in a church is a different context of separation. Women are involved in low exchange value "women's work" such as cleaning, dusting, and embroidering the altar cloths and vestments of the priest or minister. This is work that women do, often anonymously, that does not affect the economic activities of others, except in releasing males from this time investment in support of patriarchal religious ideology.

This is not to suggest that all women's organizations are economically inconsequential. Unions, political caucuses, and community activist organizations can have significant effects on voting outcomes, on focusing attention on child-care and maternity issues at the workplace, and on businesses through local and national boycotts of sexist practices. Women in these organizations may want nonhierarchical structures, cooperative decision-making processes, or other activities that males might challenge. The research on male-female interaction and communication in task-oriented settings suggests that when men join an all-woman organization, the processes and participation of individual women are likely to be suppressed (Pearson, 1985). In conclusion, we may at some point have "retilled the epistemological soil sufficiently" (Bright, 1982:98) that the androcentric, class, and racial/ethnic biases are eliminated from sociology. But that is not now.

PRAXIS AND POLICY

Feminist sociology and a sociology of women assume that the questions we raise are tied to action on behalf of women in international, national, and local settings. Some sociologists interested in the application of feminist theory to sociological topics have argued against the activist assumption (Chafetz, 1984). Others note that feminism as a theory is integral to the feminist movement as practice.

Whether this feminist theory and praxis is a reform movement or a revolutionary movement depends on the frame of feminism. As Ferree and Hess (1985) indicate, the intent to change the balance of power among existing interest groups is a reform element currently attached to the liberal-feminist model. The challenge to "dislodge the existing power elites in favor of new contenders" (Ferree and Hess, 1985:171) is the hallmark of revolutionary praxis advocated by radical, Marxist, and socialist feminists.

We see sociology as potentially rooted in the activism of early practitioner-theorists. We have shifted perspective from women as objects of study and objects of discrimination within institutions to a perspective in which women participate in defining, explaining, and changing their social situation. That change in perspective must apply to the researcher-theorist as well. Theory and praxis within a sociology of women is a dialectic between ideas and action. When we teach a course in feminist theory or a general course in the sociology of women, we contribute to the expansion of ideas among our students; yet, we also gain from the interaction. Nontraditional, differently abled, lesbian and women-of-color students will challenge our perceptions and conclusions. By respecting, evaluating, and integrating those challenges into our teaching and research, we actively break down the barrier between campus and community.

To be feminist sociologists, we are attempting to change the institutions that surround us. We assume that our research, theory, and teaching provide potential for change. There are a number of ways in which this can occur— mentoring; battling against sexual harassment; fighting racism, classism, and sexism on campus; writing texts that are inclusive of cultural diversity; and participating in community activism, to name a few. In the next section, we will highlight two forms of activism in which academic women in particular have important roles. These include promoting a feminist collective decision-making process and listening to women's own voices, especially in research.

Collective Decision Making

The feminist collective decision-making process is one where all participants share equally in the decision; all members are empowered to participate; and a collective agreement is reached. It is often a long and difficult task, particularly with groups that are either large or diverse; yet, it avoids the autocratic model of leadership that silences many participants.

As we described earlier, the usefulness of women's work has been degraded by a patriarchal and colonizing culture. In effect, women have had little to say concerning work conditions, pay, benefits, and other economic rewards related to the exchange value of the work. Women's work was defined in terms of use value and controlled by a capitalist market that held little esteem for anything that was not related to exchange value. As we incorporate more collective decision making into the workplace, women's work will become redefined according to women's true value. For example, as women demand child care as a necessity to participate in the labor force, child care becomes an exchangeable commodity.

The collective decision-making process empowers women who traditionally have been silenced. Women whose use value tasks were viewed as unimportant by the exchange-dominated economic structure were not listened to and participated rarely or as tokens. A collective process gives all participants an equal voice. For women who have been silenced by the health care professions, a collective model gives voice to the patients and all health care individuals and allows some autonomy in health care decisions. A collective process may be ideal in institutions that incarcerate women. Empowering women who have had all rights, individuality, and power removed from them may lead to surprisingly positive results.

In higher education, we have a number of options for incorporating collective processes into our teaching, research, and advising roles. As women who work in academia, we encourage women to utilize a collective framework. This could take the form of alternative methods of grading, open peer review, collective evaluation of merit for salary, or an open collective process for tenure review, to mention a few.

Women's Own Voices

Women have been defined by and spoken for by other people, particularly men. It is imperative in our research agendas, our teaching, and our activism that women have the opportunity to gain their own voice. The collective process is one that clearly leads to empowering women to speak on their own. Yet, in research, male definitions and agendas are often imposed upon women's lives. In criminology, theories developed to explain male criminal behavior were transposed to women as an afterthought. It was not surprising to find that women did not fit the model. If we are to come to understand the diversity of women's lives, we need to listen to women describing their own experiences. It is only with this as a first step that we can expect to start changing the society to benefit women.

With the collective process, women have been able to express their own views on issues that directly affect their lives. This has been an important empowering step for changes in the arenas of sexuality and reproduction. It is through listening to women's own voices that the self–health care movement has become so successful and has had a tremendous impact on the policies related to birth control and abortion. Our next step is to guarantee that all voices are heard.

A sociology by, for, and about women is one element of this praxis. We require ourselves to untangle the complexity of lives with our colleagues and students by using methodologies that empower and theories that include diversity. By researching and creating policies, we raise consciousness and the level of integrity in those processes. The usefulness of these policies and practices can then be evaluated by their effects on the unequal exchange value of women, and the improvements in the lives of elderly, lesbian, poor, and working-class women across the full range of racial, cultural, local, and international situations.

References

Abel, E. 1986. "Adult daughters and care for the elderly." *Feminist Studies*. 12:479–497.

Abramovitz, M. 1988. *Regulating the Lives of Women: Social Welfare Policy from Colonial Times to the Present*. Boston, MA: South End Press.

Adams, M. 1971. "The compassion trap." Pp. 555–578, in V. Gornick and B. K. Moran (eds.), Women in Sexist Society. New York: Mentor Books.

Addams, J. 1910. *Twenty Years at Hull-House*. New York: The New American Library.

Addelson, K. P. 1994. *Moral Passages: Toward a Collectivist Moral Theory*. Boston: Routledge.

Addelson, K. P. 1991. *Impure Thoughts: Essays on Philosophy, Feminism and Ethics*. Philadelphia: Temple University Press.

Adelman, M. 1980. *Adjustment to Aging and Style of Being Gay: A Study of Older Gay Men and Lesbians*. Ph.D. Thesis, Wright University, Berkeley, CA.

Adler, F. 1980. "The interaction between women's emancipation and female criminality: A cross-cultural perspective." Pp. 150–166, in S. K. Datesman and F. R. Scarpitti (eds.), *Women, Crime and Justice*. New York: Oxford University Press.

Adler, F. 1975. *Sisters in Crime*. New York: McGraw-Hill.

Agree, E. M. 1987. *A Portrait of Older Minorities*. Washington, DC: American Association of Retired Persons, Minority Affairs Initiative.

Andre, R. 1981. *Homemakers: The Forgotten Workers*. Chicago: University of Chicago Press.

Austin, T. L. and D. C. Hummer. 1994. "'Has a decade made a difference?' Attitudes of male criminal justice majors towards female police officers." *Journal of Criminal Justice Education*, 5(2): 229–239.

Baker, E. F. 1925. *Protective Labor Station*. New York: Longman, Green.

Balzai, J. 1993. "An activist who flew close to the flame of violence." *Los Angeles Times*, August 21.

Banks, J. A. and C. A. McGee Banks. 1989. *Multicultural Education*. Boston: Allyn & Bacon.

Barrera, M. 1982. *Race and Class in the Southwest*. Chicago: University of Chicago Press.

Bart, P. 1971. "Sexism and social science: From the gilded cage to the iron cage, or the perils of Pauline." *Journal of Marriage and the Family*, 33:734–735.

Bass, A. 1992. "Women far less likely to kill than men; no one is sure why." *Boston Globe*, February 24, p. 27.

Beck, C. M. and B. P. Pearson. 1989. "Mental health of elderly women." In J. D. Garner and S. O. Mercer (eds.), *Women as They Age*. New York: Haworth Press.

Beeghley, L. 1989. *The Structure of Social Stratification*. Boston: Allyn & Bacon.

Beeson, D. 1975. "Women in studies of aging: A critique and suggestion." *Social Problems*, 23:52–59.

Belenky, M., B. Clenchy, N. Goldberger, and J. Tarule. 1986. *Women's Ways of Knowing*. New York: Basic Books.

Bell, I. P. 1976. "The double standard." In B. B. Hess (ed.), *Growing Old in America*. New Brunswick: Transaction Books.

Bem, S. L. 1976. "Probing the promise of androgyny." Pp. 47–62, in A. G. Kaplan and J. P. Bean (eds.), *Beyond Sex-Role Stereotypes: Readings Toward a Psychology of Androgyny*. Boston: Little, Brown.

Bennett C., U.S. Bureau of the Census. 1995. *The Black Population in the United States: March 1994 and 1993*. Current Population Reports, P20–480. Washington, DC: U.S. Government Printing Office.

Benston, M. 1982. "Feminism and the critique of scientific method." In A. R. Miles and G. Finn (eds.), *Feminism in Canada. Firm Pressure to Politics*. Montreal: Black Rose Books.

Benston, M. 1969. "The political economy of women's liberation." *Monthly Review* 21(4):13–27.

Berg, I. 1971. *Education and Jobs: The Great Training Robbery*. New York: Beacon Press.

Berk, R. A. and S. F. Berk. 1979. *Labor and Leisure at Home: Content and Organization of the Household Day*. Beverly Hills: Sage.

Berk, S. F. 1988. "Women's unpaid labor." Pp. 287–302, in Stromberg and Harkess (eds.), *Women Working*. Mountain View, CA: Mayfield.

Berk, S. F. 1985. *The Gender Factory: The Apportionment of Work in American Households*. New York: Plenum Press.

Bernard, J. 1987. *The Female World from a Global Perspective*. Bloomington: Indiana University Press.

Bernard, J. 1981. *The Female World*. New York: Free Press.

Best, R. 1983. *We've Got Scars: What Boys and Girls Learn in Elementary School*. Bloomington: Indiana University Press.

Bielby, W. and J. Baron. 1987. "A woman's place is with other women: Sex segregation within organizations." In B. F. Reskin (ed.), *Sex segregation in the workplace: Trends, explanations, remedies*. Washington, DC: National Academy Press.

Biklin, S. K. and M. B. Brannigan. 1980. *Women and Educational Leadership*. Lexington: Lexington Books.

Birch, E. L. 1985. *The Unsheltered Woman: Women and Housing in the 80s*. New Brunswick: Center for Urban Policy Research.

Black, D. J. 1970. "The production of crime rates." *American Sociological Review*, 35:733–748.

Blackwell, J. E. 1989. "Mentoring: An action strategy for increasing minority faculty." *Academe*, 75(5):8–14.

Blau, F. and M. Ferber. 1986. *Economics of Women, Men, and Work*. Englewood Cliffs, NJ: Prentice Hall.

Blau, F. and C. L. Jusenius. 1976. "Economists' approaches to sex segregation in the labor market: An appraisal." *Signs*, 1:181–200.

Blauner, R. 1972. *Racial Oppression in America*. New York: Basic Books.

Bloch, R. and D. Anderson. 1974. *Police Women on Patrol*. Washington, DC: Urban Institute.

Blum, L. and V. Smith. 1988. "Women's mobility in the corporation: A critique of the politics of optimism." *Signs*, 13:528–545.

Bonacich, E. 1972. "Theory of ethnic antagonism: the split labor market." *American Sociological Review*, 37(October):547–559.

Bordo, S. 1990. "Feminism, postmodernism and gender-skepticism." In L. J. Nicholson (ed.), *Feminism/Postmodernism*. New York: Routledge.

Boris, E. and P. Bardaglio. 1983. "The transformation of patriarchy: The historic role of the state." Pp. 70–93, in I. Diamond (ed.), *Families, Politics, and Public Policy*. New York: Longman.

Bose, C. 1987. "Dual spheres." Pp. 267–286, in M. M. Feree and B. Hess (eds.), *Analyzing Gender*. New York: Sage.

Bourdieu, R. and J. C. Passeron. 1977. *Reproduction in Education, Society and Culture*. New York: Sage.

Bowles, S. and H. Gintis. 1976. *Schooling in Capitalist America*. New York: Basic Books.

Bright, C. 1982. "But what about the men?" Pp. 96–100, in P. Cruikshank (ed.), *Lesbian Studies*. New York: Feminist Press.

Brownmiller, S. 1984. *Femininity*. New York: Linden Press.

Brownmiller, S. 1975. *Against Our Will*. New York: Simon & Schuster.

Bruno, R. 1996. *What's It Worth? Field of Training and Economic Status: Spring 1993*. Current Population Report, P70–51. Washington, DC: U.S. Government Printing Office.

Bunch, C. and S. Pollack. 1983. *Learning One Way: Essays in Feminist Ed*. Trumansburg, NY: Crossing Press.

Butler, J. E. 1989. "Transforming the curriculum: Teaching about women of color." Pp. 145–163, in J. A. Banks and C. A. McGee Banks, *Multicultural Education*. Boston: Allyn & Bacon.

Campbell, A. 1981. *Girl Delinquents*. Oxford: Blackwell.

Campbell, A. 1984. *The Girls in the Gang*. Oxford: Blackwell.

Carlen, P., J. Hicks, J. O'Dwyer, D. Christina, and C. Tchaikowsky. 1985. *Criminal Woman*. Cambridge: Polity Press.

Cavan, R., E. Burgess, R. Havighurst, and H. Goldhammer. 1949. *Personal Adjustment in Old Age*. Chicago: Science Research.

Chafetz, J. S. 1988. *Feminist Sociology: An Overview of Contemporary Theories*. Itasca, IL: Peacock.

Chafetz, J. S. 1984. *Sex and Advantage: A Comparative Macro-Structural Theory of Sex Stratification*. New York: Rowman & Allenheld.

Chernin, K. 1981. *The Obsession: Reflections on the Tyranny of Slenderness*. New York: Harper & Row.

Chesney-Lind, M. 1989. "Girls' crime and woman's place: Toward a feminist model of female delinquency." *Crime and Delinquency*, 35(1):5–29.

Chesney-Lind, M. 1988. "Doing feminist criminology." *The Criminologist*, 13(4)July-August:1, 3, 16–17.

Chesney-Lind, M. 1986. "Women and crime: The female offender." *Signs: Journal of Women in Culture and Society*, 12(1):78–96.

Child, I. L., E. H. Potter, and E. L. Levine. 1946. "Children's textbooks and personality development: An explanation in the social psychology of education." *Psychological Monographs*, 60:1–54.

Choi, Namkee G. 1991. "Racial differences in the determinants of living arrangements of widowed and divorced elderly women." *The Gerontologist*, 31(4):496–504.

Cloward, R. and L. Ohlin. 1960. *Delinquency and Opportunity: A Theory of Delinquent Gangs*. New York: Free Press.

Collins, P. H. 1990. *Black Feminist Thought*. Boston: Unwin Hyman.

Collins, R. 1975. *Conflict Sociology: Toward an Explanatory Science*. New York: Academic Press.

Comte, A. 1854/1877. *Systems of Positive Polity IV*. London: Longman, Green.

Conway, A. and C. Bogdan. 1977. "Sexual delinquency: The persistence of a double standard." *Crime and Delinquency*, 23(2)April:131–135.

Cook, J. and M. M. Fonow. 1988. "Am I my sister's gatekeeper?: Cautionary tales from the academic hierarchy." Pp. 201–218, in *Nebraska Sociological Feminist Collective: A Feminist Ethic for Social Science Research*. Lewiston, NY: Mellen Press.

Corley, M. C. and H. O. Mauksch. 1988. "Registered nurses, gender and commitment." In A. Statham, E. M. Miller, and H. O. Mauksch (eds.), *The Worth of Women's Work*. Albany: State University of New York Press.

Cotera, M. P. 1977. *The Chicana Feminist*. Austin, TX: Information Systems Development.

Cottrell, L. 1942. "The adjustment of the individual to his age and sex roles." *American Sociological Review*, 7:617–620.

Cronin, S. 1987. "Unequal contracting in marriage and family relationships." In J. Freeman (ed.), *Women: A Feminist Perspective*. Palo Alto, CA: Mayfield.

Cruikshank, M. (ed.). 1982. *Lesbian Studies*. New York: Feminist Press.

Cumming, E. 1963. "Further thoughts on the theory of disengagement." *International Social Science Journal*, 15(3):377–393.

Cumming, E. and W. Henry. 1961. *Growing Old. The Process of Disengagement*. New York: Basic Books.

Daly, M. 1978. *Gyn/ecology: The Metaethics of Radical Feminism*. Boston: Beacon Press.

Danylewycz, M. and A. Prentice. 1984. "Teachers—Gender and bureaucratizing school systems." *History of Education Quarterly*, 24:75–100.

Datesman, S. K. and F. R. Scarpitti (eds.). 1980. *Women, Crime and Justice*. New York: Oxford University Press.

Datesman, S. K. and L. Aicken. 1984. "Offense specialization and escalation among status offenders." *Journal of Criminal Law and Criminology*, 75:1246–1275.

Davies, M. 1975. "Women's place is at the typewriter: The feminization of the clerical labor force." Pp. 279–296, in R. C. Edwards, M. Reich, and D. M. Gordon (eds.), *Labor Market Segmentation*. Lexington, MA: Heath.

Davis, A. 1989. *Women, Culture and Politics*. New York: Random House.

Davis, K. 1937. "The Sociology of Prostitution." *American Sociological Review*, October:746.

Day, J. C., U.S. Bureau of the Census. 1996. *Projections of the Number of Households and Families: 1995 to 2010*. Current Population Reports, P 25–1129. Washington, DC: U.S. Government Printing Office.

De Beauvoir, S. 1952/1974. *The Second Sex*. New York: Vintage Books.

DeCrow, K. 1972. "Look, Jane, look! See Dick run and jump! Admire him!" In S. Anderson (ed.), *Sex Differences and Discrimination in Education*. Worthington, OH: Jones.

Deegan, M. 1988. *Jane Addams and the Men of the Chicago School. 1892–1918*. New Brunswick, NJ: Transaction Books.

Deem, R. 1978. *Women and Schooling*. London: Routledge.

Deere, C. D. and M. Leon de Leal. 1981. "Peasant production, proletarianization and the sexual division of labor in the Andes." *Signs*, 7:338–360.

Delamont, S. 1980. *Sociology of Women: An Introduction*. London: Allen & Unwin.

D'Emilio, J. and E. B. Freedman. 1988. *Intimate Matters: A History of Sexuality in America*. New York: Harper & Row.

Deming, R. 1977. *Women: The New Criminals*. Nashville, TN: Nelson.

Diamond, T. 1988. "Social policy and everyday life in nursing homes: A critical ethnography." In A. Statham, E. Miller, and H. Mauksch (eds.), *The Worth of Women's Work*. Albany: State University of New York Press.

Dill, B. T. 1983. "Race, class and gender: Prospects for an all inclusive sisterhood." *Feminist Studies*, 9:131–150.

Domhoff, G. W. 1971. *The Higher Circles*. New York: Vintage Books.

Doress, P. B., D. L. Siegal, and the Midlife and Older Women Book Project. 1987. *Ourselves, Growing Older*. New York: Simon & Schuster.

Dowd, J. 1984. "Beneficence and the aged." *Journal of Gerontology*. 39(1):102–108.

Dowd, J. 1980. *Stratification Among the Aged. An Analysis of Power and Dependence*. Pacific Grove, CA: Brooks/Cole.

Dowd, J. 1978. "Aging as exchange: A test of the distributive justice proposition." *Pacific Sociological Review*, 21:351–375.

Dowd, J. 1975. "Aging as exchange: A preface to theory." *Journal of Gerontology*, 30(September):584–594.

Dowd, J. and Bengtson, V. 1978. "Aging in minority populations: An examination of the double jeopardy hypothesis." *Journal of Gerontology*, 33:427–436.

Duggan, L. and N. Hunter. 1995. *Sex Wars: Sexual Dissent and Political Culture*. Boston: Routledge.

Durkheim, E. 1982. *The Rules of the Sociological Method*. New York: Free Press.

Durkheim, E. 1897/1963. *Suicide.* London: Routledge.

Dworkin, A. 1983. *Right Wing Women.* New York: Perigee Books.

Dworkin, A. 1981. *Pornography: Men Possessing Women.* New York: G. P. Putnam.

Dziech, B. W. and L. Weiner. 1984. *The Lecherous Professor.* Boston: Beacon Press.

Ehrenreich, B., E. Hess, and G. Jacobs. 1986. *Remaking Love: The Feminization of Sex.* New York: Doubleday.

Ehrlich, C. 1971. "The male sociologist's burden: The place of women in marriage and family texts." *Journal of Marriage and the Family,* 33(3):421–430.

Eisenstein, H. 1983. *Contemporary Feminist Thought.* Boston: G. K. Hall.

Eisenstein, Z. 1979. "Some notes on the relations of capitalist patriarchy." In Z. Eisenstein (ed.), *Capitalist Patriarchy and the Case for Socialist Feminism.* New York: Monthly Review Press.

Eisenstein, Z. R. 1981. *The Radical Future of Liberal Feminism.* New York: Longman.

Eller, T. J. and Kathleen Short. U.S. Bureau of the Census. 1996. *Dynamics of Economic Well-Being: Poverty, 1992–1993, Who Stays Poor? Who Doesn't.* Current Population Reports, P70–55. Washington, DC: U.S. Government Printing Office.

Engels, Frederick. 1884/1972. *The Origin of the Family, Private Property and the State.* New York: Pathfinder.

English, B. 1995. "Abortion doctor weary, wary." *Boston Globe,* January 9.

Espin, O. 1984. "Influences on sexuality in Hispanic/Latina women." In C. S. Vance (ed.), *Pleasure and Danger: Exploring Female Sexuality.* Boston: Routledge.

Estes, C. L., J. H. Swan, and L. E. Gerard. 1984. "Dominant and competing paradigms in gerontology: Towards a political economy of aging." In M. Minkler and C. L. Estes (eds.), *Readings in the Political Economy of Aging.* Farmingdale, NY: Baywood.

Estes, C. L., L. Gerard, and A. Clarke. 1976. "Women and the economics of aging." In B. B. Hessled, *Growing Old in America.* New Brunswick: Transaction Books.

Estler, S. 1975. "Women as leaders in public education." *Signs,* 1:363–386.

Etzioni, A. 1969. *The Semi-Professions and Their Organization.* New York: Free Press.

Evers, H. 1983. "Elderly women and disadvantage: Perceptions of daily life and support relationships." In D. Jerome (ed.), *Aging in Modern Society: Contemporary Approaches.* London: Croom Helm.

Feagin, J. R., C. Tilly, and C. Williams. 1972. *Subsidizing the Poor: A Boston Housing Experiment.* Lexington: Lexington Books.

Federman, L. 1982. "Who Hid Lesbian History?" Pp. 115–121, in M. Cruikshank, *Lesbian Studies.* New York: Feminist Press.

Feinman, C. 1986. *Women in the Criminal Justice System.* New York: Praeger.

Ferree, M. M. and B. B. Hess. 1985. *Controversy and Coalition: The New Feminist Movement.* Boston: Twayne.

Firestone, S. 1970. The *Dialectic of Sex.* New York: Bantam Books.

Foner, A. 1975. "Age in society: Structures and change." *American Behaviorist Scientist,* 19(2): 289–312.

Fontaine, C. 1982. "Teaching the psychology of women: A lesbian feminist perspective." Pp. 71–82, in M. Cruikshank (ed.), *Lesbian Studies.* New York: Feminist Press.

Fowles, D. G. 1987. *A Profile of Older Americans: 1987.* Washington, DC: American Association of Retired Persons, the U.S. Administration on Aging, and the U.S. Department of Health and Human Services.

Freedman, E. 1982. "Resources for lesbian history." Pp. 110–114, in M. Cruikshank (ed.), Lesbian Studies. New York: Feminist Press.

Friedan, B. 1981. *The Second Stage.* New York: Summit Books.

Friedan, B. 1963. *The Feminine Mystique.* New York: Norton.

Fulton, O. and M. Trow. 1975. "Students and teachers." Pp. 1–38, in M. Trow (ed.), *Teachers and Students.* New York: McGraw-Hill.

Gage, M. J. 1893/1972. *Women, Church and State,* 2nd ed. New York: Arno Press.

Gans, H. 1972. "The positive functions of poverty." *American Journal of Sociology*, 78:275–289.

Garcia, A. M. 1989. "The development of Chicana feminist discourse." *Gender and Society*, 3(2):217–238.

Garner, J. D. and S. O. Mercer (eds.). 1989. *Women as They Age: Challenge, Opportunity and Triumph.* New York: Hayworth Press.

Gilfus, M. E. 1992. "From victims to survivors to offenders: Women's routes of entry and immersion into street crime." *Women and Criminal Justice*, 4(1):63–89.

Gilligan, C. 1982. *In a Different Voice: Psychological Theory and Women's Development.* Cambridge, MA: Harvard University.

Gilman, C. R 1979. *Herland.* New York: Pantheon Books.

Glaser, B. and A. Strauss. 1971. *Status Passage.* Chicago: Aldine, Atherton.

Glenn, E. N. and R. L. Feldberg. 1989. "Clerical work: The female occupation." In J. Freeman, (ed.), *Women: A Feminist Perspective.* Palo Alto, CA: Mayfield.

Gold, D. 1971. "Women and voluntarism." In V. Gornick and E. K. Moran (eds.), *Woman in Sexist Society.* New York: Mentor Books.

Gold, M. and D. J. Reimer. 1975. "Changing patterns of delinquent behavior among Americans 13 through 16 years old: 1967–72." *Crime and Delinquency Literature*, December:483–517.

Goodwin, A. J. and L. Scott. 1987. "Sexuality in the second half of life." Pp. 79–98, in P. B. Doress, D. L. Siegel, and the Midlife and Older Women Book Project (eds.), *Ourselves, Growing Older.* New York: Simon & Schuster.

Gordon, L. 1974. *Woman's Body, Woman's Right.* New York: Penguin.

Gould, K. H. 1989. "A minority-feminist perspective on women and aging." In J. D. Garner and S. O. Mercer (eds.), *Women as They Age.* New York: Haworth Press.

Gouldner, A. W. 1960. "The norm of reciprocity." *American Sociological Review*, 25(April):161–178.

Graebner, D. B. 1972. "A decade of sexism in readers." *The Reading Teacher*, 26.

Grambs, J. D. 1989. *Women Over Forty.* New York: Springer.

Grant, L. 1986. "Training for motherwork: Socialization of white females in classrooms." American Educational Research Association Meeting, Montreal, Quebec.

Grant, L. 1984. "Black females 'place' in desegregated classrooms." *Sociology of Education*, 57: 98–111.

Grant, W., V. Grant, and T. D. Snyder. 1986. *Digest of Education Statistics.* Washington, DC: U.S. Government Printing Office.

Grau, L. 1988. "Illness engendered poverty among elderly women." Pp. 102–118, in C. A. Perales and L. S. Young (eds.), *Dealing with the Health Needs of Women in Poverty.* New York: Harrington Park Press.

Grauerholz, E. and B. Pescosolido. 1989. "Gender representation in children's literature: 1900–1984." *Gender and Society*, 3:113–126.

Gross, E. 1986. "What is feminist theory?" Pp. 190–204, in C. Pateman and E. Gross (eds.), *Feminist Challenges: Social and Political Theory.* Boston: Northeastern University Press.

Gross, E. and C. Pateman. 1986. *Feminist Challenges: Social and Political Theory.* Boston: Northeastern University Press.

Grossholtz, J. 1984. *Forging Capitalist Patriarchy.* Durham: Duke University Press.

Gubrium, J. 1975. *Living and Dying at Murray Manor.* New York: St. Martin's Press.

Gubrium, J. 1973. *The Myths of the Golden Years: A Socio-Environmental Theory of Aging.* Springfield, IL: Thomas.

Gurko, J. 1982. "Sexual energy in the classroom." Pp. 25–32, in M. Cruikshank (ed.), *Lesbian Studies.* New York: Feminist Press.

Hacker, H. 1951. "Women as a minority group." *Social Forces*. 30:60–69.

Hadjicostandi, J. 1990. "Facon: Women's formal and informal work in the garment industry in Kavala, Greece." Pp. 64–84, in K. Ward (ed.), *Women Workers and Global Restructuring.* Ithaca, NY: Cornell University Press.

Hall, M. 1994. "'Martyr' or murderer?" *U.S.A. Today*, December 7.

Hall, R. M. and B. R. Sandler. 1982. "The classroom climate: A chilly one for women?" Washington, DC: Association of American Colleges, The Project on the Status and Education of Women.

Harding, S. 1987. "Introduction: Is there a feminist method?" Pp. 1–14, in S. Harding (ed.), *Feminism and Methodology*. Bloomington: Indiana University Press.

Harding, S. 1986. "The instability of the analytical categories of feminist theories." *Signs*, 4:645–664.

Harris, L. and Associates. 1981. *Aging in the Eighties: America in Transition*. Washington, DC: National Council on Aging.

Hartmann, B. 1987. *Reproductive Rights and Wrongs*. New York: Harper & Row.

Hartmann, H. (ed.). 1981a. *Women and Revolution: The Unhappy Marriage of Marxism and Feminism*. London: Pluto Press.

Hartmann, H. 1981b. "The family as the locus of gender, class and political struggle: The example of housework." *Signs*, 6:366–394.

Havighurst, R. 1968. "Personality and patterns of aging." *The Gerontologist*, 8:20–23.

Havighurst, R. and D. Levine. 1979. *Society and Education*. Boston: Allyn & Bacon.

Hazzard, B. L. 1982. "Contributions of black women in education." In M. W. Davis (ed.), *Contributions of Black Women to America*, Vol. 2. Columbia, SC: Kenday Press.

Heidensohn, F. 1989. *Crime and Society*. London: Macmillan.

Heidensohn, F. 1968. "The deviance of women: A critique and an inquiry." *British Journal of Sociology*, 19(2):160–176.

Hindelang, M. 1979. "Sex differences in criminal activity." *Social Problems*, 27(2):143–156.

Hobbs, F. B. with B. Damon, U.S. Bureau of the Census. 1996. *65+ in the United States*. Current Population Reports, P23-190. Washington, DC: U.S. Government Printing Office.

Hochschild, A. 1989. *The Second Shift*. New York: Viking Press.

Hochschild, A. 1975. "Disengagement theory: A critique and proposal." *American Sociological Review*, 40:553–569.

Hochschild, A. 1973. "A review of sex role research." Pp. 249–267, in J. Huber (ed.), *Changing Women in a Changing Society*. Chicago: University of Chicago Press.

Hoffnung, M. 1989. "Motherhood: Contemporary conflict for women." Pp. 157–175, in J. Freeman (ed.), *Women: A Feminist Perspective*. Palo Alto, CA: Mayfield.

Holden, K. C. 1988. "Poverty and living arrangements among older women: Are changes in economic well-being underestimated?" *Journal of Gerontology*, 43(1):522–527.

Homans, G. 1974. *Social Behavior: Its Elementary Forms*, rev. ed. New York: Harcourt, Brace and World.

Homans, G. 1958. "Social behavior as exchange." *American Journal of Sociology*, 63(May):597–606.

hooks, b. 1989. *Talking Back: Thinking Feminist, Thinking Black*. Boston: South End Press.

Horner, M. 1972. "Toward an understanding of achievement related to conflict in women." *Journal of Social Issues*, 28:157–175.

Hossfeld, K. J. 1990. "'Their logic against them': Contradictions in race, sex and class in Silicon Valley." Pp. 149–178, in K. Ward (ed.), *Women Workers and Global Restructuring*. Ithaca, NY: Cornell University Press.

Howe, F. 1987. *Myths of Co-education*. Bloomington: Indiana University Press.

Howlett, D. 1995. "Incidents, reports spark FBI probe." *U.S.A. Today*, January 10.

Hull, G. T., P. B. Scott, and B. Smith. 1982. *All the Women Are White, All the Blacks Are Men, But Some of Us Are Brave*. Old Westbury, NY: Feminist Press.

Hyman, H. H. 1983. *Of Time and Widowhood*. Durham: Duke University Press.

Institute for Women's Policy Research. 1997. *The Wage Gap: Women's and Men's Earnings*. www.iwpr.org/wagegap.htm

International Federation on Aging. 1985. *Women and Aging Around the World*. Washington, DC: The

International Federation on Aging in cooperation with the American Association of Retired Persons.

International Labour Office. 1996. *Year Book of Labour Statistics, 1996* (55th Issue). Geneva, Switzerland: International Labour Organization Publications.

Jaggar, A. M. 1983. *Feminist Politics and Human Nature.* Totowa, NJ: Rowman & Allanheld.

Jaggar, A. M. and P. S. Rothenberg. 1984. *Feminist Frameworks: Alternative Theoretical Accounts of the Relations Between Women and Men,* 2nd ed. New York: McGraw-Hill.

Jimenez-Vasquez, R. 1976. "Social issues confronting Hispanic-American women." Pp. 186–212, in *Conference on the Educational and Occupational Needs of Hispanic Women.* Washington, DC: U.S. Department of Education.

Jones, J. 1985. *Labor of Love, Labor of Sorrow.* New York: Basic Books.

Kandal, T. R. 1988. *The Woman Question in Classical Sociological Theory.* Miami: Florida International University Press.

Kanter, R. M. 1977. *Men and Women of the Corporation.* New York: Basic Books.

Kart, C. S. 1990. *The Realities of Aging,* 3rd ed. Boston: Allyn & Bacon.

Kart, C. S., E. K. Metress, and S. P. Metress. 1988. *Aging, Health and Society.* New York: Jones & Bartlett.

Katz, M. 1975. *Class, Bureaucracy and the Schools.* New York: Praeger Books.

Keith, P. 1987. "Postponement of health care by unmarried older women." *Women and Health,* 12(1):47–60.

Keller, E. F. 1982. "Feminism and science." *Signs,* 7(3):589–602.

Kelly, G. P. and A. S. Nihlen. 1982. "Schooling and the reproduction of patriarchy." In M. W. Apple (ed.), *Cultural and Economic Reproduction in Education.* New York: Routledge.

Kerber, L. K. 1983. *The Impact of Women on American Education,* Washington, DC: U.S. Department of Education.

Kessler-Harris, A. 1981. *Women Have Always Worked.* New York: Feminist Press.

Kozol, J. 1988. *Rachel and Her Children: Homeless Families in America.* New York: Crown Publishers.

Lake, E. S. 1995. "Offenders' experience of violence: A comparison of male and female inmates as victims." *Deviant Behavior,* 16(3):269–290.

Lake, E. S. 1993. "An exploration of the violent victim experiences of female offenders." *Violence and Victims,* 8(1):41–51.

Langan, P. and C. W. Harlow. 1994. *Child Rape Victims, 1992.* Bureau of Justice Statistics. Washington, DC: U.S. Government Printing Office.

Langellier, K. M. 1994. "Appreciating phenomenology and feminism: Researching quiltmaking and communication." *Human Studies,* 17(1):65–80.

Lehmann, J. M. 1994. *Durkheim and Women.* Lincoln: University of Nebraska Press.

Lehmann, J. M. 1991. "Durkheim's women: Sexist ideology at the heart of sociological theory." *Current Perspectives in Social Theory,* 11:141–167.

Levine, M. P. and R. Leonard. 1984. "Discrimination against lesbians in the work force." *Signs,* 9(4):700–710.

Lewis, M. 1985. "Older women and health: An overview." Pp. 1–15, in S. Golub and R. Freedman (eds.), *Health Needs of Women as They Age.* New York: Haworth Press.

Lindgren, J. R. and N. Taub. 1988. *Sex Discrimination.* New York: West.

Lips, H. 1989. "Gender role socialization: Lessons in femininity." Pp. 197–216, in J. Freeman, *Women: A Feminist Perspective.* Palo Alto, CA: Mayfield.

Lombroso, C. 1899/1952. *The Female Offender.* New York: Wisdom Library.

Longino, C. F. and C. S. Kart. 1982. "Explicating activity theory: A formal replication," *Journal of Gerontology,* 17(6):713–722.

Lopata, H. Z. 1987a. *Widows,* Vol 1. Durham: Duke University Press.

Lopata, H. Z. 1987b. *Widows,* Vol. 2. Durham: Duke University Press.

Lopata, H. Z. 1979. *Women as Widows: Support Systems.* New York: Elsevier.

Lopata, H. Z. 1976. "Sociology." *Signs*, 2(1):165–176.

Lopata, H. Z. 1973. "Widowhood in an American City." Cambridge, MA: Scheckman.

Lopata, H. Z. 1971. *Occupation: Housewife*. Westport, CT: Greenwood Press.

Lortie, D. 1975. *School Teacher*. Chicago: University of Chicago Press.

Lowry, L. 1985. *Social Work with the Aging*. New York: Longman.

Luker, K. 1984. *Abortion and the Politics of Motherhood*. Berkeley: University of California Press.

Magaziner, J., D. A. Cadigan, J. R. Hebel, and R. E. Pauly. 1988. "Health and living arrangements among older women: Does living alone increase the risk of illness?" *Journal of Gerontology*, 43(5):l27–133.

Malz, M. D. 1975. "Crime statistics: A mathematical perspective." *Journal of Criminal Justice*, 3:177–194.

Manis, J. and B. Meltzer. 1978. *Symbolic Interaction: A Reader in Social Psychology*. Boston: Allyn & Bacon.

Marieskind, H. 1980. *Women in the Health System*. St. Louis: Mosby.

Markides, K. S. and C. J. Mindel. 1987. "Aging and ethnicity." Beverly Hills, CA: Sage.

Markson, E. 1983. *Older Women*. Lexington: Lexington Books.

Martin, S. E. 1996. *Doing Justice, Doing Gender: Women in Law and Criminal Justice Occupations*. Thousand Oaks, CA: Sage.

Martin, S. E. 1991. "The effectiveness of affirmative action: The case of women in policing." *Justice Quarterly*, 8(4):489–504.

Martin, S. E. 1980. *Breaking and Entering: Police Women on Patrol*. Berkeley: University of California Press.

Marx, K. 1849/1949. *Capital*. London: Allen & Unwin.

Marx, K. 1818–1883/1960. *The German Ideology: Part I & II*. New York: International.

Marx, K. and F. Engels. 1888/1992. *Communist Manifesto*. New York: Bantam Books.

Marx, K. and F. Engels. 1847/1970. *The Communist Manifesto*. Peking: Foreign Languages Press.

McCarthy, C. and M. Apple. 1988. "Race, class and gender in American educational research." Pp. 9–39, in L. Weis (ed.), *Class, Race and Gender in American Education*. Albany: State University of New York Press.

McCormack, A., M. D. Janus, and A. W. Burgess. 1986. "Runaway youths and sexual victimization: Gender differences in an adolescent runaway population." *Child Abuse and Neglect*, 10:387–395.

McLaren, A. T. 1987. "Rethinking 'femininity': Women in adult education." Pp. 333–350, in J. Gaskell and A. McLaren (eds.), *Women and Education: A Canadian Perspective*. Calgary, Alberta: Detselig.

McNaron, T. 1989. "Mapping a country: What lesbian students want." In C. D. Pearson, D. Shavlik, and J. Touchton (eds.), *Educating the Majority: Women Challenge Tradition in Higher Education*. New York: Macmillan.

Mead, G. H. 1934. *Mind, Self and Society from the Standpoint of a Social Behaviorist*. Chicago: University of Chicago Press.

Melendez, S. E. and J. Petrovich. 1989. "Hispanic women students in higher education." In C. Pearson, D. Shavlik, and J. Touchton (eds.), *Educating the Majority: Women Challenge Tradition in Higher Education*. New York: Macmillan.

Mies, M. 1988. "Capitalist development and subsistence production: Rural women in India." Pp. 27–50, in M. Mies, V. Bennholdt Thomsen, and C. von Werhof (eds.), *Women: The Last Colony*. London: Zed Books.

Mies, M. 1986. *Patriarchy and Accumulation on a World Scale*. London: Zed Books.

Mill, J. S. 1965. *Auguste Comte and Positivism*. Ann Arbor: University of Michigan Press.

Mill, J. S. and H. T. Mill. 1983. (originals 1869 and 1792). *The Enfranchisement of Women and the Subjection of Women*. London: Virago.

Millman, M. and R. M. Kanter. 1975. *Another Voice*. New York: Anchor Press/Doubleday.

Minkler, M. and R. Stone. 1985. "The feminization of poverty and older women." *The Gerontologist*, 25:351–357.

Mirande, A. 1985. *The Chicano Experience: An Alternative Perspective.* Notre Dame: University of Notre Dame Press.

Mirande, A. and E. Enriquez. 1979. *La Chicana.* Chicago: University of Chicago Press.

Mitchell, J. 1974. *Psychoanalysis and Feminism.* New York: Pantheon Books.

Mitchell, J. 1971. *Woman's Estate.* Harmondsworth, England: Penguin Books.

Mohr, J. C. 1978. *Abortion in America: The Origins and Evolutions of National Policy, 1800–1900.* New York: Oxford University Press.

Monge, R. H. 1975. "Structure of the self-concept from adolescence through old age." *Experimental Aging Research,* 1(2):281–291.

Moore, H. A. 1989. "Educational pluralism: Racism and sexism in Nebraska school policy." Pp. 119–138, in Bryant et al., *Nebraska Policy Choices.* Omaha: University of Nebraska Center for Public Affairs Research.

Moore, H. A. 1983. "Hispanic females: Schooling for conformity in public education." *Hispanic Journal of Behavioral Science,* 5:45–63.

Moore, H. A. and L. A. Hoover. 1987. *Contrasting Sexual Harassment in Education: Teachers, Students and Staff.* Paper presented at the National Women's Studies Association, Minneapolis, MN (June).

Moore, H. A. and D. R. Johnson. 1983. "A reexamination of teacher expectations: Evidence of sex and ethnic segmentation," *Social Science Quarterly,* 64:460–475.

Morgan, L. 1986. "The financial experience of widowed women: Evidence from the LRHS." *The Gerontologist,* 26(6):663–668.

Morris, A. 1987. *Women, Crime and Criminal Justice.* New York: Blackwell.

National Center for Education Statistics. 1994. *Digest of Education Statistics,* NCES 94–115. Washington, DC: U.S. Government Printing Office, Table 261.

National Coalition for the Homeless. 1996. *NCH Fact Sheet: Domestic Violence and Homelessness.* http://nch.ari.net/domestic.html

Navarro, V. 1984. "The political economy of government cuts for the elderly." In M. Minkler and C. L. Estes (eds.), *Readings in the Political Economy of Aging.* Farmingdale, NY: Baywood.

Nebraska Sociological Feminist Collective. 1988. *A Feminist Ethic for Social Science Research.* Lewiston, NE: Mellen Press.

Nebraska Sociological Feminist Collective. 1983. "A feminist ethic for social science research." *Women's Studies International Forum,* 6(5):535–543.

Nettler, F. 1974. *Explaining Crime.* New York: McGraw-Hill.

Nieto, C. 1980. "Chicana identity." Pp. 251–270, in *Conference on the Educational and Occupational Needs of Hispanic Women.* Washington, DC: U.S. Department of Education.

Nilson, L. B. 1981. "The social standing of a housewife." Paper presented at the 1981 American Sociological Association meeting, San Francisco (August).

Oakley, A. 1975. *Woman's Work: The Housewife, Past and Present.* New York: Pantheon Books.

Oakley, A. 1974. *The Sociology of Housework.* New York: Pantheon Books.

Oliver, J. 1983. "The caring wife." In J. Finch and D. Groves (eds.), *A Labour of Love: Women, Work and Caring.* London: Routledge.

Ollenburger, J., S. Grana, and H. A. Moore. 1989. "Labor force participation of rural farm, rural nonfarm and urban women: A panel update." *Rural Sociology,* 54(4):533–550.

Ollenburger, J. C. 1981. "Criminal victimization and fear of crime." *Research on Aging,* 3(1)March: 101–118.

Ortiz, F. I. 1988. "Hispanic-American children's experiences in classrooms." Pp. 63–86, in L. Weis (ed.), *Class, Race and Gender in American Education.* Albany: State University of New York Press.

Ovando, C. J. 1989. "Language and diversity in education." In J. A. Banks and C. A. Banks, *Multicultural Education.* Boston: Allyn & Bacon.

Palmore, E. 1968. "The effect of aging on activities and attitudes." *The Gerontologist,* 8:259–263.

Park, R. E. 1967. *The City.* Chicago: University of Chicago Press.

Parker, S. 1982. *Work and Retirement.* London: Allen & Unwin.

Parsons, T. 1959. "The school class as a social system: Some of its functions in American society." *Harvard Educational Review*, 29(4):297–313.

Parsons, T. 1949. "The social structure of the family." In Ruth Anshen (ed.), *The Family: Its Function and Destiny.* New York: Harper.

Parsons, T. and R. Bales. 1955. *Family, Socialization and Interaction Process.* Glencoe, IL: Free Press.

Pateman, C. 1988. *The Sexual Contract.* Stanford, CA: Stanford University Press.

Pateman, C. and E. Gross. 1986. *Feminist Challenges: Social and Political Theory.* Boston: Northeastern University Press.

Pearce, D. 1985. "Toil and trouble: Women workers and unemployment compensation." *Signs*, 10:439–459.

Pearce, D. and H. McAdoo. 1981. *Women and Children: Alone and in Poverty.* Washington, DC: Center for National Policy Review.

Pearson, J. 1985. *Gender and Communication.* Dubuque, IA: W. C. Brown.

Pharr, S. 1988. *Homophobia, A Weapon of Sexism.* Inverness: Chardon Press.

Phillipson, C. 1982. *Capitalism and the Construction of Old Age.* London: Macmillan.

Planned Parenthood of Idaho. 1997. "When do abortions take place?" *Perspectives/Issue Supplement* (Spring):4.

Pollak, O. 1950. *The Criminality of Women.* New York: Barnes.

Poor, M. 1982. "Older Lesbians." In M. Cruikshank (ed.), *Lesbian Studies.* New York: Feminist Press.

Post, K. and M. Lynch. 1996. "Smoke and Mirrors: Women and the Glass Ceiling." www.ideas.org/pressrel/fsheet/95–11.html

Price, B. R. and S. Gavin. 1982. "A century of women in policing." In B. R. Price and N. Sokoloff (eds.), *The Criminal Justice System and Women.* New York: Clark Boardman.

Ramirez, M. and A. Castaneda. 1974. *Cultural Democracy, Bicognitive Development and Education.* New York: Academic Press.

Rapp, R. 1982. "Family and class in contemporary America." Pp. 168–187, in B. Thorne and M. Yalom (eds.), *Rethinking the Family.* New York: Longman.

Rasche, C. E. 1993. "'Given' reasons for violence in intimate relationships." Pp. 75–100 in A. Wilson (ed.), *Homicide: The Victim/Offender Connection.* Cincinnati, OH: Anderson.

Raymond, J. 1986. *A Passion for Friends.* Boston: Beacon Press.

Reich, M. 1981. *Racial Inequality: A Political-Economic Analysis.* Princeton: Princeton University Press.

Reichard, S., F. Livson, and P. Peterson. 1962. *Aging and Personality.* New York: Wiley.

Reinharz, S. and L. Davidman. 1992. *Feminist Methods in Social Research.* New York: Oxford University Press.

Riesman, D., J. Gusfield, and Z. Gamson. 1975. *Academic Values and Mass Education.* New York: McGraw-Hill.

Riley, M. W. 1977. "Age strata in social systems." In R. Binstock and E. Shanas (eds.), *Handbook of Aging and the Social Sciences.* New York: Van Nostrand Reinhold.

Riley, M. W. 1971. "Social gerontology and the age stratification of society." *The Gerontologist*, 11:79–87.

Riley, M. W. and Foner, A. 1968. *Aging and Society: A Sociology of Age Stratification.* New York: Russell Sage Foundation.

Riley, M. W., M. Johnson, and A. Foner. 1972. *Aging and Society: A Sociology of Age Stratification.* New York: Russell Sage Foundation.

Rix, S. E. 1987. *The American Woman.* New York: Norton.

Rix, S. E. 1984. *Older Women: The Economics of Aging*, 2nd ed. Washington, DC: Women's Research and Education Institute.

Rodman, H., B. Sarvis, and J. W. Bonar. 1987. *The Abortion Question.* New York: Columbia University Press.

Rose, S. 1989. "The protest as a teaching technique in promoting feminist activism." *NWSA Journal*, 2(2):486–490.

Rosen, E. I. 1987. *Better Choices: Blue Collar Women In and Out of Work.* Chicago: University of Chicago Press.

Rosenfeld, R. 1985. *Farm Women: Work, Family and Farm in the United States.* Chapel Hill: University of North Carolina Press.

Ross, C., S. Danziger, and E. Smolensky. 1987. "The level and trend in poverty in the United States, 1939–1979." *Demography,* 24(4).

Rossi, A. (ed.). 1970. *Essays on Sex Equality by John Stuart Mill and Harriet Taylor Mill.* Chicago: University of Chicago Press.

Rossi, A. 1969. "Sex equality: The beginning of ideology." *Humanist,* September-October.

Rossides, D. W. 1978. *The History and Nature of Sociological Theory.* Boston: Houghton Mifflin.

Rowbotham, S. 1973. *Woman's Consciousness, Man's World.* Harmondsworth: Penguin.

Rubin, G. 1972. "The traffic in women: Notes on the political economy of sex." In R. Reiter, *Toward an Anthropology of Women.* New York: Monthly Review Press.

Russell, C. 1987. "Aging as a feminist issue." *Women's Studies International Forum,* 10(2):125–132.

Russell, D. 1990. *Rape in Marriage.* Bloomington, IN: Indiana University Press.

Russell, D. 1986. *The Secret Trauma.* New York: Basic Books.

Russell, D. 1984. *Sexual Exploitation.* Beverly Hills, CA: Sage.

Russell, D. 1982. *Rape and Marriage: Cross-Sex Interviewing.* New York: Macmillan.

Saari, R., A. Butler, and S. Lambert. 1983. "AFDC cuts hurt." *ISR Newsletter.* Ann Arbor, MI: Institute for Social Research.

Saario, T. N., C. N. Jacklin, and C. K. Tittle. 1973. "Sex role stereotyping in the public schools." *Harvard Educational Review,* 43(3):386–416.

Sachs, A. and J. H. Wilson. 1978. *Sexism and the Law.* New York: Free Press.

Safir, M. et al. 1985. *Women's Worlds.* New York: Praeger.

Savitz, L. D. 1982. "Official statistics." Pp. 3–16, in L. D. Savitz and N. Johnston (eds.), *Contemporary Criminology.* New York: Wiley.

Schiedewind, N. 1983. "Feminist values: Guidelines for a teaching methodology in women's studies." Pp. 261–271, in C. Bunch and S. Pollack (eds.), *Learning Our Way.* New York: Crossing Press.

Schlossman, S. and S. Wallach. 1978. "The crime of precocious sexuality: Female juvenile delinquency and the progressive era." *Harvard Educational Review* 48(1):65–94.

Schwendinger, H. and J. R. Schwendinger. 1974. *The Sociologists of the Chair: A Radical Analysis of the Formative Years of North American Sociology.* New York: Basic Books.

Scott, H. 1984. *Working Your Way to the Bottom.* Boston: Pandora Press.

Scully, D. 1980. *Men Who Control Women's Health.* Boston: Houghton Mifflin.

Seidman, D. and M. Couzens. 1974. "Getting the crime rate down: Political pressure and crime reporting." *Law and Society Review,* 8:457–493.

Seifer, N. 1976. *Nobody Speaks for Me: Sex-Portraits of American Working Class Women.* New York: Simon & Schuster.

Shanas, E. 1979. "The family as a social support system in old age." *Gerontologist,* 19:169–174.

Shanley, M. L. 1983. "Afterword: Feminism and families in a liberal polity." Pp. 357–362, in I. Diamond (ed.), *Families, Politics, and Public Policy.* New York: Longman.

Shaw, L. B. 1983. *Unplanned Careers: The Working Lives of Middle-Aged Women.* Lexington, MA: Lexington Books.

Sheffield, C. 1984. "Sexual terrorism." In J. Freeman (ed.), *Women: A Feminist Perspective.* Palo Alto, CA: Mayfield.

Sheppard, H. L. 1976. "Work and retirement." Pp. 286–309, in R. H. Binstock and E. Shanas (eds.), *Handbook of Aging and Social Sciences.* New York: Van Nostrand Reinhold.

Sichel, J., L. Friedman, J. Quint, and M. Smith. 1978. *Women on Patrol: A Pilot Study of Police Performance in New York City.* Washington, DC: National Institute of Law Enforcement and Criminal Justice.

Sidel, R. 1986. *Women and Children Last.* New York: Viking Penguin.

Simon, R. J. 1981. "American women and crime." Pp. 18–39, in L. H. Bowker (ed.), *Women and Crime in America.* New York: Macmillan.

Simon, R. J. 1975a. *The Contemporary Woman and Crime.* Washington, DC: National Institute of Mental Health.

Simon, R. J. 1975b. *Women and Crime.* Lexington: Lexington Books.

Simpson, R. L. 1976. "Sex stereotypes of secondary school teaching subjects." *Sociology of Education,* 47:388–398.

Smart, C. 1989. *Feminism and the Power of Law.* London: Routledge.

Smart, C. 1976. *Women, Crime and Criminology.* London: Routledge.

Smith, D. E. 1987. *The Everyday World as Problematic: A Feminist Sociology.* Boston: Northeastern University Press.

Smith, D. E. 1974. "Women's perspective as a radical critique of sociology." *Sociological Inquiry,* 44:7–13.

Smith, J. 1989. *Misogynies.* London: Faber and Faber.

Smolowe, J. 1994. "When violence hits home." *Time,* July 4.

Social Security Administration. 1994. *Social Security Bulletin, 1994 Annual Statistical Supplement.* Washington, DC: U.S. Government Printing Office.

Sokoloff, N. 1980. *Between Money and Love.* New York: Praeger.

Sontag, S. 1972. "The double standard of age." *Saturday Review,* 55(39):29–38.

Spencer, H. 1876/1894. *Principles of Sociology I.* New York: Appleton.

Spencer, H. 1851. *Social Statics.* New York: Appleton.

Spender, D. (ed.). 1983. *Feminist Theorists: Three Centuries of Key Women Thinkers.* New York: Pantheon Books.

Spender, D. 1982. *Invisible Women and the Schooling Scandal.* London: Women's Press.

Squirrell, G. 1989. "Teachers and issues of sexual orientation." *Gender and Education,* 1(1):17–34.

Staples, R. 1973. *Black Women in America: Sex, Marriage, and the Family.* Chicago: Nelson-Hall.

Statham, A. E., M. Miller, and H. O. Mauksch. 1988. *The Worth of Women's Work: A Qualitative Synthesis.* Albany: State University of New York Press.

Statham, A. E., M. Miller, and H. O. Mauksch. 1988. *The Worth of Women's Work: A Qualitative Synthesis.* Albany: State University of New York Press.

Steffensmeier, D. J. 1981a. "Patterns of female property crime, 1960–1978: A postscript." Pp. 59–65, in L. H. Bowker (ed.), *Women and Crime in America.* New York: Macmillan.

Steffensmeier, D. J. 1981b. "Crime and the contemporary woman: An analysis of changing levels of female property crime, 1960–1975." Pp. 39–59, in L. H. Bowker (ed.), *Women and Crime in America.* New York: Macmillan.

Steffensmeier, D. J. and M. J. Cobb. 1981. "Sex differences in urban arrest patterns, 1934–79." *Social Problems,* 29(1):37–50.

Steffensmeier, D. J., A. Rosenthal, and C. Shehan. 1980. "World War II and its effect on the sex differential in arrests: An empirical test of the sex-role equality and crime proposition." *Sociological Quarterly,* 21:403–416.

Strasser, S. 1982. *Never Done: The Story of American Housework.* New York: Pantheon Press.

Strober, M. 1982. "The MBA: Same passport to success for women and men?" Pp. 25–44, in R. Wallace (ed.), *Women in the Workplace.* Boston: Auburn House.

Strober, M. and L. Best. 1979. "The female/male salary differential in public schools." *Economic Inquiry,* 17:218–236.

Strober, M. and A. Langford. 1986. "Feminization of public school teaching." *Signs,* 11:212–235.

Sussman, M. 1976. "The family life of old people." In R. Binstock and E. Shanas (eds.), *Applied Sociology.* New York: Free Press.

Swingewood, A. 1984. *A Short History of Sociological Thought.* London: Macmillan.

Sydie, R. 1987. *Natural Women, Cultured Men.* New York: New York University Press.

Szinovacz, M. 1983. "Beyond the hearth: Older women and retirement." Pp. 93–120, in E. W. Markson (ed.), *Older Women: Issues and Perspectives.* Lexington: Heath.

Szinovacz, M. (ed.) 1982. *Women's Retirement.* Beverly Hills: Sage.

Taeuber, C. M. (ed.). 1996. *Statistical Handbook on Women in America,* 2nd ed. Phoenix: Oryx.

Task Force on Pay Equity. 1982. *Pay Equity and Public Employment.* St. Paul: Minnesota Legislature.

Taylor, D. 1985. "Women: An analysis." In *Women: An International Report.* New York: Oxford University Press.

Thomas, W. I. 1923. *The Unadjusted Girl.* Boston: Little, Brown.

Thomas, W. I. and D. S. Thomas. 1928. *The Child in America: Behavior Problems and Programs.* New York: Knopf.

Thorne, B. 1982. "Feminist rethinking of the family: An overview." Pp. 1–24, in B. Thorne and M. Yalom (eds.), *Rethinking the Family: Some Feminist Questions.* New York: Longman.

Tiano, S. 1990. "Maquiladora women: A new category of workers?" Pp. 193–224, in K. Ward (ed.), *Women Workers and Global Restructuring.* Ithaca, NY: Cornell University Press.

Tong, R. 1989. *Feminist Thought: A Comprehensive Introduction.* Boulder, CO: Westview Press.

Toren, N. 1969. "Semi-professionalism and social work: A theoretical perspective," Pp. 141–195, in A. Etzioni (ed.), *The Semi-Professions and Their Organization.* New York: Free Press.

Torrey, B. B., K. Kinsella, and C. M. Taeuber. 1987. *An Aging World.* International Population Reports, Series P-95, No. 78. Washington, DC: Bureau of the Census.

Treiman, D. J. and H. I. Hartmann. 1981. *Women, Work and Wages: Equal Pay for Jobs of Equal Value.* Washington, DC: National Academy Press.

Trow, M. 1975. *Teachers and Students.* New York: McGraw-Hill.

Tuchman, G. 1978. *Hearth and Home: Images of Women in the Mass Media.* New York: Oxford University Press.

Turner, J. and L. Beeghley. 1981. *The Emergence of Sociological Theory.* Homewood, IL: Dorsey Press.

United Nations. 1995. *The World's Women, 1995: Trends and Statistics.* Social Statistics and Indicators, Series K12 (Sales No. E.95.XVII.2). New York: United Nations Publications.

United Nations. 1989. *Levels and Trends of Contraceptive Use as Assessed in 1988.* Population Studies Series No. 110. New York: United Nations Publications.

United Nations Blue Book Series. 1996. *The United Nations and the Advancement of Women, 1945–1996.* (Volume VI, Sales No. E.96.I.9). New York: United Nations Publications.

U.S. Bureau of the Census. 1996a. *Income, Poverty, and Valuation of Non-Cash Benefits: 1994.* Current Population Reports, P60-189. Washington, DC: U.S. Government Printing Office.

U.S. Bureau of the Census. 1996b. *Statistical Abstract of the United States 1996* (116th ed.). Washington, DC: U.S. Government Printing Office.

U.S. Bureau of the Census. 1995a. *Income, Poverty, and Valuation of Non-Cash Benefits: 1993.* Current Population Reports, P60-188. Washington DC, U.S. Government Printing Office, Table C.

U.S. Bureau of the Census. 1995b. *Money Income in the United States: 1995 (with separate data on valuation of noncash benefits).* Current Population Reports, P60-193. Washington, DC: U.S. Government Printing Office.

U.S. Bureau of the Census. 1993a. Current Population Reports, P20-426. Washington, DC: U.S. Government Printing Office.

U.S. Bureau of the Census. 1993b. *Money Income of Households, Families, and Persons in the United States: 1992.* Current Population Reports, P60-184. Washington, DC: U.S. Government Printing Office.

U.S. Bureau of the Census. 1984. *Earnings and Detailed Occupations by Education and Sex,* PC-80-28. Washington, DC: U.S. Government Printing Office.

U.S. Census Bureau. 1995. Http://www.census.gov/press-release/cb96–200.html

U.S. Commission on Civil Rights. 1985. *Comparable Worth: An Analysis and Recommendations.* Washington, DC: U.S. Government Printing Office.

U.S. Department of Education. 1996. "Climate, classrooms, and diversity in educational institutions." *The Condition of Education 1996.* Washington, DC: U.S. Government Printing Office.

U.S. Department of Education. 1989. *Digest of Education Statistics 1989* (NCES 89–133). Washington, DC: U.S. Government Printing Office.

U.S. Department of Education, National Center for Education Statistics. 1996. *Digest of Education Statistics 1996* (NCES 96-133). Washington, DC: U.S. Government Printing Office.

U.S. Department of Justice, Bureau of Justice Statistics. 1996. *Sourcebook of Criminal Justice Statistics 1995.* Washington, DC: U.S. Government Printing Office.

U.S. Department of Justice, Bureau of Justice Statistics. 1993. *Sourcebook of Criminal Justice Statistics 1993.* Washington, DC: U.S. Government Printing Office.

U.S. Department of Justice, Federal Bureau of Investigation. 1997. *Hate Crime Report.* Criminal Justice Information Services (CJIS) Division. www.fbi.gov/ucr/hatecm.html

U.S. House Select Committee on Aging. 1987. *Women in Our Aging Society: Hearings.* Washington, DC: U.S. Government Printing Office.

U.S. Small Business Association. 1996. "Statistics in Women Business Ownership." www.sbaonline.sba.gov/womeninbusiness/stats96.html

Vico, G. 1744/1948. *The New Science of Giambattista Vico.* Ithaca, NY: Cornell University Press.

von Werholf, C. 1988. "Women's work: The blind spot in the critique of political economy." Pp. 13–26, in M. Mies, V. B. Thomsen, and C. von Werholf (eds.), *Women: The Last Colony.* London: Zed Books.

Walker, K. E. and M. Woods. 1976. *Time Use: A Measure of Household Production of Goods and Services.* Washington, DC: American Home Economics Association.

Wallston, B. S. 1985. "Feminist research methodology from a psychological perspective: Science is the marriage of agentic and communal." Pp. 226–233, in M. Safir et al. (eds.), *Women's Worlds: From the New Scholarship.* New York: Praeger.

Ward, K. (ed.). 1990. *Women Workers and Global Restructuring.* Ithaca, NY: Cornell University Press.

WEAL Agenda for Women's Economic Equity, 1985–1986. Vol. 14, Nos. 3 and 4.

Weber, M. 1949. *The Methodology of the Social Sciences.* New York: Free Press.

Weber, M. 1947. *The Theory of Social and Economic Organization.* New York: Free Press.

Weber, M. 1922/1968. *Economy and Society.* G. Roth and C. Wittich (eds.). New York: Bedminster Press.

Weiler, K. 1988. *Women Teaching for Change: Gender, Class and Power.* South Hadley, MA: Bergin and Garvey.

Weis, L. 1988. "High school girls in a de-industrializing society." In L. Weis (ed.), *Class, Race and Gender in American Education.* Albany: State University of New York Press.

Weitzman, L. J. 1981. *The Marriage Contract: Spouses, Lovers and the Law.* New York: Free Press.

Weitzman, L., D. Eifler, E. Hokada, and C. Ross. 1972. "Sex-role socialization in picture books for preschool children." *American Journal of Sociology,* 77:1125–1150.

Whitford, W. 1993. "Protect staff at clinics, U.S. is urged." *Atlanta Constitution,* March 12.

Williams, J. R., J. A. Vernon, M. C. Williams, and K. Malecha. 1987. "Sex role socialization in picture books: An update." *Social Science Quarterly,* 68:148–156.

Wollstonecraft, M. 1779/1977. In J. M. Todd (ed.), *A Wollstonecraft Anthology.* Bloomington: Indiana University Press.

Wylie, A., K. Okruhlik, L. Thielen-Wilson, and S. Morton. 1989. "Feminist critiques of science: The epistemological and methodological literature," *Women's Studies International Forum,* 12(3):379–388.

Youmans, E. G. 1967. "Disengagement among older rural and urban men." In E. G. Youmans (ed.), *Older Rural Americans.* Lexington: University of Kentucky Press.

Zinn, M. B. 1990. "Family, feminism and race in American society." *Gender and Society,* 4:68–83.

Zinn, M. B., L. W. Cannon, E. Higginbothan, and B. Thorntondill, 1986. "The costs of exclusionary practices in women's studies." *Signs,* 11:290–313.

Index